# TRADING
# PLACES

# TRADING
## PLACES

### THE INTERSECTING
### HISTORIES
### OF JUDAISM
### AND CHRISTIANITY

### BRUCE CHILTON
### AND JACOB NEUSNER

THE PILGRIM PRESS
CLEVELAND, OHIO

The Pilgrim Press, Cleveland, Ohio 44115
© 1996 by Bruce Chilton and Jacob Neusner
All rights reserved. Published 1996

Printed in the United States of America on acid-free paper

01  00  99  98  97  96     6  5  4  3  2  1

Library of Congress Cataloging-in-Publication Data

Chilton, Bruce.
   Trading places : the intersecting histories of Judaism and
Christianity / Bruce Chilton and Jacob Neusner.
      p.   cm.
   Includes bibliographical references and index.
   ISBN 0-8298-1141-9 (alk. paper)
   1. Judaism—History—Talmudic period, 10–425.
   2. Church history—Primitive and early church, ca. 30–600.
   3. Judaism and politics—Comparative studies.   4. Christianity and politics—Comparative studies.   I. Neusner, Jacob,
1932–     . II. Title.
   BM177.C45   1996
   261.2'6'09015—dc20                                      96-44694
                                                              CIP

# Contents

# Time Line

**721 B.C.E.**

Northern Kingdom of Israel invaded by Assyrian Empire. The Israelites are exiled and dispersed in a cultural and ethnic genocide.

**609 B.C.E.**

King Josiah killed.

**587 B.C.E.**

Siege of Jerusalem under the Babylonian Empire. Destruction of Temple.

**539–538 B.C.E.**

Babylonia falls to Cyrus the Persian and the Jewish people are allowed to return to Jerusalem.

**515 B.C.E.**

The Second Temple dedicated on the ancient site of Solomon's Temple.

**323 B.C.E.**

Alexander the Great dies.
[Successors in their rule over Israel: (1) Egyptian Ptolemies, (2) Syrian Seleucids].

**167 B.C.E.**

Jerusalem invaded under Antiochus IV, who arranges for the offering of swine in the Temple—"abomination of desolation."

**164 B.C.E.**

Restoration of worship in the Temple under the Maccabees.

**63 B.C.E.**

Pompey enters Jerusalem. Establishment of Roman rule.

**49 C.E.**

Jewish expulsion from Rome (ended by 57).

**64 C.E.**

Fire of Rome. Emperor Nero pins blame on Christians. The Romans differentiate between Christians and Jews from this time.

**66 C.E.**

Priests stop taking offerings from non-Jews, including Caesar. Rome recognizes that a revolt has begun.

**70 C.E.**

The Temple is burned down.

**73 C.E.**

Suicide of the Zealots at Masada.

**BY 85 C.E.**

Rabbinic leaders at Yavneh clearly differentiate between Judaism and Christianity.

**BY 95 C.E.**

Christians begin to consider themselves a separate religion from Judaism (see the Epistle to the Hebrews).

**111 C.E.**

Letters between Trajan and Pliny are written.

**132–135 C.E.**

Second Jewish revolt led by Simeon Bar Kokhba.

**135 C.E.**

Jews exiled from Jerusalem.

**177 C.E.**

Persecution of Christians in the Rhone Valley under Marcus Aurelius.

**200 C.E.**

Mishna.

**202 C.E.**

Severus issues an edict against proselytism.

**250 C.E.**

Emperor Decius orders all citizens to sacrifice to the gods.

**260 C.E.**

Emperor Valerian dies.

**303 C.E.**

Policy of Christian persecution reaches its height under Diocletian (land seized, rights taken away, people forced to worship gods).

**312 C.E.**

Constantine defeats Maxentius.

**315 C.E.**

Christian symbols begin to appear on coins.

**323 C.E.**

References to gods disappear from coins. Christianity is now the religion of the empire.

**361–363 C.E.**

Return to old gods attempted, authorization for the rebuilding of the Temple given (under Julian).

# PREFACE

S ome have supposed that the histories of early Christianity and Rabbinic Judaism run parallel.[1] This book challenges that conception. We argue that the histories of Judaism and Christianity[2] not only do not run parallel, but that the lines of the respective histories intersect; and further, that in all the ways that count, they have nothing in common. That may seem surprising. After all, the two took shape in the period considered here, the first four centuries of the Common Era. Much of their respective histories took place in the same country, under the same political conditions of subordination to the multicultural empire of Rome, and they were founded on the same authoritative revelation, that of ancient Israel. But these formative histories share nothing beyond that point. The one started where the other ended. The one moved out of politics as the other moved in. The one abandoned history as a mode of organizing experience, while the other found itself compelled to invent history to explain the present age.

The fundamental exchange of positions within, and upon, politics accounts for the vastly divergent histories that each worked out in ancient times, and, indeed, even until our own day: the one within, shaping history, the other without, enduring events and denying these formed history at all. It is only in the twentieth century that political change of equivalent magnitude has taken over the historical careers of each, bringing the two together again, confronting them both with a single encounter in common with a new political universe.

True, in ancient times, when Christianity and Judaism traded places, neither did so by design or even aspiration, the one to es-

xi

cape history, the other to make it. But that is how in the formative age of each religion matters took their course, and the comparisons and contrasts set forth in these pages spell out the three fundamental fields in which the two traded places: politics, values, and teleology. In a fourth field, as we shall see, each worked out against the perspectives of Scripture, particularly prophesy, a theology of history.

How to explain the exchange? It came about not because either party intended to exchange positions, but through the response of both parties to events that expressed the will of other people altogether. How both groups that called themselves "Israel" responded to events beyond the control of either shows us the power of religion to take over and reshape what to begin with lies beyond control. In the end, Judaism found success in making the best of what it could not change, and Christianity entered public discourse in a bid to transform the world.

The exchange proved not only formal but profound and substantive. As the one (Judaism), formerly public and institutional, formed a private vision of a disempowered community, the other (Christianity), formerly taking shelter in the locus of mutual help and home and family and small communities, assumed the risk and responsibility of a public conception of a newly empowered faith. In political change, in the transformation of the realities of power, we discern the foundations for the various other profound alterations in the very character of Judaic and Christian religious consciousness and character. Between the first and the fourth centuries, changes began in politics, and they worked their way through the entire system of the faith. They affected media of divine worship. For example, in the first century Judaism focused on the Temple in Jerusalem, which conducted public worship, including an elaborate sacrificial cult, under political auspices, through a regime of priests supported by a native political authority. By the end of the fourth century—the Temple now long in ruins and evidently not likely to be restored in the foreseeable future—Judaism found its center in the Torah, as taught and enforced by sages governing a community lacking access to most forms of the legitimate violence that constitute politics. For its part, Christianity in the first century comprised small groups meeting in homes, but by the turn of the fifth century it defined the public life of the great empire.

With the conversion of Constantine, Christianity gained a politics—that is, a strategy as well as the power for public action—and entered into events in such a way as to form events into history and draw lessons therefrom. Judaism turned from a politics of power to a morality of self-abnegation; Christianity ended up in command of what would evolve into Western civilization. Starting as outsiders, Christians emerged from the catacombs fully at home in exercising power. That is the story told in these pages, which narrate how the two foundational religions of the West traded places.

If that is the principal way in which the two religions traded places—the public and political becoming private and communal, and vice versa—there were other major changes, and in time to come, consideration must be given to further points in the transformation of Judaism and Christianity precipitated by the political fortunes confronted by each.

1. In the encounter with God, Judaism moved from Temple and synagogue worship to an encounter with God in the Torah; Christianity turned God incarnate in Jesus Christ into the idea of divine reality within history.

2. The canon, for Judaism, changed from tradition to the dual Torah; in the history of Christianity the canon moved from the Torah to the Bible (including the New Testament).

3. The sage in Judaism changed from a faceless example of virtue to a highly individuated personality; Christianity changed from a community of saints to the institutional and social structure formed around the bishop, conveyed in church orders defined by councils and stated as creeds.

In these and other ways, Judaism and Christianity took intersecting paths, the one ending up in the situation from which the other took off.

But the fields we have chosen for close exposition—politics, values, teleology, history—strike us as urgent, important in understanding what is happening even now. For today the two great religions once more redefine their stance toward the world—and one another. Judaism reemerges as a religion of politics, and Christianity reconsiders its engagement in worldly affairs. In the State of Israel the religion, Judaism, joins debates on public policy and seeks political power to accomplish its goals. In the many countries in which Christianity has enjoyed political power, Christians in the church's hierarchy and elsewhere try to find the path between religious coercion and complete abdication of religious participation in the formation of public policy. And both religions contemplate renascent Islam, also engaged in a vast and complex labor of sorting out the religious responsibilities of the Muslim state. Accordingly, this project in the comparative history of religions is particularly timely on the eve of the third millennium, because in these very years Judaism has regained a political vision of itself in the State of Israel, at the very moment at which, in many nations possessed of large populations of faithful Christians, Protestants and Catholics and Orthodox alike, churches seek new ways to negotiate their relationships with states, no longer conceiving that the state forms the medium for attaining the churches' sacred goals or realizing their tasks. Political change, bearing in its wake profound revisions in symbolic systems and structures such as those of a religious character, marks the end of the old millennium and the beginning of the new. We do well at this turning in the public consciousness to reconsider an earlier moment of transformation—the age of transposition when the now-prevailing conception of matters took shape.

Given the complexity of the religious situation in the first four Christian centuries—marked as they were by diversity in both Judaism and Christianity such that we do well to speak of Judaisms and Christianities—which Judaism do we compare with which Christianity?[3] The sole Judaism under discussion is the only Judaism amply documented by the writings of these centuries, which is Rabbinic Judaism. In the shank of the book, that Judaism is defined, and the story of its transformation, as set forth in its documents, is spelled out in the comparison and contrast with Christianity's history over the same centuries.

That being said, a direct comparison of Christianity with Rabbinic Judaism is impossible because Christianity is rooted in a movement whose place in Judaism was a matter of contention from the outset. That contention generated several different Christianities. Jesus' position focused on the transforming reality of the "kingdom of God," an Aramaic phrase he was familiar with from the prayers and the translations of the Hebrew Bible that were current in his time.[4] His speaking of God as king, and his preaching of that kingdom on God's behalf, involved Jesus in disputes regarding the grounds of his authority, disputes that mounted in intensity. The acknowledged cultic authorities in Jerusalem even held that his teaching subverted the authority of the Temple. When Jesus occupied that Temple and expelled those who were trading in animals, he directly opposed the unusual arrangement Caiaphas (the high priest) had sanctioned, which provided for trade within the great court of the Temple.[5]

Jesus acted as he did, not to prevent sacrifice as such, but to insist that what was offered in the Temple should belong to Israel, and not be a matter of simply paying for the property of priests. Jesus' vision was of the accessibility of sacrificial worship, such that one would have no need of commercialism. His statement in Mark 11:17 puts the matter starkly: trade in the house of God is theft. But Jesus' stance is no less radical than the book of Zechariah (14:20–21), which predicts that the goods in Jerusalem will be ready for sacrifice, without commercial transaction.

In Jesus radical theology, the kingdom of God was restructuring the principal institution of Israel in his time: the Temple. It was natural that the authorities there would resist him. Given that Jesus' activity extended to the use of physical force, it was also inevitable that the full power of the high priest would be brought to bear against him. But did his position make him a blasphemer, or a prophet of God's ultimate aim for his people? One's answer to that question, around the year 30 C.E. in Jerusalem, told the difference between those whose loyalty was to the Temple as sanctioned by God and those who shared Jesus' vision of the kingdom.[6] Jesus himself, however, did not finally locate himself as outside Judaism, and the authorities who sympathized with Caiaphas were only able to dispatch with him through the intermediary of Pilate, the Roman governor.

Jesus' occupation of the Temple did not result in the definitive expulsion of traders at the time. Caiaphas was able to restore order, along with his own preferred arrangements. But the true resolution of the dispute, in his mind, required the execution of Jesus, which he achieved by means of Pilate (whose likely role in the proceedings is described below). The teaching of Jesus after his occupation of the Temple, and specifically his reference to his meals of fellowship as a replacement of sacrifice in the Temple, played into Caiaphas' hands.

However they learned of Jesus' new interpretation of his meals of fellowship, the authorities arrested him just after the supper we call last. Jesus continued to celebrate fellowship at table as a foretaste of the kingdom, just as he had before. As before, the promise of drinking new wine in the kingdom of God joined his followers in an anticipatory celebration of that kingdom (see Matt. 26:29; Mark 14:25; Luke 22:18). But he also added a new and scandalous dimension of meaning. His occupation of the Temple having failed, Jesus said over the wine, "This is my blood," and over the bread, "This is my flesh" (Matt. 26:26, 28; Mark 14:22, 24; Luke 22:19–20; 1 Cor. 11:24–25; Justin, *Apology* I.66.3).

In Jesus' context, the context of his confrontation with the authorities of the Temple, his words can have had only one meaning. He cannot have meant, "Here are my personal body and blood"; that is an interpretation that only makes sense at a later stage in the development of Christianity. Jesus' point was rather that, in the absence of a Temple that permitted his view of purity to be practiced, wine was his blood of sacrifice, and bread was his flesh of sacrifice. In Aramaic, "blood" (*dema*) and "flesh" (*bisra,* which may also be rendered as "body") can carry such a sacrificial meaning, and in Jesus' context, that is the most natural meaning.

The meaning of "the last supper," then, actually evolved over a series of meals after Jesus' occupation of the Temple. During that period, Jesus claimed that wine and bread were a better sacrifice than what was offered in the Temple, a foretaste of new wine in the kingdom of God. At least wine and bread were Israel's own, not tokens of priestly dominance. (For a history of the development of the meanings and practices of eucharist in primitive Christianity, see Chilton, *A Feast of Meanings: Eucharistic Theologies from Jesus through Johannine Circles—Supplements to* Novum Testamentum 72 [Leiden: Brill, 1994].) No wonder the opposition to him, even among the Twelve (in the shape of Judas, according to the Gospels), became deadly. In essence, Jesus made his meals into a rival altar.

That final gesture of protest gave Caiaphas what he needed. Jesus could be charged with blasphemy before those with an interest in the Temple. The issue now was not simply Jesus' opposition to the siting of vendors of animals, but his creation of an alternative sacrifice. He blasphemed the law of Moses. The accusation concerned the Temple, in which Rome also had a vested interest.

Pilate had no regard for issues of purity as such; Acts 18:14–16 reflects the attitude of an official in a similar position, and Josephus shows that Pilate was without sympathy for Judaism. But the Temple in Jerusalem had come to symbolize Roman power, as well as the devotion of Israel. Imperial funds actually paid for some sacrifices in Jerusalem, so that the Empire would become part of the prosperity that was prayed for in the Temple. Rome jealously guarded the sacrifices that the Emperor financed in Jerusalem; when they were spurned in the year 66, the act was taken as a declaration of war (see Josephus, *Jewish War* II, §409). The Romans were engaged in the cult because they wished for political reasons to protect the operation of the Temple. They saw sacrifice there as a symbol of their tolerant acceptance of Jews as loyal subjects, and their arrangement to pay for some of the offerings was a matter of record (see Josephus, *Jewish War* II, §197 and 409; *Against Apion* II, §77; Philo, *Embassy to Gaius* 157, 317). The same Temple that was for the priestly class a divine privilege was for the Romans the seal of imperial hegemony. Jesus stood accused of creating a disturbance in that Temple (during his occupation) and of fomenting disloyalty to it and (therefore) to Caesar. Pilate did what he had to do. Jesus' persis-

xvii

tent reference to a "kingdom" that Caesar did not rule, and his repute among some as messiah or prophet, only made Pilate's order more likely. It all was probably done without a hearing; Jesus was not a Roman citizen. He was a nuisance, dispensed with under a military jurisdiction.

In this preface we have focused on the dispute at the end of Jesus' life in order to set the stage for the developments that followed. None of them can be understood unless and until it is appreciated what a radical and contentious figure Jesus was. His perspective was so thoroughly determined by his understanding of the kingdom of God, there was no room for the consideration of another authority. His terms of reference were given by the Judaism of his time, yet he offered no compromise with the institutions of Judaism. That provided the occasion for competing definitions of Christianity among Jesus' most prominent followers.

James, the brother of Jesus, practiced devotion to the Temple as well as to Jesus' teaching. A reintegration with the sacrificial cult had become possible for Jesus' followers generally, because the vendors of animals were restored to their usual position: not in the Temple, but on the Mount of Olives on the opposite side of the Kidron Valley. James shared this welcome reintegration into the ordinary worship of Israel with Peter, Jesus' most famous disciple. But James' devotion to the Temple was such that he claimed that Jesus' purpose was the restoration of the house of David, and insisted that non-Jews who wished to follow his brother's teaching should keep certain elementary laws of purity (see Acts 15:15–21). Still, his requirements were less stringent than the requirements of those who insisted that any male who sought baptism should first be circumcised (see Acts 15:1). Baptism for James could be offered to those outside the usual definition of "Israel," but there was still a position of privilege for those who accepted the law of Moses. It was within his circle that Jesus' "last supper" was strictly associated with Passover (see Matt. 26:17–19; Mark 14: 12–16; Luke 22:7–13). Because only those who were circumcised were to eat of Passover (see Exod. 12:48), the limiting implications of such a presentation—for liturgy and for the leadership of Jesus' movement—are evident.

In that same Temple, Peter and those of his circle were also sometimes to be found. Unlike James, however, Peter associated with non-Jews for the purpose of baptizing them (which took him far from Jerusalem). On his understanding, the same spirit that was active among Jesus' first followers was available to non-Jews who believed in him, so that ordinary requirements of purity could be suspended (see Acts 10:1–48). Peter did not deny the law of Moses, but he held that the same spirit that was active in the case of Moses was also available in the case of Jesus. Eucharist was a celebration of the covenant mediated by Moses *and* Jesus in the understanding of Peter. Just as there were circumcisers to the right of James, there were what we might call socializers to the left of Peter. Paul is the most famous example of a radical application of Peter's approach: those who believed in Jesus were the true sons of Abraham, and the law of Moses was only a way station on the road to that realization (see Gal. 3).

The differences among the circumcisers, the followers of James, the followers of Peter, and Paulinists cannot be pursued here. (For a discussion, see Chilton and Neusner, *Judaism in the New Testament* [London: Routledge, 1995].) The present observation is simply that, given the radical, contentious perspective of Jesus, it was inevitable that his followers would develop disagreements over the fundamental question of their relationship to "Israel" as most people understood that term. Some would insist, with the circumcisers, that the movement was for Israel alone; others, with James, would see Israel at the center of the movement, supported by pious non-Jews; the Petrine vision involved an accommodation among Jews and non-Jews; and Paul envisaged old Israel virtually swallowed up in a new effulgence of faith. Those differences could and did lead to the most profound disputes, so that the very concept of a "church," a unified body of faithful people, was itself the source of heated, sometimes violent, contention.

The story of how Judaism and Christianity traded places is also the story of how the pluralism of Jesus' movement learned the art of unity by means of consensus. That story, among others, will be pursued in the chapters that follow.

Jesus' message of what he called "the kingdom of God" caused offense to many people in his time. He insisted that no secular institution (not even the Roman Empire) could displace God's power, and that no religious institution (not even the Temple in Jerusalem) could compete with God's authority. That vision of God at the center of all things, and of God resolved to embrace all things, was at the heart of Jesus' teaching. Today, Jesus' language can continue to cause offense. Governments are no longer "kingdoms," and the divine center of creation is no longer assumed to be masculine. For the purposes of prayer and communicating the gospel, replacements for "kingdom (of God)" have been sought. Among them are "reign," "realm," "imperial rule," "dominion," "monarchy," "rule." In this study, however, we give precedence to Jesus' own usage.

He spoke of the "kingdom" (*malkhutha* in Aramaic, *basileia* in Greek) because he wished to refer to God's activity as "king" (*malkha* in Aramaic, *basileus* in Greek). The symmetry with "kingdom" in English is precise. More important, Jesus wished to make it clear he was using a personal metaphor to refer to God's care and power at the center and on the horizon of our lives. That was why he could speak of God as a strangely forgiving king (see Matt. 18:23–35), but also as a woman baking bread (see Luke 13:20–21). The focus of the kingdom was God's own identity (as "king"), not an abstraction. All the terms that have been suggested as a replacement for kingdom can be misunderstood in much the way that "kingdom" is. And all of them lack the direct reference to "king" which was the point of Jesus' metaphor. We lose some capacity for metaphorical speech if we press too quickly for standardized replacements of Jesus' frequently playful use of language. Once the message of Jesus has been understood, of course, we will naturally transfer it into our own experience. But we must understand him first, or we run the risk of projecting our own agenda on to him.

This book took shape in the classrooms of Bard College from 1994 to 1996, where the two of us together taught a course (1994) on Judeo-Christian relations through history, as well as another (1995, 1996) bearing the same title as this book. Students read the book and helped us clarify our thought. They also discussed the sources collected in the companion sourcebook. There in the Bard classroom we pursued discussions of comparisons and contrasts, allowing us to solidify our thoughts in amiable argument with one another. Our students, indeed, accused us of never holding conflicting opinions on anything. But that judgment pertains to certain intellectual matters; we do differ in politics and, after all, an Episcopal priest and a rabbi of Judaism cannot concur on absolutely everything and remain true to their deepest convictions. We share not only collegiality and friendship but learning, and if we concur on many things it is because of a shared reason that unites us.

We take this occasion also to express our shared respect for Bard College, which made our work together possible. In that context we thank the president of Bard College, Leon Botstein, for bringing about the appointment that resulted in the collaborative venture that has proved so stimulating for us both. This book is only one of the projects contemplated in consequence.

We express our thanks to Pilgrim Press for serving us so well as publisher, and our high esteem for Richard Brown, our editor. If he has referred to us as an editor's dream authors, we reciprocate and conceive him to be the ideal editor for an academic religious book such as this one.

It was at the University of Göttingen in the summer semester of 1995 that Jacob Neusner wrote the first draft of his half of the book, as Von Humboldt Research Professor in the faculty of theology. He thanks his principal host, Professor Gerd Lüdemann, as well as other colleagues in the faculty of theology for their hospitality and friendly interest in his work. He further expresses his thanks to the University of South Florida for the research chair that he occupies there. No one in the academic world enjoys more favorable circumstances for scholarship than does one with the advantage of a distinguished research professorship in the Florida state university system. He expresses further thanks for a substantial research expense fund, ample research time, and stimulating, straightforward, and cordial colleagues, many of

✡

xxi

✞

whom are also cherished friends. As noted, in the time in which this work was done, he served also as Visiting Professor of Religion at Bard College, which awarded a further research grant. These visits to Bard proved intellectually stimulating and rewarding, and he expresses thanks for the college's supererogatory support of his work.

Bruce Chilton acknowledges an old debt, to his teachers at the General Theological Seminary in New York City. He has benefited from several different sorts of education over the years, but in no other place was the critical vision as global and as chronological as it was at GTS. Such an engagement with the pluralism of human experience is a testament to the faith that God's word yearns to become flesh, and gives grounds to hope that the voice of genuinely Christian theology might be heard in our land again.

*Bruce Chilton*
*Bernard Iddings Bell Professor of Religion*
*Bard College*
*Annandale-on-Hudson, New York*


*Jacob Neusner*
*Distinguished Research Professor of Religious Studies*
*University of South Florida*
*Professor of Religion*
*Bard College*
*Von Humboldt Research Professor Abt. Antikes Judentum*
*Georg-August-Universität Göttingen*

# INTRODUCTION

## THE POLITICAL FOUNDATIONS OF RELIGIOUS HISTORY

We live in a century in which political changes have provoked profound change in the condition and character of religion. When empires fall and rise, vast revolutions in public policy encompass, also, the way in which people work out their traditions of eternity in this-worldly terms. While, to take a particularly Western case, people seek to live in the "kingdom of God" (for Christianity) or under the authority and sovereignty of the "kingdom of heaven" (for Judaism), they also respond out of the resources of religion to the politics of empires, kingdoms, republics, and nation-states. And that response spills over into the politics of the divine with which they are principally concerned.

Take the effect of political change on the condition of Judaism—not only the Jews as an ethnic group but Judaism, the religion—in the past two, catastrophic centuries. Until World War I Judaism flourished in the multicultural empires of Russia, Austria-Hungary, and Germany; but all have collapsed, and with them perished, in the greatest disaster Judaism has ever known, the vast reservoir of the faithful that endured in them. The end of imperialism has opened the way for Islam to reconsider its political condition. Islam has found renewal in the political revolutions that accompanied the demise of European rule over vast Muslim population in India, the Near and Middle East, North Africa, Malaya and Indonesia, and elsewhere. Christianity, giving up state support or sponsorship, has gained new vitality in the competition with both

1

other faiths and, more so, with militant secularism. Because of political changes, relationships among the three monotheisms have altered, in the case of Christianity and Judaism, for the better, but between Islam and Judaism, much for the worse. It follows that, over the span of a hundred years, vast revisions in political arrangements affecting nations have brought about a counterpart revolution in the condition of religions, and that revolution extends not only to institutional structures—the advent of massive state support for Judaism in the State of Israel, for instance—but also to issues of theology and religious law and practice as well. No one cognizant of the condition of Judaism in 1900 can have anticipated its public expression in 2000, and the same is so for Christianity and Islam.

We have to look backward through time to the fourth century to locate a change in politics that brought about an equivalently profound and far-reaching revolution in the character and condition of two religions. One is Christianity, which survived persecution for three centuries and emerged from the catacombs to the court of the Roman Empire, as the government of Constantine first declared Christianity licit and then made it the religion of the state. In our own century, we may imagine an equivalent event. Had Leo Baeck, the leading Reform rabbi of Germany in the National Socialist period, who was imprisoned in the model concentration camp, Theresienstadt, been snatched from near death to be appointed Reichsführer of Nazi Germany in place of Adolph Hitler, or had Hitler been succeeded by Joseph Goebbels, who thereupon had himself circumcised and baptized into Judaism, we should not have confronted a more amazing, stupefying event than Christianity then confronted.

But Christianity was not alone in having to sort out the meaning of such remarkable political changes. Judaism too faced the crisis of faith, but in a different way. Having spent three hundred years ignoring the advent of a religious community competing for the patrimony of ancient Israel's heritage—Scripture and the self-revelation of God conveyed therein; the genealogy of faith announced in its pages; the account of creation, revelation, and coming redemption, and the conditions thereof—Judaism now could no longer dismiss the Christian challenge. Having lost its political foundations, Judaism faced a Christianity not only licit but in command. The condition of Judaism, no less than that of Christianity, was vastly altered by reason of events of a political character. As in our own day, longstanding arrangements, looking backward for a thousand years, gave way to new modes of defining the social order in which Judaism would endure, so in the fourth century, enduring patterns of politics recast the realities with which the faith would have to cope. And, it turned out, the new political order would endure and dictate the relationship of Christianity with other religions and with politics as well, an order so sturdy as to deal with the long-term challenge of Islam as much as that of Judaism—until our own day.

That is the context in which we undertake, at the end of this, our own century of radical change, the comparison and contrast of the formative histories of Judaism and Christianity, which played themselves out over the first through the fourth centuries. This comparison yields a complex pattern. In some ways the two histories run in opposite directions, for in these pages we spell out some of the important ways in which Judaism by the fourth century had entered into the situation of the Christianity of the first century, and Christianity in that same span of time assumed the position of political Judaism at the outset. And that is what we mean by "trading places." But in other ways, we shall see, the two histories yield parallel events, as the framers of both traditions reached common conclusions (with divergent concrete results, to be sure) in connection with issues confronting them both in common. The final chapter draws the historical parallel in religious structures that both religions organized for themselves. Obviously, comparisons and contrasts between the two religions' histories do not exhaust themselves with those treated here, but, in our view, when one is comparing histories of religions, the categories analyzed here—politics, values (in the concrete sense: that which is valued), teleology, doctrine of history, and, finally, the formation of authoritative structures—prove fundamental.

Why identify as the generative cause the political revolution of the fourth Christian century, which, we now recognize, marks also the first century of Western civilization as the work of Christianity in succession to Greco-Roman culture? It is not only because politics redefined the circumstances in which Christianity would work out its history, but also because politics had redefined the condition of Judaism as well, and, in the fourth century, underscored the reversal. Specifically, in the first century Jews governed themselves as a state within the Roman imperial system and conceived of Israel as a political entity. Christians for their part bore no political vision, never framing a theory of how they would govern because politics lay beyond the bounds of their imagination. Over the next four hundred years, the very shape of the two great religions changed so that the one assumed the traits as to politics and much else that characterized the other at the outset. They traded places. When Christianity began, it had no politics or economics. The faithful looked to heaven, expecting God's dominion, not their own, to rule. Judaism before the year 70, by contrast, framed its vision in terms of a politics of the holy people, realizing the vision of Moses to form a political entity, the dominion of priests. The religious message came to be expressed also in economics. By the end of the fourth century, with Christianity in command of the Roman Empire, Jews had turned inward, the family and corporate but essentially voluntary community forming the outer limits of their social world. By contrast, Christians now worked out the vision of a Christian state, governed in Christ's name by the Christian emperor and his court. So the political Israel of the first century would give up politics for the duration, envisioning the restoration only with the Messiah's coming, and apolitical Christianity would find itself required to frame a profoundly political conception not only of law but, in Augustine's recapitulation, of the very meaning of politics.

## WHAT DO WE MEAN BY "JUDAISM"?

No single Judaism, beginning with Abraham and continuing in a single linear and unitary history to the present time, has ever existed,[1] though nearly every Judaism over time has represented itself in exactly that way, alleging that it is the sole, the only

Judaism now and always. But, faced with the diversity of the contradictory claimants, all of them claiming to authenticity and unique standing as not *a* Judaism but *the* Judaism, we can hardly favor one Judaism over another.[2] Nonetheless, all Judaisms form species of a single genus, Judaism. Defining the genus, Judaism, in distinction from all other genera of religion, poses no difficulty. By a Judaism we mean a religious system that deems the Torah, commencing with the Pentateuch (the five books of Moses), properly interpreted, to convey the entirety of God's will for humanity, beginning to end. Only (a) Judaism may make that statement. The kindred religious genera, Christianity and Islam, affirm the Pentateuch or the Torah but deem that document insufficient, the one adding the New Testament, the other, the Qur'an to the record of divine self-manifestation.

Through recorded history, many such Judaic religious systems, or Judaisms, have taken shape and left solid evidence of their presence. Each framed the self-understanding of an identifiable social group or entity of Jews, who, by the conventions of the system, invariably then called themselves Israel. But for all of them the Torah—always meaning a privileged position for the Pentateuch, or the five books of Moses, revealed by God to Moses and set forth by Ezra in c. 450 B.C.E.—formed the single reference point. A variety of kindred Judaic religious systems or Judaisms concurred on that one point, if not on many others. Each of these systems, or Judaisms, set forth its distinctive and coherent statement of the social order formed by its faithful, comprising an account of (1) the social group that embodied that order or the particular Israel, (2) the worldview of that Israel, and (3) the way of life of the same. All together these Judaisms may be said to comprise a family of kindred religious systems, but the conception of a single Judaism—harmonious, linear in its history, cogent in its theology, uniform in its way of life—contradicts all the facts we have out of antiquity (as much as such a unitary Judaism would conflict with the facts of everyday Judaisms in the world today). To be sure, each of these religious systems appealed to the Torah of Moses or revelation and self-manifestation of God at Sinai, and all of them shared that common Scripture.

The definition of the genus in hand, we turn to the speciation thereof. Distinguished in detail but also in fundamental conviction, generative myth and symbol, and consequent modes of exegetical thought and expression, each such system, or Judaism, formed a self-contained community of Jews. Every Judaism defined its social order, the social group of the participants, and indicated also the boundaries beyond its social limits. So we know one Judaism from another, to begin with, when we can identify the group defined by that Judaism as Israel. Some Judaisms imposed narrow, and others broad, constructions on the meaning of Israel; for some, belief formed the key, for others, behavior. But all of these systems possessed distinctive and distinguishing traditions, laws, or doctrines of their own. Each of the various Judaisms put forth its own writings or oral traditions, represented by the Elephantine papyri, the Dead Sea Scrolls, documents now collected as Old Testament pseudepigrapha, and the like; for their part synagogues exhibit decorations that do not correlate well with existing writings; the later history of at least one subdivision among Judaisms, the Christian one, obscures its origins within, and (in more accurate language) as, a Judaism. When, therefore, we speak of Judaism, we have to specify which one, and indicate, in concrete terms, the specific body of evidence to which we appeal in formulating a linear and harmonious history of a Judaism.

Which Judaism, then, produced the history that we propose to contrast with that of (a) Christianity? A particular Judaism comes under study in these pages, the one represented by a distinctive corpus of writing. It is the Judaism that came to full exposure in exactly the same centuries that witnessed the formation of Christianity in all its forms, that is, the first six centuries of the Common Era. Comparing two religions that emerged in the same time, in much the same groups of people, and in the same general region, certainly presents a straightforward opportunity for comparison. Not only so but, as we shall see, the religious history of the two religions treated here exhibits interest in a shared agenda of religious thought and expression, institutional and intellectual alike, so that we contrast one kind against another kind of the same genus, in this case, religions that appeal to the Hebrew Scriptures as divine revelation. But as we shall see at some length, whatever the commonalities, the two religions would follow historical paths that ran not parallel but in opposite directions altogether, the one starting in the politics at which the other concluded its formative history.

Before the destruction of the Temple in Jerusalem by Rome in 70 C.E., several Judaisms flourished and left written or material evidence for their systems. But from that time to the conquest of the Near and Middle East by Islam six centuries later, one particular Judaism, which produced a vast volume of preserved writings, takes pride of place. Specifically, we select the best-documented and most influential and (as it turned out) the one enduring Judaism to emerge in ancient times. That is the Judaism represented here in its historical unfolding in comparison with and contrast to the Christianity of the same period—Rabbinic Judaism. It is easily defined by appeal to its generative myth that at Sinai God revealed the Torah in two media, written and oral. The written part of the Torah corresponds to the Hebrew Scriptures, or Old Testament, or "Tanakh" (the neologism formed of the first letter of the Hebrew words for Torah, *Nebi'im,* "Prophets," and *Ketubim,* "Writings"). The oral part of the Torah reaches us in written form in the Rabbinic canon, as we shall see in a moment. Hence the Judaism under study here may be called "the Judaism of the dual Torah."

The Judaism of the dual Torah is also called Rabbinic Judaism, from the title of its principal figures, sages called rabbis. It is best documented in the pages of a vast law code and commentary, the Talmud of Babylonia, and hence is also known as Talmudic Judaism. It would define the paramount Judaism from its own day to ours and therefore is called "normative" or "classical" Judaism.

After Scripture, the canonical writing to come to closure first was the Mishnah, a philosophy in the form of a law code that concluded in c. 200 C.E., encompassing sayings attributed to authorities who flourished in the preceding two hundred years. The Mishnah formed one of Rabbinic Judaism's two foundation documents, Scripture being the other. The Mishnah was in time characterized as the outcome of oral tradition commencing with God's instruction to Moses at Sinai, hence "oral Torah," and Scripture, by contrast, was known as "written Torah." The Mishnah was supplemented by a collection of sayings called the Tosefta, or supplements, which are assigned to authorities who also appear in the Mishnah; the Talmud of the Land of Israel (c. 400), the first systematic reading of the Mishnah; and the second Talmud, the one of Babylonia (c. 600).

Alongside developed the exegeses of Scripture, called Midrash, which served in a way parallel to that of the Mishnah. Formed into compilations, these Scripture exegeses began with verse-by-verse readings but, over time, evolved into large-scale documents, each with its own character. The important ones were: (1) in the first set, Sifra to Leviticus; Sifré to Numbers; and another Sifré, to Deuteronomy, (2) in the second set, Genesis Rabbah, to Genesis; and Leviticus Rabbah, to Leviticus, (3) in the third set, Lamentations Rabbati, Esther Rabbah I, Song of Songs Rabbah, and Ruth Rabbah, for the named scrolls of the Torah read in the synagogue at certain liturgical seasons. Another important testimony to the system and structure of the religious worldview of the time, the Prayerbook, may or may not have originated among rabbis in particular but certainly expresses their convictions and contains prayers written by them and valued within their circles.

What does it mean to allege that a religious system has had a history, and how do we propose to trace the history of the particular Judaism we address in these pages? In the case of Rabbinic Judaism, we compare the traits of its earlier documents with those of the later ones, noting contrasts as well as points of continuity. Since we are treating a religious system, not an ethnic group, this inquiry into the twists and turns of critical conceptions as they work their way through one writing after another indeed yields the history of the important ideas of a given religious canon, stage by stage, from the formative to the final statement. We know little of the state of opinion among Jews in general or even among those Jews who identified with the Torah as the sages of the dual Torah taught it. When we speak of this Judaism, that is all that we mean. Therefore, our evidence derives from the examination of the principal ideas and concerns of the documents of Rabbinic Judaism, read in sequence from start to finish, from the Mishnah through the Talmud of Babylonia, along with the parallel sequence from the earliest to the latest Midrash-compilations, that we come to understand the religious system that animates the whole.

Specifically, in this book we compare and contrast the Judaic religious system put forth in the earlier documents, the Mishnah and associated Midrash-compilations, with that represented in the later writings of Rabbinic Judaism, thus following the transformation of Rabbinic Judaism in the unfolding of the first six centuries of the Common Era.[3] In this way we see how a statement made at the end of the second century, looking backward toward an empowered Israel with a government and public institutions, compares with a statement shaped after the rise to power of triumphant Christianity in the fourth century. The contrast shows how one system not only provided the foundations for another but also revised and recast the main structures of the received system in response to radical changes in the political universe confronting its framers. The history of the Judaism treated here then intersects with the history of the Christianity represented in these pages.

## WHAT DO WE MEAN BY CHRISTIANITY?

Primitive Christianity might be described as a series of Judaic movements centered on Jesus. That primitive phase is described in the Preface, pp. xviii–xix. By the end of the period of the New Testament (which is also the end of the first century), outside observers and those who were baptized began to agree that the church was autonomous of Judaism. The shift to early Christianity had been accomplished. No document illuminates that shift more clearly than the Epistle to the Hebrews.

The Epistle to the Hebrews has long stood as an enigma within the New Testament. "Who knows who wrote the Epistle?" asked Origen in the third century; he answered the question himself, "God knows!"[4] But the enigma of Hebrews goes beyond the question of who wrote it; when and where it was written, and to whom, are also issues of lively debate.[5]

The epistle has been compared to a homily,[6] and calls itself a "word of exhortation" in 13:22. "Word" here (*logos*, as in John's Gospel) bears the meaning of "discourse," and the choice of diction declares Hebrews' homiletic intent. It is a sustained argument on the basis of authoritative tradition, which intends to convince its readers and hearers to embrace a fresh position and an invigorated sense of purpose in the world. Hebrews engages in a series of scriptural identifications of Jesus: both Scripture (in the form of the Septuagint, the translation of the Hebrew Bible into Greek) and God's Son are the authoritative point of departure.

Scripture is held to show that the Son, and the Son's announcement of salvation, are superior to the angels and their message (Heb. 1:1–2:18, see especially 2:1–4). Jesus is also held to be superior to Moses and Joshua, who did not truly bring those who left Egypt into the full rest promised by God (3:1–4:13). Having set up a general assertion of the Son's superiority on the basis of Scripture, the author proceeds to his main theme (4:14): "Having, then, a great high priest who has passed into the heavens, Jesus the Son of God, let us hold the confession fast." That statement is the key to the central argument of Hebrews, and therefore to an understanding of the epistle.

Two terms of reference in the statement are used freshly and—on first acquaintance with the epistle—somewhat unexpectedly. Jesus, whom we have known as Son, is now "great high priest." The term "high priest" is in fact used earlier, to speak of his having expiated sin (2:17),[7] and in that role Jesus is also called the "apostle and high priest of our confession" (3:1). But now, in 4:14, Jesus is the "great high priest," whose position is heavenly. Now, too, the emphatic confession of his heavenly location is the only means of obtaining divine mercy. Recognizing Jesus' true stature permits believers to approach the throne of divine grace and obtain mercy (see Heb. 4:16).

Jesus' suffering is invoked again in 4:15 in order to make the link to what was said earlier, of Jesus' expiation. But then 4:16 spells out the ethical point of the entire epistle: "Let us then draw near with assurance to the throne of grace, so that we might receive mercy and find grace in time of need." With bold calculation,

Jesus is presented as the unique means of access to God in the only sanctuary that matters, the divine throne in heaven.

The portrayal of Jesus as great high priest, exalted in heaven, proves to be the center of the epistle (Heb. 4–7). At first, the argument may seem abstruse, turning as it does on Melchizedek, a relatively obscure figure in Genesis 14. In Genesis, Abram[8] is met by Melchizedek after his defeat of the king of Elam. Melchizedek is identified as king of Salem, and as priest of God Most High (Gen. 14:18). He brings bread and wine, and blesses Abram; in return, Abram gives Melchizedek one-tenth of what he has in hand after the victory (Gen. 14:18–20).

The author of Hebrews hammers out a principle and a corollary from this narrative. First, "It is beyond all dispute that the lesser is blessed by the greater" (Heb. 7:7). From that straightforward assertion, the superiority of Melchizedek to Levitical priests is deduced. Levi, the founding father of the priesthood, was still in Abram's loins at the time Abram paid his tithe to Melchizedek. In that sense, the Levitical priests who were to receive tithes were themselves tithed by the greater priest (Heb. 7:8–10).

The importance of Melchizedek to the author of Hebrews, of course, is that he resembles Jesus, the Son of God. His very name means "king of righteousness" (*zedek* in Hebrew), and he is also "king of peace," or Salem in Hebrew. There is no reference to his genealogy, and his birth and death are not recorded (Heb. 7:2b–4). In all these details, he adumbrates Jesus, true king of righteousness and peace, from a descent which is not priestly in a Levitical sense, of whom David prophesied in the Psalms, "You are a priest for ever, after the order of Melchizedek" (Heb. 7:11–25, citing Psalm 110:4 on several occasions, cf. 7:11, 15, 17, 21).[9] Jesus is the guarantor by God's own promise of a better, everlasting covenant (7:22). His surety is linked to Melchizedek's as clearly as they share a single enacted symbol (or sacrament) of God's effective presence: both of them use bread and wine as the seal of God's promise and blessing.[10]

The superiority of the better covenant is spelled out in what follows in Hebrews through chapter 9, again relying on the attachment to Jesus of God's promise in Psalm 110 (Heb. 7:28): "For

✿
**11**
✠

the law appoints men having weakness as high priests, but the word of the oath which is after the law appoints a son for ever perfected." Perfection implies that daily offerings are beside the point. The son was perfect "once for all, when he offered himself up" (7:26–27).

The author leaves nothing to implication: Moses' prescriptions for the sanctuary were a pale imitation of the heavenly sanctuary that Jesus has actually entered (8:1–6). Accordingly, the covenant mediated by Jesus is "better," the "second" replacing the "first," the "new" replacing what is now "obsolete" (8:6–13).

Chapter 9 simply puts the cap on an argument that is already clear. In its elaboration of a self-consciously christological interpretation, Hebrews develops a theory of the relationship between Jesus and the Scriptures of Israel. The devotion to detail involved attests the concern to develop that theory fully. The chapter begins with the "first" covenant's regulations for sacrifice, involving the Temple in Jerusalem. The objects of worship are used to set the scene: specific mention is made of the menorah, the table and presented bread in the holy place, with the holy of holies empty but for the gold censer and the ark.[11] The reference to the censer as being in the holy of holies fixes the point in time of which the author speaks: it can only be the day of atonement, when the high priest made his single visit of the year to that sanctum, censer in hand.[12]

That precise moment is only specified in order to be fixed, frozen forever. For Hebrews, what was a fleeting movement in the case of the high priest was an eternal truth in the case of Jesus. The movement of ordinary priests, in and out of the holy place, the "first tabernacle" (9:6) while the high priest could only enter "the second tabernacle," the holy of holies (9:7), once a year, was designed by the spirit of God as a parable: the way into the holy of holies could not be revealed while the First Temple, the first tabernacle and its service, continued (9:8–10). That way could only be opened, after the Temple was destroyed, by Christ, who became high priest and passed through "the greater and more perfect tabernacle" of his body (9:11) by the power of his own blood (9:12) so that he could find eternal redemption in the sanctuary.

Signal motifs within the Gospels are developed in the passage. Jesus' death and the destruction of the Temple had been associated in the Gospels, in their reference to the tearing of the great veil in the Temple at the time Jesus died (see Matt. 27:51; Mark 15:38; Luke 23:45). But in Hebrews, it is as if Jesus' death (c. 30 C.E.) and the burning of the Temple under Titus (70 C.E.) happened at the same time! It is not clear what exactly the author made of the interim of forty years between the two events: they are conflated in the central focus on the eternal significance of what Jesus accomplished.

Moreover, the passage takes it for granted that Jesus' body was a kind of "tabernacle," an instrument of sacrifice (9:11). Hebrews makes that specification of the cultic meaning of Jesus because the Gospels speak of his referring to his "body" and his "blood" in the words of the institution of the eucharist. Similarly, John's Gospel actually has Jesus refer to "the temple of his body" in 2:21;[13] it would seem that Hebrews is continuing to explore that sacrificial meaning. "Body" and "blood" here are Jesus' self-immolating means to his end as high priest. The Temple in Jerusalem has in Hebrews been replaced by a purely theological construct. The true high priest has entered once for all (9:12) within the innermost recess of sanctity, so that no further sacrificial action is necessary or appropriate.

In Hebrews the homiletic conviction of Luke, that Scripture finds its purpose in Jesus, is elevated to the status of a theory. Hermeneutics that had attested the resurrection (for example in Luke 24:25–27) have now become the hermeneutics of preexistence. Jesus lives because he was always alive, and in the light of his activity one can finally understand what Scripture was speaking of. The destruction of the Temple in 70 C.E. was an advantage, because it enables us to distinguish the image from the reflection.

In the conception of Hebrews, the Temple on earth was a copy and shadow of the heavenly sanctuary, of which Moses had seen "types."[14] A type (*tupos,* "impression" in Greek) is an impress, a derived version of a reality (the anti-type). Moses had seen the very throne of God, which was then approximated on earth in the sacrificial cult. That approximation is called the "first covenant" (9:1), but the heavenly sanctuary, into which Christ has entered (9:24),

✡
**13**
✝

offers us a "new covenant" (9:15) that is the truth that has been palely reflected all along.

The concluding three chapters of Hebrews shape all that has preceded into an ethical appeal in order to influence the behavior of those who read and hear the epistle. Literal sacrifice is to be eschewed (10:1–18), and the approach to God in purity is now by means of Jesus (10:19–22). The confession is to be maintained, love and good works are to be encouraged, communal gatherings are to continue as the day of the Sovereign approaches (10:23–25).

Above all, there is to be no turning back, no matter what the incentives (10:26–39). Faith in that sense is praised as the virtue of the patriarchs, prophets, and martyrs of old, although they were not perfected (11:1–40). Jesus alone offers perfection, as "the pioneer and perfecter of our faith" (12:1–3). Many incidental commandments follow: do not be afraid of shedding your blood (12:4), do not become immoral or irreligious in leaving old ways behind (12:16), give hospitality and care for prisoners and those who are mistreated (13:1–3), honor marriage and do not love money (13:4–5), respect leaders and beware false teaching (13:7, 9, 17), remember to share and to pray (13:16, 18). Interesting as those commands are individually (especially in drawing a social profile of the community addressed [see below]), the overriding theme is evident and carries the weight of the argument (12:14): "Pursue peace with all, and sanctification, apart from which no one will see God." Divine vision, the sanctification to stand before God, is in Hebrews the goal of human life, and the only means to such perfection is loyalty to Jesus as the great high priest.

The sense of finality, of a perfection from which one must not defect, is deliberately emphasized (12:22–24): "But you have come to Mount Zion and the city of the living God, the heavenly Jerusalem, and to myriads of angels in festal gathering, and to the assembly of firstborn enrolled in heaven, and to a judge—God of all, and to the spirits of the just who are made perfect, and to Jesus the mediator of a new covenant, and to sprinkled blood which speaks better than the blood of Abel." Jesus, the only mediator of perfection, provides access to that heavenly place, which is the city of the faithful, the heart's only sanctuary.

## HEBREWS' NEW RELIGION

The themes of Hebrews were to become the themes of catholic Christianity. The Son of God would be understood as inherently and obviously superior to the angels, to Moses and Joshua, as the great high priest who alone provides access to the only sanctuary that matters. Framing a single confession of his heavenly location in relation to the divine throne was to require literally centuries of discussion within the church, but the necessity of such a confession was axiomatic.

Because Hebrews' themes became widespread, their development in the epistle will strike most readers as needlessly elaborate. But those themes were discovered only because the author maintained his rigorously christological focus on Melchizedek, so that the bread, the wine, and the blessing he gave Abram became the key to Jesus' superiority in the bread and the wine of a new and better covenant. Moses' prescriptions are shadows, imitations of the heavenly sanctuary, which Jesus has actually entered. The Temple in Jerusalem has in Hebrews been replaced by a conception of the divine throne in heaven and the faithful congregation on earth, and Jesus' perfect sacrifice is the unique and perfect link between the two.

Hebrews so centrally locates Jesus as the locus of revelation that it became inevitable to ask about his nature(s) and his consciousness in a way that was not current before, *because Hebrews develops a religious system that derives completely from Jesus.*

Comparison with the earlier systems of Christian Judaism enables us clearly to characterize the achievement of Hebrews. Where the obvious question in Christian Judaism was the nature of Israel, the natural question that emerges from Hebrews is the nature(s) of Christ. We can see an indication of that change immediately by placing the "Israel" of Hebrews in the context of the often divisive concern to define Israel within the movement of Jesus from its earliest phase.

Jesus had insisted on a policy of treating all of Israel as Israel, as was seen in the Preface (pp. xv–xix). God's people were in the classic sense "pure"—ready by celebration and customary practice

✿

15

✞

to accept and enter the kingdom of God. For Peter, that made Jesus a new Moses, as may be seen in the narrative of the Transfiguration (Matt. 17:1–9; Mark 9:2–10; Luke 9:28–36). Just as there is an implicit comparison between the followers of Jesus and the Israel that followed Moses out of Egypt, the prophetic covenant of Moses and the divine sonship of Jesus stand side by side. James's point of departure was David, rather than Moses. Here, the belief of Gentiles causes, not the redefinition of Israel, but the restoration of the house of David, which is committed to preserve Israel in its purity (see Acts 15:13–21). But Paul began with Abraham, who in his theology embodied a principle of believing that was best fulfilled by means of faith in and through Jesus Christ (see Gal. 3). The synoptic Gospels, in their variety, posit an *analogy* between Jesus and the figures of the Hebrew Bible: Christ becomes the standard by which Israel's Scripture is experienced, corrected, and understood to have been fulfilled. This development of interpretation is explained below in "The Power of Analogy in Primitive Christianity and Early Christianity." An excellent example is provided by the way in which the story of Peter's confession of Jesus at Caesarea Philippi (Matt. 16:13–23; Mark 8:27–33; Luke 9:18–22) rejects any simple identification of Jesus in biblical terms. John's nuance is sophisticated, but plain: Jesus is the true Israel, attested by the angels of God, by whom all the families of the earth will be blessed (see John 1:51, in comparison with Gen. 28:10–22).

All such options are brushed aside in Hebrews. The author understands Israel, literally, as a thing of the past, the husk of the first, now antiquated covenant. He says the word "Israel" just three times. Twice in chapter 8 he refers to Israel, but simply as part of his quotation of Jeremiah 31:31–34, where to his mind a completely new covenant is promised (Heb. 8:8, 10). The point of that citation, as elaborated by the author, is that the new covenant makes the former covenant obsolete (8:13). Accordingly, when the author speaks of Israel in his own voice, it is simply to refer to "the sons of Israel" in the past, at the time of the exodus from Egypt (11:22).[15] Melchizedek is a positive, theological category. Israel is no longer, and remains only as a cautionary tale from history.

The ability of the author of Hebrews to relegate Israel to history is related to the insistence, from the outset of the epistle, that the Son's authority is greater than that of the Scripture. Once, God spoke in many and various ways through the prophets; now, at the end of days, God speaks to us by a son (Heb. 1:1, 2). The comparative judgment is reinforced, when the author observes that, if the word delivered by angels (that is, the Torah[16]) carried with it retribution for transgression, how much more should we attend to what we have heard concerning the Son (Heb. 2:1–4). The implication of both statements is clear: Scripture is only authoritative to the extent that it attests the salvation mediated by the Son (1:14; 2:3–4). The typology that is framed later in the epistle between Jesus and the Temple derives directly from the conviction of the prior authority of the Son of God in relation to Scripture.[17]

The dual reevaluation, of Israel and of Israel's Scripture, is what permits Hebrews to trace its theology of Christ's replacement of every major institution, every principal term of reference, within the Judaisms of its time. Before Hebrews, there were Christian Judaisms, in which Christ was in various ways conceived of as the key to the promises to Israel. Hebrews' theology proceeds from those earlier theologies, and it remains a Christian Judaism, in the sense that all of its vocabulary of salvation is drawn from the same Scriptures that were axiomatic within the earlier circles.

But the Christian Judaism of Hebrews is also and self-consciously a system of Christianity, because all that is Judaic is held to have been provisional until the coming of the Son, after which point it is no longer meaningful. There is a single center within the theology of Hebrews. It is not Christ with Moses, Christ with Temple, Christ with David, Christ with Abraham, Christ with Scripture, Christ with Israel. In the end, the center is not really even Christ with Melchizedek, because Melchizedek disappears in the glory of his heavenly archetype. Christ is the beginning, middle, and end of theology in Hebrews, just as he is the same yesterday, today, and forever (Heb. 13:8). Everything else is provisional—and expendable—within the consuming fire that is God (12:29).

The intellectual achievement of Hebrews may be gauged by comparing its insistence on Christ as the unique center of faith

✿

✞

with the presentations of previous circles of thought and practice. The care with which the Petrine circle presented Jesus with Moses in the Transfiguration (see Mark 9:4) is simply abandoned, when the author of Hebrews remarks, as if in passing, that Jesus was counted worthy of more glory than Moses was (Heb. 3:2–6). Similarly, James's emphasis on the Davidic promise in Jesus (see Acts 15:13–21) is all but ignored in Hebrews, as David appears only as the author of Psalms (Heb. 4:7) and as one of a string of heroes from the past (11:32). And chapter 9 of Hebrews, of course, sets aside any continuing interest in the Temple in Jerusalem, where James's authority was centered (see Acts 21:17–26).

Comparison between Paul and Hebrews is natural.[18] Paul presented Jesus as the fulfillment of God's promises to Abraham (Gal. 3:6–9), and argued that the fulfillment of the promise meant that Torah could no longer be looked on as a requirement (Gal. 3:19–29). Paul brands any attempt to require non-Jews to keep the Torah as a consequence of baptism as "Judaizing" (Gal. 2:14). That theology is obviously a precedent for the author of Hebrews, who proceeds to refer openly to a new covenant superseding the old (8:13).

But for Paul "all Israel" was the object of God's salvation (Rom. 11:26), just as the covenant fulfilled by Jesus was nothing other than the covenant with Abraham (so Gal. 3:15–18). For that reason, Scripture in Paul's thought is a constant term of reference; from it derives the coherent narrative of a covenant revealed to Abraham, guarded under Moses, and fulfilled in Christ. By contrast, Christ is the only coherent principle in Hebrews, and Scripture is a mine from which types may be quarried.

Hebrews' technique of argumentation is a logical extension of the allegorical and symbolic readings presented in the synoptics and in John. But the synoptics and John accept, in the manner of Philo of Alexandria, that Scripture is to be used—at least for some—to regulate behavior, as well as to uncover divine truth. When the synoptics compare Jesus to Elijah (see Matt. 16:14; Mark 8:28; Luke 9:19), and when John presents him as Jacob (John 1:51), the assumption is that Elijah and Jacob have their own meaning, and that some people will live loyally within their understandings of Elijah's or Jacob's presentation of the God of Israel. In Hebrews, the past is of interest principally as a counterexample to the city that is to come (see Heb. 13:14), and old ways are to be left behind (Heb. 10:1–18).

Instead of invoking Scripture, or even an account (such as Paul's) of the covenantal meaning of Scripture, the author of Hebrews ties his ethical imperatives directly to the example of Jesus. The community is to overcome its fear of shedding blood (Heb. 12:4) by considering the perfection of Jesus (12:1–3). That perfection is held to exclude immoral or irreligious ways, because they are not compatible with the grace of God (12:15–17). The perspective on social policy is strikingly more assured than in any other document in the New Testament: the author of Hebrews can say precisely and without argument, when most of his predecessors could not, just how Jesus' example is to be followed and what behavior causes God to withdraw God's grace.

Hebrews is written to a community that views the teaching of Jesus alone as regulative. Scripture, the Old Testament (the only form of Scripture then available[19]), is simply the foreshadowed truth of what Jesus the great high priest fully reveals. The community is addressed as a whole; most of its people have already received baptism (6:1–3), and they know right from wrong in the light of Jesus' teaching. They need to be urged to continue meeting together (10:25), despite what is called "the custom of some." The existence of factions within a community in which there is general consensus is therefore suggested, and that impression is confirmed by the particular appeal to obey leaders (13:17).

With Hebrews a Christian Judaism becomes a closed system, Christianity complete within its own terms of reference. The epistle does not deal with circumcision, with a Temple that is standing, or in particular with any contemporary synagogue of Judaism. Its orientation is global. Primitive Christianity here becomes, before the reader's eyes, early Christianity. After Hebrews, it will be apparent to Christians that any loyalty to Judaism is a throwback, to be tolerated or not, but always off the center of the religious system. Before Hebrews, there were Christian Judaisms; after Hebrews, the appearance of any institution of Judaism within the church will be seen to be a form of Jewish Christianity.

The early Christianity of Hebrews was not yet in the classical mode that emerged during the second century, within the terms of reference of popular philosophical discussion. Hebrews' Christianity is "early," not classical. Although it replaces the institutions of Israel with Christ, that replacement is taken to be complete in itself, without the addition of other forms of thought. Interpretation here makes an early Christianity out of the Christian Judaism of its community, and offers the result to those who followed, and wrestled in philosophical terms with this Son of God who also suffered for humanity as a whole. Hebrews represents the early Christianity that was to become catholic Christianity, the target of our discussion here.

## PUBLIC JUDAISM, PRIVATE CHRISTIANITY

At the beginning of the Common Era, the Judaism that the ancient world encountered presented a view of God so appealing in its rationality and accessibility as to compete with various philosophical schools for the loyalty of educated people in the Greco-Roman world. Christianity, for its part, formed a marginal group, neither fully Judaic nor seriously philosophical. Judaism formed part of the established comity of the Roman Empire; its adherents enjoyed the protection of the state for the free exercises of their particular rites, not to mention for the abstinences that distinguished them from others. By contrast, Christianity identified with a convicted criminal, who perished in an odious form of execution. It presented the world with stories of its founder, martyred and risen from the dead. Judaism, represented by the Mishnah, set forth a doctrine of the social order encompassing a politics, an economics, and a philosophy that involved philosophical method to attain philosophical standing for its theological convictions.[20] Christianity's founder dismissed politics, presented no economic system as part of his message but only a certain attitude toward wealth as ephemeral, and neither in modes of thought nor, indeed, even in concerns of reflection could he have been confused with the philosophers of the day.

Over the next four centuries, Judaism and Christianity traded places. Judaism no longer addressed the world at large with propositions of generally intelligible truth attained through broadly accepted modes of inquiry and analysis, but made its statement in another idiom altogether, one that was inner-facing and framed in details. Economics in the conventional sense no longer served as a principal medium for systemic expression. Politics conceived "Israel" not as a state possessed of legitimacy, including access to legitimate violence, but now as a supernatural community, exempt from history. Exegesis of a received text, a particular kind of exegesis of a rather private set of revealed texts, took the place of a public, generally accessible philosophy, method and substance alike. And, at the end, Christianity put forth a new history of humanity, from Adam forward, in light of what had now taken place; it announced principles of politics serving to govern all of humanity; and it conceived of itself as bearer of a general truth, capable of philosophical re-presentation. So Christianity formulated its truth in generally accessible terms and framed its statement in philosophically accessible language.

Along these same lines, too, at the beginning Judaism was a licit, Christianity an illicit, religion; at the end, Judaism was (at best) tolerated, and Christianity governed. In the beginning, Christians conceived not of power but of martyrdom, invoking not this-worldly but supernatural and moral force. In the end, "Israel" had become an enchanted world, and Christianity, a fully empowered and paramount presence in Greco-Roman, hence in Western, civilization. In the beginning Judaism actively sought converts, while Christianity for a brief time actually contemplated limiting its appeal to those already within Israel; in the end Judaism withdrew from the competition for converts, accepting without vigorous encouragement the few who persisted.

## Symbol Change and Social Change

Symbol change, such as we consider here, ratifies social and political change; we do not invoke otherworldly or mysterious considerations in explaining how the religions changed places. Changes did not take place incrementally but drastically, again because of sudden political change bearing profound and long-term consequences. Specifically, the status of Israel, viewed as the holy people, changed as its rival for the patrimony of Scripture, Christianity, gained power.[21] If Christianity set forth a politics in the fourth century but not in the first, if Judaism did so in the earlier time but not later on, it is because power relationships demanded a Christian politics and made moot a Judaic one. The two religions changed places, the one taking at the end the positions of the other at the outset, because at the end the situation of each, defined by its relationship to political power, came to correspond with that of the other at the outset. The histories "intersected"— rather than running parallel—because at a determinate point, the conditions to which they accommodated drastically changed. The weak became strong, the established lost its position, and—and this is the point of this book—the rest followed. So this is a book about what happens when the oppressed and persecuted take power, and when disestablishment defines the destiny of a formerly confident and capable political community.

Take the case of the canon, for example. Between the second and fourth centuries Christianity added to the received Torah a further authoritative, divinely inspired Scripture, forming the New Testament, and so created the Bible. The Hebrew Scriptures, the written Torah, now demanded a reading as the Old Testament, predicting the New. Why? Because political change now proved that Scripture's prophetic promises of a king-Messiah had pointed toward Jesus, now Christ enthroned. Concomitantly, the teleology of the Israelite system of old, focused as it was on the coming of the Messiah, now found confirmation and realization in the rule of Jesus, again, Christ enthroned. And the symbol of the whole— hermeneutics, teleology alike—rose in heaven's heights: the cross that had triumphed at the Milvian Bridge (see chap. 1, pp. 57–58). For its part, the Mishnah's Judaism, which had formerly treated the Messiah theme in the context of the hierarchization of leadership—priest, general, and politician ("king") alike—now accorded to the Messiah theme remarkable prominence. The heirs of the Mishnah, Rabbinic Judaism's sages, now pointed toward an eschatological teleology, to be realized in the coming of the Messiah when Israel's condition, defined by the one whole Torah of Sinai, itself warranted. And, it would necessarily follow, the symbol of the Torah would expand to encompass the teleology and hermeneutic at hand. Salvation comes from the Torah, not the cross. So point by point, the principles of the Judaism turn out in the fresh reading of the Talmud of the Land of Israel, coming to closure at the end of the fourth century, to respond point by point to the particular challenge of the principal event of that century.

## THE POWER OF ANALOGY IN PRIMITIVE CHRISTIANITY AND EARLY CHRISTIANITY

As discussed above, the Epistle to the Hebrews provides us with a lens through which to view the emergence of early Christianity: a religious system in which the major terms of reference of Judaism were subsumed by Christ, and therefore effectively replaced. What occurred in that epistle was momentous, and no one can take away the achievement of its anonymous author. At the same time, it is obvious that Hebrews was building on a symbolic language that had begun to move in the direction that the epistle followed. Moreover, Hebrews must have struck a deep chord already within primitive Christianity, in order for it to become the best representative of the new phenomenon, early Christianity, which can be said to exist from its time.

The first three Gospels (Matthew, Mark, and Luke) provide the best examples of the symbolic language that Hebrews took up, refined, and made the very basis of the fledgling movement. These Gospels represent a standard for the preparation of candidates for baptism within the new movement.

The first three Gospels are called synoptic in scholarly discussion because they may be viewed together when they are printed in columns. Unfortunately, their obviously literary relationship has caused scholars to assume that they were composed by scribes working in isolation who copied one from another. A comparative approach,[22] served by an understanding of the development of tradition into documents both within early Judaism and early Christianity, has brought us to the point where deviations of one document from another, related document are not as-

✿
23
✞

sumed to be purely scribal changes. After all, the Gospels were not written by individual scholars for a learned public; the synoptics rather represent how distinct communities, in contact with one another directly and indirectly, nurtured new members. Agreements and disagreements among the synoptic Gospels provide a way to see how different communities of Christians pursued a common program of catechism, but in distinctive ways.

The story of the confession of Peter at Caesarea Philippi (Matt. 16:13–23; Mark 8:27–33; Luke 9:18–22) presents an example of synoptic instruction in how to understand Jesus through the lens of the faith that is confessed at baptism. Jesus himself poses the question of his identity in the opening ("Who do people say I am?" in Mark), and the disciples reply with a startling range of biblically based answers, in which Jesus is identified in prophetic terms. He is said to be John the baptizer,[23] Elijah, or one of the prophets. In seeing Jesus in the Bible, and the Bible in Jesus, the disciples' response to Jesus' question immediately introduces us to a use of Scripture that is out of the ordinary. The prophets are not referred to as purely from the past, but are taken to be alive and effective in the ministry of Jesus.

The common element in these understandings is that they involve an approach to the Bible as a matter of experience. Jesus is seen in immediately prophetic terms; the prophets' activity lives on in the case of Jesus. Jesus was a catalyst for his followers and in the memory of the church; he set off a reaction between the Bible of the time and those who read the Bible. The experience of him was such that in the synoptic Gospels biblical language and imagery became the vehicle of understanding and expressing what was happening in the case of Jesus. Jesus had taken his principal theme, the kingdom of God, from the Bible of his day (the Aramaic paraphrases known as the Targums). For him, however, the kingdom was not simply a promise contained in the Bible, but a reality that was changing the world. The principle that the Scripture refers to facts of experience was accepted by those who tried to understand Jesus as one of the prophets.

But Jesus in the synoptic narrative is not content with a simple identification of himself with one of the prophets of old; he replies, "But who do you yourselves say I am?" The question is also a demand. The demand of Jesus is to use the measure of Scripture in a critical way, not only as a matter of experience. His disciples are to see him as important, like John, Elijah, or another prophet, but also as crucially different.

By refusing to embrace any one prophetic designation in the story, Jesus presses Peter on to use the title "Christ" or "Messiah," one of the most flexible terms in the Hebrew Bible.[24] It might refer, depending on context, to a king in the line of David, to a high priest readied for his office, or to a prophet commissioned to convey his message. The associations of the term with empowered anointing are evident, but Jesus then proceeds to relate the term to his own suffering. A criticism of the received understanding of Scripture is obvious here: it simply will not do to identify Jesus directly with the charisma of the prophets, with the might of kings, or with the dignity of priests. Jesus in the story insists on his difference from such figures.

His difference, his individuality, does not reside in his claim to be greater than an Elijah or any anticipated Messiah. After all, Jesus did not expect to be taken up alive into heaven, as was said of Elijah (see 2 Kings 2:9–12), and no one ever said that he actually ruled as the Messiah of Israel. Jesus' distinctiveness is a matter of his suffering, which the story of Caesarea Philippi places alongside the prophetic and messianic designations as the key to Jesus' identity. The synoptic Jesus insists not only that Scripture be seen as a matter of experience, but that the critical difference between present experience and the biblical testimony is as important for our understanding of God as the similarity between the two.

In a single word, there is an *analogy* between Jesus and the figures of the Hebrew Bible. He is experienced in terms of what they were, and yet he is also seen as different; and in that difference lies the meaning of his teaching and his action. Jesus liked to refer to Scripture as fulfilled in his ministry.[25] He called attention to both similarities and critical distinctions between what was said of God in Scripture and what he saw of God as a matter of experience. The promises to Israel might lead you to expect that the feast of the kingdom was to exclude those outside the nation, but Jesus

✡

**25**

♰

anticipated that people would stream in from everywhere and that the exclusions that took place would be surprising (see Matt. 8:11, 12; Luke 13:28, 29). The analogy between Scripture and experience is rooted in the sensibility that a given biblical text is identifying and describing the God we experience. But under Jesus' approach there is no sense in which Scripture can be said to limit what God does and is about to do. In the synoptic development of that approach, there is a stable analogy, not an identity, between Jesus and Scripture.

The experience of God as biblical is only the beginning, or the occasion, of the Bible's authority. Jesus refused to limit himself to the repetition of the biblical text: he was noted (and notorious) for departing from agreed norms in order to speak of God. Who else within his time and setting would compare the kingdom of the one, almighty God with a woman baking bread (Luke 13:20–21)? In addition to being experiential in reference to Scripture, Jesus was also critical. His critical perspective, of course, was not historical; rather, his creative adaptation of biblical language and imagery evidences an awareness that God in the text and God in experience do not entirely coincide. The synoptics honor that awareness in their analogical presentation of Jesus and Scripture.

Because the God of the Bible is experienced, and yet—as experienced—may not be contained within the biblical text, the trademark of Jesus' instrumental use of Scripture is "fulfillment." By referring to Scripture as fulfilled, Jesus claimed to resolve the tension between the coincidence and the distance of the biblical God from his own experience. When, for example, Jesus says in the synagogue in Nazareth, "Today this Scripture has been fulfilled in your ears," he does not literally mean that he did everything referred to in the passage from Isaiah he has just read (see Luke 4:16–21). The simple facts are that Isaiah 61:1, 2 refers to things Jesus never did, such as releasing prisoners from jail, and that Jesus did things the text makes no mention of, such as declaring people free of impurity (see Matt. 8:2–4; Mark 1:40–45; Luke 5:12–16).

By means of their example, the synoptic Gospels establish a thoroughly christological technique in the interpretation of Scripture as fulfilled. Christ, the guarantor of the kingdom, is the standard by which Scripture is experienced, corrected, and understood to have been fulfilled. There is here still no articulated theory of the relationship between Christ and Scripture; that would come later. But the synoptics did insist that the catechesis of believers who sought baptism should include the christological technique of understanding the Scriptures.

Inevitably, social questions emerged in a movement that included Jews and non-Jews: did the acceptance of non-Jews imply their full fellowship with Jewish believers? Could they, for example, eat together (in breach of most understandings of Jewish rules concerning the preparation of food)? In their response to that question, such principal leaders of the movement as Peter, James, and Paul went their separate ways. Paul reports favorably on the practice in Antioch before emissaries from James came, when meals could be conducted with common fellowship among Jewish and non-Jewish followers of Jesus (see Gal. 2:12). According to Paul, the arrival of those emissaries caused Peter to separate from non-Jews, and even Barnabas confirmed the policy of separation (Gal. 2:12–13). The tendency of Hellenistic communities of Christians to mix their Jewish and non-Jewish constituencies, and therefore to relax or ignore issues of purity in foods, is here documented by Paul (c. 53 C.E.).

Within the synoptic Gospels, Jesus himself is portrayed as resolving the question of fellowship at meals by means of two meals whose presentation is laden with symbolism. That is an example of how the synoptics reflect the catechesis of the early followers of Jesus. The symbolic recitation of the synoptic communities presents two stories of feeding, one of five thousand people and one of four thousand. In the first story (Matt. 14:13–21; Mark 6:32–44; Luke 9:10b–17), the eucharistic associations are plain: Jesus blesses and breaks the bread prior to distribution (Matt. 14:19; Mark 6:41; Luke 9:16). That emphasis so consumes the story, the fish—characteristic among Christian eucharistic symbols—are of subsidiary significance by the end of the story (compare Mark 6:43 with Matt. 14:20 and Luke 9:17). Whatever the pericope represented originally, it becomes a eucharistic narrative in the meaning of the synoptics. Jesus gathers people in an orderly way (see Matt. 14:19; Mark 6:39, 40; Luke 9:14, 15), by "symposia" as Mark literally has it (6:39); without that order, they might be described as sheep without a shepherd (Mark 6:34).

A valuable literary source from the turn of the first and second centuries relates the prayer that, just as bread is scattered on the mountains (in the form of wheat)[26] and yet is gathered into one, so the church might be gathered into the Father's kingdom (*Didache* 9:4). The 5,000 congregate in such a manner, their very number a multiple of the prophetic gathering in 2 Kings 4:42–44,[27] and Luke 9:11 has Jesus speaking to them concerning the kingdom, making the same connection that the *Didache* does.

The authority of the Twelve is a marked concern within the story. Their return in Matt. 14:12b, 13; Mark 6:30, 31; and Luke 9:10a after their commission (see Matt. 10:1–42; Mark 6:7–13; Luke 9:1–6) is what occasions the feeding, and their function in the proceedings is definite: Jesus gives them the bread, to give it to others (Matt. 14:19; Mark 6:41; Luke 9:16). Their place here is cognate with their position within another pericope (from the cycle of James's teaching), which features the Twelve, the parable of the sower, its interpretation, and the assertion that only the Twelve possess the mystery of the dominion (Matt. 13:1–23; Mark 4:1–20; Luke 8:4–15).[28] Such a mystery is also conveyed here, in the assertion that twelve baskets of fragments were gathered after the five thousand ate. The lesson is evident: the Twelve will always have enough to feed the church, and the church itself corresponds to the twelve tribes of Israel.

The story of the feeding of the four thousand (Matt. 15:32–39; Mark 8:1–10) follows so exactly that of the five thousand that its omission by Luke—perhaps as a redundant doublet—may seem understandable. The four thousand are a multiple of the four points of the compass, the story follows that of the Canaanite or Syrophoenician woman (Matt. 15:21–28; Mark 7:24–30), and concerns a throng from a number of different areas and backgrounds (see Matt. 15:21, 29; Mark 7:24, 31). Likewise, the number 7, the number of bushels of fragments here collected, corresponds to the deacons of the Hellenists in the church of Jerusalem (cf. Acts

6:1–6), and is related to the traditional number of the seventy nations within Judaism.[29]

Moreover, the reference to Jesus as "giving thanks" over the bread in Matt. 15:36 and Mark 8:6 better corresponds to the Hellenistic version of the eucharist in Luke 22:17, 19 and 1 Corinthians 11:24 than does "blessed" in Matthew 14:19 or Mark 6:39, which better corresponds to the earlier formula in Matthew 26:26 and Mark 14:22.

After the second feeding, Jesus rebukes his disciples for a failure to understand when he warns them about the leaven of the Pharisees and others, and asks whether they truly grasp the relationship between the number 12 and the 5,000 and the number 7 and the 4,000 (Matt. 16:5–12; Mark 8:14–21). In the Hellenistic catechesis, the meaning is clear, and its implications for eucharistic discipline are evident.[30] Full celebration of eucharist is neither to be limited to Jews, as the program of James would have it, nor to be forced upon communities in a way that would require Jews to accept reduced standards of purity, as the Pauline program would have it. There is for the Hellenistic catechesis, of which the synoptic transformation is a monument, an ongoing apostolate for Jews and Gentiles, prepared to feed as many of the church that gather.

## THE EMERGENCE OF THE CANON
## OF THE NEW TESTAMENT

Having Gospels is not the same thing as reading them alongside the acknowledged Bible of Israel. The Bible of the earliest church, from the time of Jesus until much later, consisted first and foremost of the Scriptures of Judaism (only later known commonly as the Old Testament). The books that were to be included in the Old Testament were a matter of general agreement. The book of Jesus ben Sira, also known as Ecclesiasticus, already refers in its prologue (written around 132 B.C.E.) to the Law, the Prophets, and other books. Its division of the Bible corresponds to the threefold division that became conventional among the rabbis. The first five books (the Pentateuch) were known as the Law proper. "Prophets" designated both the classical prophetic writings and what we think of as historical works (such as the books of Kings). "Writings" referred to the remainder. Luke 24:44 similarly refers to the Law of Moses, the Prophets, and the psalms. But there was considerable debate among Jews and Christians throughout the period of the New Testament concerning exactly which books did and did not qualify for reading in synagogue. The Song of Songs, for instance, caused great doubt. But Josephus, the Jewish historian of the first century, shows that by that time the contents of the Bible were a matter of broad agreement.[31]

Other writings were greatly revered, but they did not come to be included within the Hebrew Bible. Some of them were included in the Greek translation of the Scriptures of Israel known as the Septuagint (because it was held to be the work of some seventy Hebrew translators working in Egypt). One of these is the book of Jesus ben Sira, which has already been mentioned; another is the Wisdom of Solomon.

At the time of the Reformation, these works were treated differently from the rest of the Old Testament, because the Hebrew Bible did not include them. They were called the Apocrypha (a term used long before by St. Jerome), "hidden," "secret," or "obscure" works of uncertain origin. The designation is still commonly used, although it seems clear that Hebrew originals of at least some of these works once did exist; fragments of ben Sira discovered at Masada prove that point.[32] In any case, it is important to bear in mind that early Christians did not think of these Scriptures as "apocryphal"; the book of Jesus ben Sira (11:18, 19), for example, finds an echo in the New Testament (Luke 12:16–21).

In addition to the Apocrypha, other works were read by many Jews, even though they were not included in the Hebrew Bible or the Septuagint. Among the best known of them is the Book of Enoch (or 1 Enoch, to distinguish it from other works in Enoch's name), parts of which were found at Qumran. Books of this sort are known as the pseudepigrapha because many of them were falsely attributed to ancient authorities (such as Enoch himself). Again, however, it would be rash to suppose that the first Christians would have been happy with our modern category: 1 Enoch 1:9 is cited as Scripture in the New Testament's brief letter of Jude

(14–15). The general picture that emerges is that Christians were happy to read the Scriptures of Israel, the "Old Testament," as normally recognized, and that therefore the list of the books that were accepted varied from church to church.

The drastic step that Christians took from the point of view of Judaism was the reading of other works alongside the Scriptures of Israel during the course of worship and instruction. From the time of the mission of Paul as remembered in Acts (see 13:13–43), Christians had been given the opportunity to speak in synagogues after the Bible had been read. They took that opportunity to relate the Scriptures to Jesus, the object of their faith. But in their worship apart from synagogues, Christians developed their own practices. Justin Martyr, a writer of the second century, refers to memoirs of the apostles as well as writings of the prophets being read in churches (*Apology,* 67). Such "memoirs," which we would recognize as the Gospels of the New Testament, already had a long history by the time of Justin, as has been discussed in the last section. The apostles had been sent by Jesus himself to spread his message, and their remembrance of Jesus and their understanding of him were recollected, developed, and treasured in the early church. By the second century, the apostolic memoirs and letters were read in churches as a matter of course alongside or instead of Scripture; effectively, they *were* Scripture.

Christian writers from the second century, such as Justin, amply attest the esteem in which various documents of the New Testament were held. Indeed, there is even reference within the New Testament itself (2 Pet. 3:15–16) to the reading of Paul's letters. But only gradually did there emerge a standard, or canon (from the Greek *kanon,* "measure"), of which documents were to be used in public worship and instruction. The canon of the New Testament was formed less because there was a positive desire for a published list than because the fluid situation of early Christianity permitted certain groups to deviate unacceptably from normal practice.

During the second century, catholic Christianity came to define itself over and against Gnosticism. Gnosticism will be discussed further in chapters 2 and 3, but for the moment we may describe it as a movement that claimed that knowledge (*gnosis*) held

31

the secret to an existence of pure spirit, outside the constraints of human flesh. Marcion was among the most prominent of Gnostic teachers; he came from Asia Minor to Rome and founded his own community there during the middle of the second century.

He opposed the God of Jesus to the God of the Jews, and repudiated the use of the Hebrew Bible. Because the Scriptures of Israel also feature prominently within the document of the New Testament, Marcion also rejected the majority of them. His collection of acceptable works included only Luke's Gospel and ten letters of Paul, and even then, Marcion expunged what he considered to be Jewish additions to the texts.

Another immigrant to Rome (this time from Egypt), named Valentinus, was also a Gnostic. He was not the organizer Marcion was, but his teaching was very influential. He represents the wing of Gnosticism that was concerned with the existence of the present, evil world: how could it derive from God, who is truly good? Valentinus argued that the Father is transcendent, quite apart from and other than what we can see around us. The world came into existence after a series of quasi-divine beings were generated from the Father; the last of these was Wisdom. Wisdom desired to find her way back to the Father, but her ignorance led to spirit being imprisoned in matter. Such, according to Valentinus, is the predicament of spiritual people, who are trapped in the false world of matter, and only knowledge of the Father can save them.

Schemes of this kind may seem abstract and complicated, but they enjoyed a tremendous appeal during the second century. For all their complexity, they offered a theological account of the very human feeling of being trapped in an evil world, far from a remote spiritual home.

The early church tolerated a great deal of variety, but teachers such as Marcion and Valentinus appeared to catholics to remove too much of the God and the Scriptures of Israel, and to insist too much on their own, specialist readings of the New Testament. An early response to Marcionite and Valentinian teaching is contained in what is known as the Muratorian Canon after its discoverer (Lodovico Antonio Muratori). The dating of the document is still under discussion, but it addresses conditions of the second century in Rome, and expressly repudiates Marcion and Valentinus. The canon is little more than a list that names most of the works of what we now know as the New Testament, and makes some comments on the derivation of the documents from the apostles and their followers.

The canon has some remarkable inclusions and omissions, and its fragmentary condition fully explains neither. Although possibly in error, the Wisdom of Solomon is listed, a fact that may suggest that the debate about the canon fundamentally concerned Scripture as a whole in the mind of the anonymous writer, not the New Testament as a separate work. After the Revelation of John, he mentions a Revelation of Peter, but points out that it is not permitted to be read throughout the church. In other words, a principle of universal acceptance (catholicity) is set alongside a principle of apostolicity (the authorship of apostles or apostolic successors). A popular document called *The Shepherd of Hermas,* which features a series of angelic visions, is not to be read publicly, according to the canon, although it may be read privately. The canon recognized that *The Shepherd* was written recently in Rome, and was neither prophetic (in the sense of the Scriptures of Israel) nor apostolic. There is no apparent mention of 1 Peter or 2 Peter (unless the work called the Revelation of Peter has something to do with one or both of them), and none at all of Hebrews, James, or 3 John (unless it had been included in one of the earlier letters).

The Muratorian list reflects a canon that is provisional, and discussion concerning whether certain books should be included stretched out over centuries after the time the author of the list compiled his work. Hebrews and the Revelation were special objects of dispute, largely because their apostolic origin was seriously questioned. But in 367 C.E., Athanasius, bishop of the churches in Alexandria, wrote a festal letter that designates the canon of the New Testament as the twenty-seven books known today. The matter was not definitively settled by Athanasius, but his position was gradually accepted, both in the Greek-speaking east and the Latin-speaking west of the Christian world. It is notable that the formulation of the canon lagged behind the formulation of creeds; the fluidity of an earlier period was easier to tolerate in literary terms than it was in doctrinal terms. Nonetheless, the twin principles of apostolicity and catholicity were commonly agreed upon; it was in applying these principles that disputes arose.

The canon that emerged amounted to a refusal of some works, and an insistence that others should be recognized. *The Shepherd of Hermas* was rejected in spite of its popularity. Other works were also excluded, even though apostolic authorship was claimed for them. Most famous among them today is the *Gospel according to Thomas,* which was composed in a form in which we would recognize it during the second century. The "Judas Thomas" of whom the Gospel speaks is Judas, the brother of Jesus (see Mark 6:3). The term *Thomas* means "twin" in Aramaic, and this Judas was considered Jesus' twin brother in some Syriac traditions. But that identification was not widely accepted, and the *Gospel according to Thomas* was not considered as canonical, although it was in fact cited by theologians. The rejection of such works from the canon resulted not only from doubts about their actual authorship, but also from their lack of general acceptance. On the other hand, although the authorship of Hebrews was unknown, the wide acceptance of the epistle, and its general consistency with Paul's thought, meant that it was eventually included in the canon.

The terms "Apocrypha" and "pseudepigrapha" have been applied to early Christian documents outside the New Testament. The usage is perhaps unfortunate, since these terms are applied very differently in respect to the Hebrew Bible. The adjective "noncanonical" might be recommended as being more descriptive, and less prejudicial. In any case, it must be borne in mind that the canonical writings were by no means the only ones read by early Christians. The religious atmosphere of Christianity in Rome, for example, is better reflected in *The Shepherd of Hermas* than it is, say, in Matthew's Gospel. And although the *Gospel according to Thomas* seems to rely on the canonical Gospels for many of the sayings of Jesus it presents, some appear quite independent and may be authentic. And apart from its historical value in that sense, Thomas informs us in a unique way of the Syriac Christian ethos as it was moving in the direction of Gnosticism.

"Canon" is not essentially a historical category, whether by "history" we have in mind the story of Jesus or the experiences of early Christians. Sometimes, noncanonical works will tell us more about some activities of Jesus, and about certain communities of Christians, than do canonical documents. On the whole, the New Testament is earlier than the New Testament "Apocrypha" and "pseudepigrapha," but that does not make it more "historical" all of the time.

If the canon is not a historical category, what is it? It is the collection of those works which, after long and considered discussion, the church understood as so basic to its faith as to amount to a publishable standard of practice and belief. There has been a perennial debate between Protestants and Catholics whether the canon created the church or vice versa. Both positions are only partly true. It would be better to say that the various documents of the New Testament shaped the faith of the church, and that the church's understanding of its apostolic and catholic faith then determined the precise canon of the New Testament. For this reason, the canon as a whole reflects the faith of the church, as an index of its public theology.

# 1

# TRADING POLITICS

## HISTORICAL SURVEY: ROMAN IMPERIAL POLICY AND THE JUDEO-CHRISTIAN REVERSAL OF FORTUNES

In order to understand the magnitude of the changes confronting Judaism and Christianity during the period that concerns us, it will help to have clearly in mind the official policies and public circumstances that affected the treatment of both groups. Neither was immune from prejudice, but each enjoyed at least some degree of tolerance (if not actual toleration) within the Roman Empire, even during difficult times. And both came to know how the open encouragement of imperial officers could transform their fortunes.

### ISRAEL PRIOR TO CONTACT WITH THE ROMANS

The beginning of Roman contact with Judaism seemed to bode well for their relationship. The contact occurred just as the people of Judaea were recovering from a crisis that had threatened their survival. Indeed, their survival had by then been in question for a long time. By the year 721 B.C.E., the northern kingdom of Israel had been invaded by the Assyrian Empire; the most prominent people were sent into exile, and that Israel simply ceased to exist as a culture (see 2 Kings 17:6).

Spurred on by the demise of Israel in the north, whose people were lost to history, the prophets in the southern kingdom of Judah attempted to purify the life of their people. Isaiah urgently argued against foreign alliances, and insisted that fidelity to God alone would save Jerusalem; Jeremiah ceaselessly denounced faithlessness, and was prosecuted for his trouble; Ezekiel's enactments of coming disaster won him a reputation as a crank. But during the reign of Josiah, a royal reformation backed much of the critique of the prophets (cf. 2 Kings 22:1–23:30; 2 Chron. 34:1–35:27). Josiah established worship in the Temple according to covenantal norms; he centralized sacrifices, even of the Passover, in Jerusalem; he tolerated no foreign incursions. In his program, he was guided by a scroll of the Law, which was found in the Temple during the extensive work authorized by Josiah, a scroll that has, since antiquity, been associated with the present book of Deuteronomy.

Deuteronomy presses an agenda of radical centralization and separation from foreign nations such as impelled Josiah. But in 609 B.C.E., Josiah was killed in battle in an attempt to block the alliance between Pharaoh Neco and the Assyrians at a place called Megiddo. The impact of his death may be gauged by the impact of that name upon the apocalyptic tradition, in the form "Armageddon" (Rev. 16:16; see also Zech. 12:11).

The end of the kingdom of Judah came quickly after the death of Josiah. Culminating in 587 B.C.E., the Babylonian Empire, which had succeeded the Assyrians (cf. the book of Nahum), implemented a policy of exile, subsequent to their siege of Jerusalem and their destruction of the Temple. Had the course of events then followed what happened to Israel (that is, the northern kingdom, similarly exiled in 721 B.C.E.), there would today be no Judaism to study. The policy of exile involved the removal of royalty, priesthood, and aristocracy far from Jerusalem, with the intent that they would be absorbed by the culture of Babylon (see 2 Kings 24:10–17; 25:27–30).

Paradoxically, however, just the forces that must have seemed sure to destroy the religion of the covenant with God instead assured its survival, and provided for its international dimension. During the Babylonian exile, the priestly and prophetic movements joined forces to form a united program of restoration, which put a form of Israel back on the map within a generation. Even more influentially, they memorialized their vision of that Israel in a book, and made it classic ever after. The Pentateuch as we know it was completed during the fifth century. With the emergence of the Pentateuch, an ideal Israel, attributed to the regulations of Moses, emerged as a truly canonical standard.

The dispossession of Judah to Babylon, then, contributed to the priestly and prophetic hegemony that made restoration possible. But just as particularly priestly concerns are represented in the Pentateuch, the prophetic movement also brought a distinctive message to the canon. The prophets generally agreed with their priestly confederates that the land was to be possessed again, and post-exilic additions to the books of Isaiah (40–55), Jeremiah (23:1–8; 31), and Ezekiel (40–48) constitute eloquent propaganda of return. But the previous abuses of the kings and their sanctuaries made the prophetic movement insist that righteousness was the prior requirement of sacrifice, and that the events of the recent past were a warning. A Zechariah might be happy to set out the hope of a priestly Messiah beside the Davidic king who was to rule (chapters 3, 4, and 6), but the predominant emphasis fell on the crucial necessity of the removal of injustice (chapters 5, 7, and 8).

Moreover, eschatology became characteristic of the prophetic movement, both in additions to biblical prophets such as Isaiah and Ezekiel, and in fresh works such as Joel and Malachi: the contemporary governance, whether Persian, Ptolemaic, or Seleucid, and the present Temple were provisional, until an anointed king and an anointed priest would rule properly. Just the image of a priestly orientation redefined by the prophets is projected into the career of Ezra in the books of Ezra and Nehemiah: prophet, priest, and scribe become one in their insistence on the vision of classic Israel, centered on the restored Temple.

The great shift in policy that permitted the actual rebuilding of the Temple could not have been more dramatic. The Babylonian Empire fell to Cyrus the Persian, who in 538 B.C.E. permitted the people of Judah to return to their land. No wonder Cyrus is referred to as God's anointed, his "Messiah," in Isaiah 45:1! Although the politics of restoration proved complicated, a new Temple was dedicated on the ancient Solomonic site around 515 B.C.E.

The Temple as restored was, however, far from ideal. Some who remembered the splendor of Solomon's edifice are reported to have wept when they saw the results of the first efforts of restoration (Ezra 3:10–13). That imperfect focus nonetheless served to attract a permanent priesthood, and the notion of a canon provided focus to the prophetic movement: now a body of literature, which could be interpreted, was held to provide the guidance that individual prophets formerly gave. Indeed, it is notable that Ezra's own ministry involved guiding Israel on the basis of scriptural interpretation: the scribe emerges as the dominant religious personality, as the warrant of true prophecy and the arbiter of priestly conduct (see Neh. 8). But the appearance that scribal leadership was settled is more superficial than representative. Battles concerning the proper conduct of the cult, and the proper personnel of the priesthood, raged during the period of restored Israel, and powerful movements produced literatures outside scribal control. While the Pentateuch and what are called the Former Prophets (Joshua—2 Kings) and the Latter Prophets within Judaism may be attributed to the hegemony of priestly and prophet interests that has been described above, the category of "Writings" (the last in the three biblical divisions of traditional Judaism), together with the "Apocrypha" and the "pseudepigrapha," best characterizes other facets of the religion.

The book of Psalms represents a cultic piety centered on just those aspects that the book of Leviticus does not engage: the music, dance, poetry, prayer, and praise (the term "psalms," *tehillim,* means "songs of praise") that the Temple attracted. They speak more eloquently of the emotional effect of and popular participation in sacrificial worship than any other document in the Bible. Proverbs also represents a non-priestly, non-prophetic focus of piety in restored Israel, defined by prudential wisdom. Job and Ecclesiastes are other examples of the literature of divine wisdom within the canon. Initially, Wisdom is understood to be an aspect of God, which by knowing one can become familiar with God. "Wisdom" is a feminine noun, and came to be personified as a woman; by the time of Ecclesiasticus and *The Wisdom of Solomon,* she is considered a fundamental means of access to God.

*The Wisdom of Solomon* was composed in Greek during the first century B.C.E., but the focus on Wisdom is by no means unique to what is commonly called Hellenistic Judaism: contacts with Egyptian and Babylonian inquiries into divine Wisdom probably date from the time of the Israelite and Judean kings, as part of their characteristic syncretism. But unlike idolatry and polygyny, which were adamantly rejected by the prophets, Wisdom survived and prospered; Wisdom was embraced by Judaism as a suitable and fertile means of communion with God after the notion of the unique covenant with Israel had triumphed. In the case of Philo of Alexandria, whose lifetime straddled the end of the last era and the beginning of our own (25 B.C.E.–45 C.E.), the pursuit of Wisdom became a philosophical articulation of Judaism; he contributed an awareness of how Judaism and Hellenistic culture—whose contact is already obvious in the "Apocrypha" and "Pseudepigrapha"— might be related. Philo is unusually learned in his representation of a basic development of the Judaism of his period. His simultaneously Greco-Roman and Judaic notion of the *logos* (the "word" of God) is a case in point (see *On the Creation of the World*).

The legitimacy of the priesthood in the restored Temple, meanwhile, became increasingly disputed. The Persian regime gave way to Alexander the Great: among the dynasties of the generals who succeeded him (after his death in 323 B.C.E.), first the Egyptian Ptolemies and then the Syrian Seleucids largely maintained the enlightened settlement of the Persians in regard to Israel. The Seleucid monarch Antiochus IV (called Antiochus Epiphanes) is commonly portrayed as a great exception to the policy, and he did unquestionably occupy Jerusalem and arrange for a foreign cult in the sanctuary, which included the sacrifice of swine (a Hellenistic delicacy; 1 Macc. 1:20-64; Josephus, *Antiquities* 12 §248–56). But Antiochus entered the city as the protector of a high-priestly family, the Tobiads, who were then in dispute with the Oniad family (Josephus, *The Jewish War* 1 §31-35). Dispossessed, the latter group moved to Egypt, where a temple was built at Heliopolis, in a form different from the restored Temple in Jerusalem (*The Jewish War*

✡
**41**
✟

1 §33; 7 §420–32). The cult of Onias appears to have been of limited influence, but the mere existence in the period of restored Israel of an alternative cult, manned by legitimate pretenders to the high priesthood in Jerusalem, is eloquent testimony of deep divisions within the sacerdotal ranks, and within Judaism generally.

### EARLY JUDAISM AND THE ROMANS

"Early Judaism" may conveniently be dated from 167 B.C.E., with the entry of Antiochus IV into Jerusalem and his desecration of the Temple, but it is evident that the radical pluralization of Judaism prior to Jesus, of which Jesus was both a symptom and a result, is rooted in the flawed unity of restored Israel during the previous period. But Antiochus's campaign triggered both a fissure of interests and a reconfiguration of those interests, in a way that made pluralism the order of the day. The temple of Onias is only one example, but one that shows that the way in which sacrifice was offered, and by whom, was held by one familial group to be a better measure of the acceptability of worship than where sacrifice was offered. The definition of what truly made for Israel had by the second century B.C.E. separated various groups within Judaism from one another.

During the same period there was another group, defined by a desire to remain faithful to sacrifice in Jerusalem by an appropriate priesthood and a resistance to the demands of Antiochus. This group was known as "the faithful" (the famous *hasidim*). Among them was Mattathias, a country priest from Modin, whose son, Judas Maccabeus ("the hammer"), introduced the most powerful priestly rule Judaism has ever known. The family became known as the Maccabees and also as the Hasmoneans, after Hasmon, Mattathias's ancestor. Judas, as is well known, turned piety into disciplined revolt, including an alliance with Rome (1 Macc. 8) and a willingness to break the Sabbath for military reasons (1 Macc. 2:41), which saw the restoration of worship within the covenant in the Temple in 164 B.C.E. (1 Macc. 4:36–61). After Judas's death, his brother Jonathan was named high priest (10:20), and from that time until the period of Roman rule, the high priesthood was a Hasmonean prerogative.

Judas's treaty with the Roman republic (as it then was) involved mutual defense (see 1 Macc. 8). His success resided in his combination of priestly prerogatives and political acumen. That combination of priestly and royal power was too rapid for some, and simply unacceptable in the view of others. In strictly familial terms, the Hasmoneans could not claim the high priesthood as a right, and therefore competition with other families of priests was a factor in resistance to them. Moreover, the suspension of the Sabbath for military purposes and the arrogation of the high priesthood and the monarchy by the non-Davidic Hasmoneans seemed particularly vicious to many Jews. Antiochus had sanctioned apostasy, but the Hasmonean regime appeared to be compounding apostasy both in its initial resistance (breaking the Sabbath) and in its consolidation of power (compounding seizure of the high priesthood with the claim of monarchy).

The Book of Daniel certainly does not express overt opposition to the Hasmoneans, but it does represent the less activist, apocalyptic stance of many faithful Jews of the second century B.C.E. The eschatology of the prophets during the period of restored Israel is transformed into a scenario of the end time, in which the Temple would be restored by miraculous means, with the archangel Michael's triumph capped by the resurrection of the just and the unjust (cf. Dan. 12). Folk Judaism of the period also anticipated providential interventions (cf. Tobit), but Daniel elevates and specifies that anticipation until it becomes a program of patient attention and fidelity, warranted by both heavenly vision and the pseudepigraphical ascription to the sage of the Babylonian period.

In the case of the Essenes, opposition to the Hasmoneans became overt. They pursued their own system of purity, ethics, and initiation; they followed their own calendar; and they withdrew into their own communities, either within cities or in isolated sites such as Qumran. There they awaited a coming, apocalyptic war, when they, as "the sons of light," would triumph over "the sons of darkness," meaning not only the Gentiles, but anyone not of their vision. Their insistence upon a doctrine of two Messiahs, one of Israel and one of Aaron, would suggest that it was particularly the Hasmoneans' arrogation of priestly and royal powers that alienated the Essenes.

Most of those who resisted the Seleucids, or who sympathized with the resistance, were neither of priestly families nor of Essene temperament. Nonetheless, the unchecked rule of the Hasmonean priests in the Temple was not entirely acceptable to them. For that large group, the Pharisaic movement held a great attraction. The Pharisees, in their attempt to influence what the Hasmoneans did rather than to replace them definitively, appear as much more conservative than the Essenes or competing, priestly families. Their focus was on the issue of purity, as defined principally in their oral tradition, and their interpretation of scripture, and since issues of purity were bound to be complicated in the Hasmonean combination of secular government and sacrificial worship, disputes were inevitable. Paradoxically, the willingness of the Pharisees to consider the Hasmoneans in their priestly function involved them in the most vocal and bloody disputes of all. The Hasmonean king Alexander Jannaeus is reported to have executed by crucifixion eight hundred opponents, either Pharisees or those with whom the Pharisees sympathized, and to have slaughtered their families. Alexander Jannaeus died in 76 B.C.E. and was succeeded by his wife Salome Alexandra, who came to an accommodation with the Pharisees that guaranteed them considerable influence (see Josephus, *Jewish War,* 1 §96–114). It appears clear that, within the Hasmonean period, purity was a political issue and a symbol: the acquiescence of one of the dynasty to any Pharisaic stricture implicitly acknowledged that the Hasmonean priesthood was provisional, and the Pharisaic movement probably found its original, political expression in opposition to that priesthood.

The Pharisees accepted and developed the notion that, with the end of the canon, the age of prophecy in the classical sense had ceased (see 1 Macc. 4:46). For that reason, they plausibly saw Ezra and the men of his "great assembly" as their precedent, and their own, interpretative movement as an extension of that program of restoration. But in two vital respects the Pharisees need to be distinguished from the reforms of Ezra. First, they identified themselves with no specific priestly or political figure (Ezra included): their program was its own guide, and was not to be subservient to any particular family or dynasty. Second, Pharisaic interpretation was not limited to the Scriptures, nor was its characteristic focus scriptural: the principal point of departure was the recollection of the earlier teachings of those called "sages."

Ultimately, after the period of the New Testament, the ideology of the rabbis (as the Pharisees came to be designated) had it that Moses conveyed Torah on Sinai in two media, one written and one oral. Even before that understanding, however, the sages treated the teachings of their predecessors in "chains" of tradition as normative. It was not so much that oral tradition was set alongside Scripture, as that oral tradition *was* Scripture until the canon itself could no longer be ignored as the functional standard of Judaism. At that stage, Midrash emerged as an attempt to correlate the dual Torah, written and oral.

Factionalism among the Hasmoneans, which resulted in rival claims to the high priesthood between Aristobulus and Hyrcanus (the sons of Salome Alexandra), culminated in an appeal by both sides to the Roman general Pompey, who obliged by taking Jerusalem for Rome and entering the sanctuary. The Psalms of Solomon represents a common, pious expression of horror at the events of 63 B.C.E., which was probably shared by most Pharisees (whether or not the Psalms should be taken as specifically Pharisaic).

From that period, and all through the reign of Herod and his relatives, the Pharisees' attitude to the government was ambivalent. Some appear to have engaged in a principled opposition to Roman rule and its representatives as such. Today, that group is known as the Zealots, but the term is a misnomer. The Zealots were a priestly group of revolutionaries, not rebellious Pharisees, who were associated with Eleazar, son of Simon, during the revolt of 66–70 C.E. The rebellious Pharisees are also to be distinguished from the movements of prophetic pretenders, who claimed divine inspiration for their efforts to free the land from the Romans. Other Pharisees normally accommodated to the new regime, but resisted—sometimes violently—Herodian excesses, such as the erection of a golden eagle on a gate of the Temple (War 1 §648–55).

Nonetheless, an apparently Pharisaic group is called the Herodians, which presumably signals its partisanship of the interests of the royal family as the best support of their teaching of purity (see Mark 3:6). They may be associated with rabbis who enjoyed the protection of Herod and his house; the authorities referred to in Rabbinic literature as the "sons of Bathyra" may have been such a group. Other Pharisees still largely cooperated with the Romans, and with the priestly administration of the Temple, although they might fall out regarding such questions as whether the priestly vestments should be kept under Roman or local control, or the price of doves for sacrifice.

The priesthood itself, meanwhile, was fractured further in its response to the fact of Roman governance. Some priests, especially among the privileged families in Jerusalem, were notoriously pro-Roman. The story of sons of the high priest having the surgery called epispasm, in order to restore the appearance of a foreskin (for gymnastic purposes), is well known. There is little doubt but that such families, the most prominent of which were members of the Sadducees and Boethusians, were not highly regarded by most Jews. They are typically portrayed in a negative light, as not teaching the resurrection of the dead; but the issue may have been one of emphasis: the Torah had stressed that correct worship in the Temple would bring with it material prosperity, and the elite priests attempted to realize that promise in the terms and conditions of this world.

The arrangement gave them such consistent control that they became known as "high priests," although there was in fact only one high priest. But Josephus indulges in the usage of the plural, as do the Gospels, so it should not be taken as an inaccuracy: the plural is a cultic mistake, but a sociological fact. Caiaphas held a historically long tenure as high priest during the period. But the normally frequent turnover reflects the collective nature of the priestly leadership, as well as Roman caution in respect of a post that might have produced a national leader.

Herod the Great himself understood the possibilities of the high priesthood in that regard, which is why he had Jonathan and Hyrcanus, potential rivals (albeit relatives by marriage), murdered, and why he married Mariamme. His ambition was for a new

Hasmonean dynasty, and it appears that only the notorious greed of his sons, combined with his willingness to have them executed, thwarted its realization. As it was, Herod's grandson and namesake, who was king of Chalcis, did maintain the residual power of selecting the high priest, although as king of Chalcis he had no ordinary authority over Jerusalem.

Several priests were also prominent in the revolt against Rome, however, and it should not be thought that such priestly nationalists, among whom were Joseph bar Matthias, better known as Flavius Josephus (who lived from 37 C.E. until after the turn of the century), emerged only at the end of the sixties. The precedent of the Hasmoneans was there for any priestly family to see as a possible alternative to Roman rule, direct or indirect. Josephus, with his characteristic lack of modesty (false or otherwise), referred to his own relationship to that dynasty. Indeed, some priests were not only nationalists, but revolutionaries, who joined with the Essenes, or with rebellious Pharisees, although any alliance with a prophetic pretender is, perhaps, not a likely supposition.

The Pharisees' mastery of the oral medium made them the most successful—in terms of popularity—of the tendencies within pluralized Judaism. In the period before written communication was standard among the generality of Jews, the use of memorization and recitation was far more prominent. The Pharisees were in a position to communicate guidance in respect of purity, an emerging understanding of scripture (in Aramic translation, the Targumim, whose development they influenced), and their own sense of the authority of the sages, without requiring general literacy. There is no reason to suppose, for example, that rabbis of the first century, such as Hillel and Hanina ben Dosa, were able to read fluently, although each was a formative member of the Pharisaic, and therefore later of the Rabbinic, movements. The Pharisees' willingness to live by craft rather than by status—the most prominent example being Hillel's menial labor—also meant that they could move from town to town, promulgating their views. In some respects, their occasional itinerancy was comparable in Israel to that of the Greco-Roman philosophers of the Mediterranean world (Stoic, Pythagorean, and/or Cynic).

The success of the Pharisees in small towns became all the more pronounced as their power was largely ceded to priestly interests in Jerusalem. Many local scribes, but not all, were likely Pharisees, and the majority would have to account for Pharisaic views. Scribes are, strictly speaking, simply men who can read and write, a skill that in antiquity represented some social and educational attainment. In Israel, given the Roman encouragement of local government, scribes emerged in towns and villages as a focus of judicial and religious power. From the time of the writing of the Torah itself, it was accepted that both aspects of God's rule, the legal and the cultic, were articulated by Moses. The ability of the scribes to read and write made them ideal judges, adjuncts to priests, teachers, and leaders of worship.

Indeed, those various functions were probably discharged by an interactive group of scribes, people of priestly lineage, Pharisees and other elders, in any given village. And it was likely in the same place in a town that cases were settled, purity or impurity declared, lessons given, and the Torah recited from the written form and from memory in Aramaic. There too, disputes would take place among scribes, judges, priests, Pharisees, and elders, concerning how the Torah was to be understood and applied. Later Rabbinic literature tends to reduce the disputes of the period to the "houses" of Hillel and Shammai, but that is quite evidently a simplification; because they lacked any central leadership in the period before 70 C.E. Pharisees differed from movement to movement, town to town, rabbi to rabbi, and even day to day.

The structure of a local council also prevailed under Roman rule in Jerusalem. The Greek term *sunedrion* was applied to it, and it has become known as "the Sanhedrin," largely as a result of the Mishnah. Mishnah, a document of the second century, cannot be taken as a sure guide to events and institutions during the first century, but it does seem clear from the Gospels and Josephus, along with the Mishnah, that the council in Jerusalem was largely controlled by the high priests. But elders or aristocrats of the city also participated, among whom were Pharisees (and, of course, some scribes, who may or may not have been priests, elders, or Pharisees). Whether there were actually seventy-one members of the Sanhedrin (as in Rabbinic literature; see Sanhedrin 1:6 in the Mishnah) cannot be said with certainty, and the extent of its capital jurisdiction is not known. But the Romans appear to have given the council the authority to execute perpetrators of blatant sacrilege. The authority of the council of Jerusalem outside the city followed the prestige of the city itself, and the acknowledged centrality of the Temple. But a ruling of the council there was not automatically binding upon those in the countryside and in other major cities; acceptance of a given teaching, precept by precept, was the path of influence. Pharisees also taught in and around the Temple, the focus of their discussion of purity, and the Pharisees in Jerusalem were the most prestigious in the movement.

The social development of Christianity resulted in a tendency to cast scribes, Pharisees, and lawyers into a single category of persecutors and hypocrites, like the "Jews" themselves, and that influence is evident in the text of the Gospels. But the realities of a radically pluralized Judaism in which Jesus was a vigorous participant also shine through the text as it may be read today.

The references within the Gospels to the groups and movements within Judaism become quite explicable within the social history sketched here. Priests appear locally, in adjudications of purity, while high priests are essentially limited to Jerusalem, or use Jerusalem as a base of power.

Jesus himself enters into disputes with Pharisees and finally teaches in the Temple itself and occupies the holy precincts, where high priests, particularly Sadducees, find him guilty of blasphemy and denounce him to the council of Jerusalem, which makes its recommendation to Pilate. Scribes appear both in a local context (even as a part of Jesus' movement), and in Jerusalem during the final confrontation. They are probably to be identified with references to "lawyers" in the Gospels. The Pharisees engage in vigorous debate with Jesus because he is also interested in developing teaching in respect of purity, but Jesus himself is to be understood in relation to that movement. He is called "rabbi," has close followers, deliberately promulgates his teaching by travel and sending his disciples to teach, and attempts to influence the conduct of worship in the Temple.

From the point of view of official Roman policies, the conflicts among the Jews, as well as their niceties and nuances, were beside the point. They had made a special provision for Jews during the time of the Republic (see below), and they honored it. What the different groups did with and to one another only mattered from the point of view of the public order. The Roman attitude is accurately represented in the book of Acts, which was written around 90 C.E., in the scene when the apostle Paul is denounced by some Jewish opponents before the Roman official Gallio (Acts 18:12–17; in that Gallio left an inscription behind, we can date this event to the year 52 C.E.). Gallio explicitly and firmly refuses to adjudicate the dispute, on the grounds that his concerns are with breaches of the Roman law, not with the Torah.

## ROME AND THE PROBLEMS OF CHRISTIANITY AND REVOLUTION

The emergence of a group of followers around a Galilean rabbi named Jesus seems to have occasioned no official concern from the Romans prior to Jesus' action in the Temple, with one exception. Herod Antipas ruled Galilee and Peraea (east of the Jordan) as a client king of Rome, in succession to his father, Herod the Great (who died in 4 B.C.E.). His reign was notably stable, largely because he assiduously repressed critics. John the Baptist denounced Antipas's marriage to his brother's former wife, and Antipas had him beheaded (see Mark 6:17–29). John was not placing an unusual requirement on Antipas, but insisting Antipas keep the Torah of purity as any person might understand it (see Lev. 20:21). When Jesus, who had been a disciple of John's for a time, enjoyed popular success, Antipas' suspicion turned to him (see Matt. 14:1–2; Mark 6:14–16; Luke 9:7–9). One saying of Jesus probably reflects a period in which he fled from Antipas, and that may have been a reason for his final visit to Jerusalem (see Luke 13:31–33).

But the execution of John the Baptist by Herod Antipas, and the execution of Jesus by Pontius Pilate, were not examples of religious oppression. In each case, the representative of Roman power was insisting (from his own point of view) upon recognition of the legitimacy of the Roman settlement. Herod's marriage was a public arrangement; the good order of the Temple was part and parcel of the Roman recognition of Judaism as a sanctioned religion (see Preface, pp. xvii–xviii). Provided routine worship in the Temple continued, and imperial sacrifices were accepted there, the old alliance from the time of Judas Maccabeus was remembered (see 1 Macc. 8), and Judaism would enjoy the status of *religio licita,* legal religion.[1]

The value of being considered licit was the avoidance of the potential or actual danger of being violently repressed as a conspiratorial threat. Within the active memory of writers during the first century, the bloody removal of those who practiced the Bacchanalia in 186 B.C.E. was vivid. During the reign of Claudius (41–54 C.E.), a Roman officer who attended the imperial court was immediately sentenced to death because he wore a Druid talisman. Since the Druids of Britain remained an untamed and rebellious people, their very symbols were considered a threat.

Followers of Jesus, especially those who had long practiced Judaism (and continued to do so after baptism), naturally assumed that their meetings were as licit as Judaism itself. After the Sabbath closed at sunset, which was seen as the end of one day and the beginning of another, followers of Jesus would continue their observance, concluding at dawn on Sunday, the day and the time of the resurrection. The rising of the heaven's sun corresponded to the rising of God's son within this practice.

With the inclusion of non-Jews within their community by baptism, and with their refusal to require circumcision and (in some cases) the observance of other laws of purity, followers of Jesus ran the risk of being denounced as followers of a *superstitio,* rather than as practitioners of a *religio licita.* The book of Acts consistently presents Paul as hounded by leaders of synagogues who, having given him a hearing, resisted his message (see, for example, Acts 13–14). The very name given to Jesus' followers, *Christiani,* was a sign of coming trouble. Adherents of the movement came to be known as "Christians," meaning partisans of Christ, in Antioch by around the year 40 C.E., and they embraced that term of intended ridicule.[2] The use of the term by outsiders highlights the marginal status of non-Jews who accepted baptism. Without conversion to Judaism, they were not Jews in the usual understanding; having rejected the gods of Hellenism by being baptized, they were also no longer representative of the Greco-Roman syncretism that was then fashionable. By calling disciples *Christiani,* a term analogous to *Caesariani* and *Pompeiani,* outsiders compared the movement more to a political faction than to a religion. (It would be as if, in English, we called a disciple a "Christite," on the model of Thatcherite, Reaganite, or Clintonite.)

In the year 64 C.E., the emperor Nero used the marginal status of Christians to get out of a difficult political situation of his own. In that year, the great fire of Rome broke out, and it was rumored that it had been set at Nero's order. There is no doubt but that the opportunity for him to rebuild Rome along the lines he preferred was one he exploited to the greatest possible extent. Nero attempted to deflect suspicion from himself by fastening blame for the fire on Christians. They were rounded up, interrogated, and slaughtered, often with elaborate means of torture. Nero's excesses in regard to the Christians were obvious even to those who held that their religion was superstitious. The result seems to have been a reduction of attacks upon Christians for several decades.

In Jerusalem, meanwhile, trouble of a different kind was brewing for both Judaism and Christianity. A new spirit of nationalism influenced the priestly aristocracy. Josephus reports that James, the brother of Jesus, was killed in the Temple c. 62 at the instigation of the high priest Ananus during the interregnum between the Roman governors Festus and Albinus (*Antiquities* 20 §197–203). To have the most prominent leader within Christian Judaism removed was obviously a momentous event within Christianity, but arguably the execution was even more ominous for the prospects of Judaism within the empire. Ananus was deposed from the high priesthood for his action, but Josephus's account of the period makes it clear that, from the time of Albinus onward, Rome had to contend with a rising tide of nationalistic violence in and around Jerusalem.

The tide rose fatefully in the year 66 C.E., when Eleazar (the *sagan,* or manager of the Temple) convinced priests not to accept offerings from non-Jews. That included the sacrifices paid for by Rome: the authorities of the Temple were breaching terms basic to the recognition of Judaism as *religio licita.* Insurgents took the

Antonia, the fortress adjacent to the Temple, and killed the soldiers within. War had been irrevocably declared, and the victor could only have been Rome. The Temple itself was destroyed by fire in 70 C.E. after a protracted siege, and the suicide of the Zealots at Masada in 73 C.E. was the last public act of the revolt.

The strategy of the empire in the wake of the revolt was simple, direct, and punitive. The *fiscus Iudaicus,* a tax that adult males had paid for the maintenance of the Temple, was now demanded by Rome to be paid to the Temple of Jupiter Capitolinus in Rome. Moreover, the Roman version of *fiscus Iudaicus* was to be paid by all Jews, minors and women included, not only by adult males.[3] It is not surprising that, in the wake of those events, Judaic hopes centered on the restoration of the Temple. Works such as 2 Esdras (in the Apocrypha, also known as 4 Ezra), written around 100 C.E., openly represent the messianic vindication that was the object of much prayer and action. Such hopes were in cruel contrast to the political reality that the *fiscus Iudaicus* was now the price of being considered *religio licita.*

That period also saw much unrest among Jews outside geographical Israel, especially during the reign of Trajan (98–117 C.E.). Trajan also had to deal with the question of what to do with Christians. Although Nero had discredited vigorous persecution, the association of Christianity with Judaism raised the question of Christian loyalty to Rome anew. Even within the New Testament, there are hints of an unwillingness of the new community to pay the *fiscus Iudaicus* (see Matt. 17:24–27, from a Gospel composed c. 80 C.E.). Moreover, the Davidic descent of Jesus and his relatives could easily be understood as a challenge to Roman hegemony. During the time of the emperor Domitian (81–96 C.E.), the surviving relatives of Jesus, grandsons of Jesus' brother Judas, were interrogated concerning their understanding of the reign of God preached by Jesus. So Trajan inevitably had to deal with the issue of Christians.

In a letter written in 111 C.E. to Pliny, governor of Bithynia and Pontus in Asia Minor, Trajan sets out a moderating policy. Recognition of the gods of Rome (including the emperor as *divi filius,* son of god) is said by Trajan to be all that should be required of those denounced as Christians. The question was not their identity or their practice as such, only whether they were loyal to the empire. By this time, there is no question of Christianity as such being included under the umbrella of Judaism.

Indeed, the empire may be said to have recognized a separation between Judaism and Christianity before Jews and Christians did.[4] Nero never considered extending the rights of a *religio licita* to Christians in 64, when followers of Jesus still worshiped in the Temple in Jerusalem. Not until around 85 C.E. would the framers of a principal prayer of Judaism, the "Eighteen Benedictions," compose a curse to be included against the "Nazoraeans," followers of Jesus. On the Christian side, as we have already seen, the claim to replace Judaism came by the time of the Epistle to the Hebrews in its present form, around 95 C.E. Trajan simply takes the separation for granted, but in effect treats Christianity as a harmless superstition.

By contrast, it is obvious that there was still considerable advantage for Judaism in being considered *religio licita*. Jews could not be required to recognize what they saw as idolatrous gods by Roman magistrates. But the relative peace of the early years of the century in geographical Israel did not last. Between 132 and 135 C.E., a second revolt broke out, and the Temple was again its focus. Led by an able general named Simeon bar Kosiba, whose letters to his commanders have recently been discovered, a new regime was established in Jerusalem and plans were made for the restoration of the Temple. Simeon took the name Bar Kokhba, "son of the star," from the oracle of Balaam in Numbers 24:17, which promises the vindication of Jacob (Israel's original name). He even enjoyed the support of one of the greatest rabbis of his time, Aqiba.[5]

The precise sequence of events leading up to the war is a matter of dispute among scholars. But the immediate cause seems to have been Hadrian's edict prohibiting circumcision. The real point of the edict was to stop the practice of castration within religious settings, a feature of some religions known as Mysteries. Castration was abhorrent to the Romans, and circumcision seemed a close enough analogy to warrant concern. The intent of the edict was perhaps to prevent the circumcision of proselytes, since Judaism still retained the protection of *religio licita.*[6]

## JUDAISM AND CHRISTIANITY IN A HOSTILE EMPIRE

Although this second great revolt against the Romans was better organized than the first, its consequences were even more disastrous. The remnants of the Temple were removed, and a new temple erected: to Jupiter Capitolinus. Jerusalem was renamed Aelia Capitolina, and Jews were forbidden to live there. The Rabbinic response is evident in the Mishnah, which was promulgated c. 200 C.E. under the aegis of Judah ha-Nasi. By this time, of course, Judaism could no longer center on Jerusalem. After the first revolt, a rabbi named Yoḥaanan ben Zakkai had been given permission to establish an academy of rabbis in Yavneh, near Jerusalem. But by the second century, even Yavneh was eclipsed by centers in prosperous Galilee, such as Usha and Beth She'arim. Later, metropolitan cities such as Sepphoris and Tiberias were the foci of leadership.[7] The farming communities of Galilee provided the support for the Rabbinic enterprise of framing a philosophy out of the Pharisaic concern for the purity of Israel. Reference to the Messiah in the Mishnah is, for all practical purposes, absent.

✡
55
☦

While Judaism continued as *religio licita,* its association with revolt, the Roman categorization of circumcision with castration, and the definitive destruction of the Temple (recognized as one of the greatest buildings of its time), vastly undermined the public standing of Judaism in the Roman world. At the same time, attention focused more on Christians in any case.

The relative tolerance of Trajan's policy, as articulated to Pliny, ironically resulted in the extraordinary phenomenon of Christian martyrdom. In effect, Trajan stood down from the open persecution of a Nero, and simply insisted upon the equivalent of an oath of loyalty. But the loyalty involved was to the gods of Rome, and to the emperor as divine son. In good conscience, Christians could not comply with the relatively lenient policy, especially since swearing allegiance to the emperor as *divi filius* was an act performed before his image, with an oblation of wine and the burning of incense. It was, however perfunctory, an imperial sacrifice, and an obvious example of idolatry. Ignatius of Antioch was put to death during the reign of Trajan, and he encouraged others to follow his example of holy obstinacy. On the other hand, Roman devotion to the divine ideal of the empire could also lead to the use of the loyalty test to seek out and kill Christians. That occurred in 177 C.E. in the Rhone valley, at the instigation of the emperor (and noted Stoic philosopher) Marcus Aurelius.

Still, the emperor Severus issued an edict against Christians making converts (and against Jewish proselytism, as well) in 202 C.E. Apparently the former policy, ultimately derived from Trajan, was not an effective instrument of repression. It is of note that Severus's edict also included Judaism: for the first time, Judaism was classed with Christianity (instead of the reverse, as in the first century). The Severine persecution that followed was severe but short-lived. One unfortunate effect (from the Roman point of view) was that it provoked Tertullian in North Africa to write his encouragement of martyrdom, and to utter the words that were to prove prophetic: "The blood of the martyrs is the seed of the Church."[8] Others in North Africa, such as Cyprian, were later to wrestle with the truth of those words.

In 250 C.E., the emperor Decius decreed that all citizens were to take part in sacrifice to the gods, and the inevitable result was a widespread persecution of Christians. During that persecution, the greatest theologian of the time, Origen, was imprisoned and tortured. Origen died during the reign of Valerian (253–260), who attempted to suppress Christian worship itself for the first time. But Valerian was captured and killed by Shapur, the Sassanid monarch. In important rescripts, the emperor Gallien actually restored Christian churches and cemeteries. Valerian's death is therefore an important transitional point from the point of view of official policy toward Christianity: it marks the moment from which Christians will begin to acquire formal rights. At the same time, Valerian's death marks the importance of the Sassanid Empire as a counterweight to the Roman Empire. The transition of Rabbinic authority from Galilee to Babylonia is to some extent explicable on that basis.

The emperor Diocletian (284–305) was the last great persecutor of Christianity during the period of the empire. His motives appear to have been patriotic. After all, he branded the Manichaeans[9] as criminal (in an edict of 297) before he acted against the Christians. But when his persecution came, it was systematic and savage. Beginning in 303, property was seized and clergy were arrested. Trajan's old test, of offering sacrifice to the gods, was resumed and made universal. Diocletian himself abdicated in 305, but the persecution went on until 313. It was the last gasp of the ideal of a universal civic religion of the Roman Empire based on the ancestral gods.

### THE CONSTANTINIAN SETTLEMENT

Among the rivals for the title of emperor in the chaotic wake of Diocletian was Constantine, who defeated Maxentius at the Milvian Bridge in 312. Legend has it that as a result of a vision, Constantine permitted the display of crosses on shields within his army. His victory assured the restoration of Christian worship and Christian property. Christian symbols even appear on coins from 315, and the older references to the gods disappear from 323. Constantine would accept baptism himself only at the time of his death, but there was no question but that Christianity was now, de facto, the religion of the empire.

A brief coda marks the extraordinary reversal of fortunes experienced by Judaism and Christianity between the first and the fourth centuries. Under the emperor Julian (361–363), a return to the old gods was attempted, and authorization for the rebuilding of the Temple in Jerusalem was given. Here Judaism is treated as belonging to the category of ancestral religion, rather than one of the new movements such as Christianity and Manichaeanism. An earthquake greeted the attempt to bring the project off, which only encouraged the Christian mobs that resisted the policies of Julian. The emperor himself was killed in battle with the Sassanids. His death left Rome to the Christians, and Jewish hopes for the restoration of the Temple in ruins. Babylonia, which had long offered a more congenial environment than Rome for a Judaism that would order its own affairs, now appeared to be no less a land of promise to the Rabbis than was a Jerusalem that could not longer host the Temple.

## THE JEWISH STATE BECOMES THE HOUSE OF ISRAEL AND THE CHRISTIAN CHURCH BECOMES THE HOLY ROMAN EMPIRE

The single most interesting exchange in the intersecting histories of Judaism and Christianity saw the Jewish state turn into the House of Israel, and the church take over and transform itself into what became the Holy Roman Empire. Emerging from the catacombs to the imperial court, Christians formed a new vision of history, and their place in it. The great historical theologian Eusebius of Caesarea, writing in Constantine's shadow, to make sense of events had to recast the entire history of the world from creation to the present moment, thus responding to the new politics in which Christianity found itself.

For their part it was long ago that the Jews had had a state and lost it. The Judaic politician-historian Josephus told his story on the premise that the Jews retained political options, and should exercise the politics of alliance with Rome that had served for nearly two centuries (from Maccabean times when Israel allied itself with Rome). The initial statement of Rabbinic Judaism in the Mishnah looked backward toward a political Israel, possessed of a state governed by a king, a politically founded Temple governed by a high priest comparable in his domain to the king in his, and a court system in the hands of sages backed up by the government. The final statement in the Talmuds and associated Midrash-compilations later on conceived of Israel not as state but as household. Then the Judaic conception of state and official government (high priest, king, sage) gave way to the corporate community with a government subordinated to a higher authority (patriarch in the Land of Israel, exilarch in Babylonia, both ruling by the authority of the empires, Roman and Iranian, respectively). A free-standing group of sages ("our sages of blessed memory") was to govern the community in practical ways through the authority of the patriarch or exilarch, but they claimed to form God's ministry and to govern by reason of mastery of the Torah, and that alone. So for the Judaism of the dual Torah, Israel at the end became what Christianity had formed at the outset, not a government but a community; impelled not by coercive but by essentially voluntary media for the realization of the myth of supernatural "Israel."

The philosopher-jurisprudents who produced the Mishnah shared the prevailing assumption that, while public policy had changed for Israel, Israel remained a political entity. The Mishnah, which reached closure more than a century and a quarter after the destruction of the Temple and three-quarters of a century after the definitive closure of Jerusalem to Jews and suppression of the quasi-independent Jewish administration in the Land of Israel, invented a politics to serve—to make the statement of—its system. To be sure, its initial politics in no way replicated the facts of the Jewish government prior to 70, and instead fabricated a political fantasy. But the holy Israel of the Mishnah, hierarchically arranged in ascending order and aiming on high, remained a state. Politics in the commonplace sense—the doctrine of legitimate violence, of who may do what to whom and for how long and in what institutions— remained a constitutive component of the Judaic religious system that the Mishnah put forth.

But that is not how matters were to conclude in the system's second and final formative statement. The documents that recast the Rabbinic system, and reached closure after the conversion of Rome to Christianity in the fourth century, also recast politics. Now, instead of a state with its king, high priest, and sages' administration, Israel was represented in the form of a corporate community, addressing some few matters of purely local concern, with sages in charge. And sages were represented as not essentially political figures in any this-worldly sense but rather as holy men whose power extended beyond the here and now and who could inflict supernatural penalties as readily as worldly ones. They did not coalesce into a coherent government, a permanent institution, but were portrayed as governing episodically and notionally, anecdotally. And Israel itself formed a supernatural community, a vast, extended, holy family, children of Abraham, Isaac, and Jacob; but this Israel then formed no foreign policy—Josephus in the fourth century would have little to say of current interest at all—and fought no wars.

Why did the initial statement of the Rabbinic system, that of the Mishnah, require politics as a medium for setting forth its message, while the later statement of the same system did not? How is it that deep thought within Christianity about the relationship between the city of God and the city of this world waited until the late fourth-century theologian Augustine? Now the inclusion of a politics in the Mishnah, and the reframing of politics into a supernatural venture in the hands of holy men, demands an explanation of its own, not appeal to a simple, causal relationship between events and ideas. The politicization of Christianity—not merely the advent of a new political situation with which Christians would deal—likewise requires its own framework of analysis. For while Christians could never have imagined the course that history actually took—not a shred of evidence suggests that any Christian anticipated the emperor's conversion before it took place!—from early times they proselytized with the aim of converting the ruler, and his people with him, the legendary correspondence between Abgar of Edessa and Jesus suggesting a politics in place long before actualities provoked reflection on such matters. Hence the apolitical life of the church in its earliest centuries contrasts with at least one early aspiration to realize the Gospel through legitimate violence, such as, from the fourth century, would take place.

## Political Israel in the Initial Statement of Rabbinic Judaism

When setting forth its view of power—the legitimate use of violence—and the disposition of power in society, the Mishnah's authorship describes matters in a manner that is fundamentally political, inventing a political structure and system integral to its plan for the social order. The Mishnah's Israel forms a political entity, fully empowered in an entirely secular sense, just as Scripture had described matters. To political institutions of the social order, king, priest, and court or civil administration, each in its jurisdiction, is assigned the right legitimately to exercise violence here on earth, corresponding to, and shared with, the same empowerment accorded to institutions of heaven. Moreover, these institutions are conceived permanently to ration and rationalize the uses of that power. The picture, of course, is this-worldly, but, not distinguishing crime from sin, it is not secular, since the same system that legitimates king, high priest, and court posits in heaven a corresponding politics, with God and the court on high exercising jurisdiction for some crimes or sins, and the king, priesthood, or court down below for others.

Among prior Judaisms only the Torah's—that is, the scriptural system finally defined with the closure of the Pentateuch in the time of Ezra—had set forth a politics at all. The appeal to politics in setting forth a theory of the social order of their particular "Israel" will have provoked some curiosity among, for one example, the framers of the Judaism portrayed by the Essene library uncovered at Qumran, and, for another, the framers of the Christianity of the Land of Israel in the first century. Both groups, heirs of the ancient Scriptures as much as were the framers of the Mishnah, found in politics no important component of the systemic structure they set forth. Nor did the apostle Paul and those Jews who produced the Gospels invoke the category of politics to convey their systemic message; for them, politics was declared by Christianity's founder to be quite beyond the limits of the Gospel.

By contrast, the integration of a politics within a systematic account of the social order will not have surprised the great figures of Greco-Roman philosophy, Plato and Aristotle, for example. That fact takes on consequence when we note that the Pentateuch simply does not prepare us to make sense of the institutions that the politics of Judaism for its part designs. The Pentateuchal politics invokes priest and prophet, Aaron and Moses, but knows nothing of a tripartite government involving king, priest, and sage; nor do the royal narratives concede empowerment to the priest or sage. On the other hand, as we shall see, knowledge of the *Politics* of Aristotle and the *Republic* of Plato gives perspective upon the politics of the Mishnah. The Pentateuch contributes nothing to the Mishnah's scheme of routine government by king and high priest and sages' court. The Pentateuch's prophetic rule and constant appeal to God's immediate participation in the political process, and, in particular, its administration of sanctions and acts of legitimate violence, falls into the category of a politics of charisma. For the Mishnah, ad hoc intervention from Heaven lay beyond all imagining. The difference is not merely that the Pentateuchal institutions appeal to prophet and priest; there also is a difference in how the structure works as a political system. For the Pentateuchal myth that serves to legitimate coercion—rule by God's prophet, in the model of Moses, governance through explicitly revealed laws that God has dictated for the occasion—plays no active and systemic role whatsoever in the formulation and presentation of the politics of Judaism. Philosophical systems use politics, by contrast, to set forth the rules and unchanging order of legitimate exercise of power, its teleology and its structure. Plato and Aristotle make no place for godly intervention on any particular occasion.

And for their part, among the types of political authority contained within the scriptural repertoire, the one that the Mishnah's philosophers reject is the prophetic and charismatic, and the one that they deem critical is the authority governing and governed by rules in an orderly, rational way. The principal political figures—king, high priest, the disciple of the sage—are carefully nurtured through the learning of rules, not through cultivation of gifts of the spirit. The authority of sages in the politics of Judaism in particular does not derive from charisma, e.g., revelation by God to the sage, who makes a ruling in a given case, or even general access to God for the sage. So the politics of the Pentateuch—structure and system alike—in no way forms the model for the politics of the Mishnah. Hence the correct context for the classification of the Mishnah's politics must be located elsewhere than in a Judaism between the Pentateuch's and the Mishnah's, c. 500 B.C.E. to 200 C.E. But what about the Greco-Roman tradition of philosophical politics?

With the Pentateuchal precedent in mind, we can hardly consider the mere presence of a highly orderly and systematic political structure and system to be an indicator of the peculiarly philosophical character of the Mishnah's politics. Two specific traits, however, direct our attention toward the philosophical classification for the Mishnah's politics in framing a systemic composition, even though, to be sure, the parallels prove structural and general, rather than detailed and doctrinal. First, like the politics of Plato and Aristotle, the Mishnah's politics describes only a utopian politics, a structure and system of a fictive and a fabricated kind: an intellectuals' conception of a politics. Serving the larger purpose of system construction, politics of necessity emerges as invention, e.g., by heaven or in the model of heaven, not as a secular revision and reform of an existing system. In the middle of the second century, Rome incorporated their country, which they called the Land of Israel and the Romans called Palestine, into its imperial system, denying Jews access to their capital, Jerusalem, and permanently closing their cult center, its Temple. Nevertheless, the authorship of the Mishnah described a government of a king and a high priest and an administration fully empowered to carry out the Law through legitimate violence. So the two politics—the Mishnah's and the Greco-Roman tradition represented by Plato's and Aristotle's—share in common their origins in intellectuals' theoretical and imaginative life and form an instance, within that life, of the concrete realization of a larger theory of matters. In strange and odd forms, the Mishnah's politics falls into the class of the *Staatsroman*, the classification that encompasses, also, Plato's *Republic* and Aristotle's *Politics*. But, admittedly, the same may be said for the strange politics of the Pentateuch.

Second and more to the point, the Mishnah's sages stand well within the philosophical mode of political thought that begins with Aristotle, who sees politics as a fundamental component of his system when he says, "political science . . . legislates as to what we are to do and what we are to abstain from"; and, as to the institutionalization of power, we cannot imagine a more ample definition of the Mishnah's system's utilization of politics than that.[10]

While that statement, also, applies to the Pentateuchal politics, the systemic message borne by politics within the Pentateuchal system and that carried by politics in the Mishnah's system do not correspond in any important ways. Aristotle and the philosophers of the Mishnah utilize politics to make systemic statements that correspond to one another, in that both comparison and contrast prove apt and pointed. Both spoke of an empowered social entity; both took for granted that ongoing institutions legitimately exercise governance in accord with a rationality discerned by distinguishing among those empowered to inflict sanctions. Both see politics as a medium for accomplishing systemic goals, and the goals derive from the larger purpose of the social order, to which politics is subordinated and merely instrumental.

What, precisely, was the systemic message assigned to the political components by the system-builders of the Mishnah? It concerned the hierarchical classification of society. Since society is viewed as classified and hierarchized, the task of politics is to designate who is on top, who in the middle, and who on the bottom. Who does what to whom in that well-ordered social structure that the Mishnah's framers envisaged? The hierarchical ordering of power through a theory of politics comes to expression in a political myth, one that we discern when we identify, in particular, what differentiates the sanctions—that is to say, power in its brute and pure form—among the several jurisdictions. Then how do we differentiate jurisdictions, which is to say, how do we discern the hierarchical ordering effected through politics, which is to say, systemically expressed through the imagined structure and system embodied in legitimate sanctions?

When we understand the differentiating force of myth that imparts to politics its activity and dynamism, we shall grasp the systemic message, conveyed through the political component of the system, that animates the structures of the politics and propels the system. Appealing to a myth of taxonomy, the politics of the system accomplishes its tasks by explaining why this, not that, telling as its foundation story a myth of classification of power. The myth appeals in the end to the critical bases for the taxonomy, among institutions, of a generalized power to coerce. When we move from sanctions to the myth expressed in the application and legitimation of those sanctions, we see a complex but cogent politics sustained by a simple myth. Specifically, the encompassing framework of rules and institutions and sanctions is explained and validated by the myth of God's shared rule, counterpart to God's shared ownership of land.

That dominion, exercised by God and surrogates on earth, is focused partly in the royal palace, partly in the Temple, and partly in the court. But which part falls where and why? The political myth of Judaism answers that particular question, and, consequently, the Judaic political myth comes to expression in its details of differentiation, which permit us to answer the generative question of politics, Who imposes which sanction and why?

Four types of sanctions are to be differentiated, deriving from four distinct institutions of political power, each bearing its own mythic explanation. When we follow these points of differentiation, we shall be prepared to recognize how vastly the politics changed in the successor documents, for, as we shall see, the later politics makes no such differentiation but recognizes only one legitimate political institution on earth. For the Mishnah's politics, the first is what God and the heavenly court can do to people. The second is what the earthly court can do to people, and that type of sanction embodies the legitimate violence of which political theory ordinarily speaks. The third is the sanction imposed by the cult's requirements, which can deprive people of their property as legitimately as can a court.

The fourth is the sanction that is self-imposed: conformity to consensus. Then the issue becomes, whose consensus? Defined by whom? Four types of coercion, including violence of various kinds, psychological and social as much as physical, are in play. The types of sanction within the system that are exercised by other than judicial-political agencies surely prove violent and legitimately coercive, even though the violence and coercion are not the same as those carried out by courts.

The exercise of power, invariably and undifferentiatedly in the name and by the authority of God in heaven to be sure, is kept distinct. Concrete application of legitimate violence by (1) Heaven covers different matters from parts of the political and social world governed by the policy and coercion of (2) the this-worldly political classes. And both sorts of violence have to be kept distinct from the sanction effected by (3) the community, not through institutional force and expression, but through the weight of attitude and public opinion. The politics works in such a way that all political institutions, God and the court and the Temple and the monarchy, the agencies with the power to bestow or take away life or property or to inflict physical pain and suffering, work together in a single continuum and in important ways so cooperate as to deal with the same crimes or sins.

The orderly character of the hierarchization of power is shown by a simple fact. Quite absent from the politics is God's direct intervention, and that difference decisively distinguishes the Mishnah's from the Pentateuch's political theory. For in the Mishnah's system God's intervention on an ad hoc and episodic basis in the life of the community does not serve to explain obedience to the Law in the here and now. What sort of evidence would indicate that God intervenes in such wise as to explain the obedience to the Law on an everyday basis? Invoking God's immediate presence, a word said, a miracle performed, would suffice. But in the entirety of the more than five hundred fifty chapters of the Mishnah and the much larger corpus of the Tosefta, no one ever prays to have God supply a decision in a particular case. There is no counterpart to Moses' asking God whether women can inherit, absent a male heir, for instance. Since a paraphrase of the later position that, anyhow, prophecy had ceased, can readily account for that fact, it is more to the point to observe that no judge appeals to God to put to death a convicted felon. If the judge wants the felon killed, he kills him. But, it may be argued, the Mishnah's system indeed does appeal to extirpation, meaning that Heaven too participates in the system. That is quite so, but because of the hierarchical order that is set forth, when God intervenes, it is on the jurisdiction assigned to God, not the court. And then the penalty is a different one from execution.

Penalties fall into four classifications: (1) what Heaven does, (2) what cultic institutions do, (3) what the civil administration and court system does, and (4) what is left to the coercion of public opinion, that is, consensus, with special attention to the definition of that "public" that has effective opinion to begin with. That final realm of power, conferring or withholding approval, proves constricted. The first three prove critical. (1) God takes care of *deliberate* violation of God's wishes. If a sin or crime is inadvertent, the penalties are of one order, if it is deliberate, they are of a different order. The most serious infraction of the Law of the Torah is identified not by what is done but by the attitude of the sinner or criminal. If one has deliberately violated God's rule, then God intervenes. If the violation is inadvertent, then (2) the Temple imposes the sanction. And the difference is considerable. In the former case, God through the heavenly court ends the felon's or sinner's life. Then a person who defies the laws as these concern one's sexual conduct, attitude toward God, or relationships within the family, will be penalized either (if necessary) by God or (if possible) by the earthly court. That means that (3) the earthly court exercises God's power, and the myth of the system as a whole, so far as the earthly court forms the principal institutional form of the system, emerges not merely in a generality but in all its specificity. These particular judges, here and now, stand for God and exercise the power of God. In the latter case, the Temple takes over jurisdiction; a particular offering is called for, as the Book of Leviticus specifies. But there is no need for God or the earthly court in God's name to take a position. The power of social coercion, e.g., ostracism, is systemically unimportant.

✡

67

✝

Power therefore flows through three distinct but intersecting dominions, each with its own concern, all sharing some interests in common. The heavenly court attends to *deliberate* defiance of Heaven, the Temple to *inadvertent* contradiction—therefore not defiance—of Heaven. The earthly court attends to matters subject to its jurisdiction, by reason of sufficient evidence, proper witnesses, and the like, and these same matters will come under heavenly jurisdiction when the earthly court finds itself unable to act. Who then tells whom to do what? Power comes from two conflicting forces: the commanding will of God and the free will of the human being. Power expressed in immediate sanctions is mediated, too, through these same forces: heaven above, human beings below, with the Temple mediating between the two. And that brings us to the politics portrayed in the successor writings, with the difference simply characterized in this way: From a realm of order and hierarchy (in this context, a redundant combination) in which power is diffused but well focused, we turn to a disorderly politics indeed.

## DISEMPOWERED ISRAEL IN THE POST-CONSTANTINIAN STATEMENT OF RABBINIC JUDAISM

The successor system, speaking on its own and not in response to the Mishnah, exhibits none of the traits of the Mishnah's politics, but sets forth those of its own. Where the Mishnah's politics is orderly and hierarchical, the Yerushalmi's scarcely effects differentiation within the Israelite sphere at all; it has one political entity and a single political class, not three on earth. There is Israel on earth, undifferentiated, corresponding to the one in heaven. It knows not the marvelously differentiated and classified penalties and sanctions on which the Mishnah's authorship lovingly dwells in such tractates as Keritot and Sanhedrin, but a quite undifferentiated system of sanctions, each serving for the correct context. And context is always the point of differentiation: doing what one can, when one can, where one can, appealing to Heaven to do the rest. The Mishnah's and the Yerushalmi's politics had little in common, except so far as the latter simply paraphrased and clarified details of the former.

The Talmud of the Land of Israel and related writings portray not the (imagined) orderly and inner-facing politics of Israel living by themselves under God, king, priest, and sage, but the palpable chaos of Jews living among gentiles, governed by a diversity of authorities, lacking all order and arrangement.[11] The politics of the Mishnah is classified with that of philosophers, in abstract terms thinking about logic and order. The politics of the successor documents shows us politicians deeply involved in the administration of the concrete social group, describing its "Israel" as a real-life community. The later authorships, in the fourth and fifth centuries, prove analogous not to philosophers but to men of affairs: judges, lawyers, bureaucrats, heads of local governments.

True, both the Mishnah's and the successor documents' politics in the end put sages in charge of everything. But in the first system sages formed one component of a well-ordered structure, in which monarchy, priesthood, and clerkdom formed a cogent whole and together, each doing its assigned task, administered an orderly world in an orderly way. In the second, sages are represented as the sole legitimate authority, competing to be sure with such illegitimate authorities as the patriarch within and the gentile government of Rome beyond. The practical politics then dealt with Jews who lived under both rabbis near at hand, settling everyday disputes of streets and households, and also distant archons of a nameless state, to be manipulated and placated on earth as in heaven. But the Yerushalmi's portrait of legitimate power, as distinct from illegitimate violence, appeals then to the legitimation of the Torah serving solely for the sages, while the Mishnah's account differs in ways now entirely obvious.

Indeed, what we find most striking as we look back upon the Mishnah's politics is that while legitimate power is carefully parceled out, illegitimate power is ignored. In the Yerushalmi's politics, by contrast, the issue is the distinction between illegitimate power, worked by patriarch within and Rome beyond, and legitimate power, focused solely upon sages. The issues thus shift, even while the category remains the same. That shift seems to us to indicate a decay in categorical cogency; the Mishnah's category of politics is preserved but then bypassed, as issues not formerly considered intervene and drastically revise the character of the whole—even in its initial context and definition.

The Mishnah's politics breathes the pure air of public piazza and stoa, while the politics of the Talmud of the Land of Israel and its associated Midrash-compilations exudes the ripe stench of private alleyway and courtyard. That is why the comparison of the Mishnah's politics with philosophical politics, the Yerushalmi's with an other-than-philosophical politics, is amply justified. The image of the Mishnah's politics is evoked by the majestic Parthenon, perfect in all its proportions, conceived in a single moment of pure rationality. The successor system is a scarcely choate cathedral in process, the labor of many generations, each of its parts the conception of diverse moments of devotion, all of them the culmination of an ongoing and evolving process of revelation in the here and now. The Mishnah's system presents a counterpart to Plato's *Republic* and Aristotle's *Politics,* a noble theory of it all. In literary terms, in the transition from the Mishnah to the successor writings we leave behind the strict and formal classicism of the Mishnah, like Plato's *Republic* describing for no one in particular an ideal society never, in its day (or indeed, in any other), to be seen. We come, rather, to focus on the disorderly detail of the workaday world, to be sure taking the utopian Mishnah along with us in our descent into the streets, where people really do commit acts of violence against one another, and where authority really does have to sort out legitimate acts and ongoing institutions able to perform such acts from illegitimate ones.

In the later system do we find recognition of other authorities able to coerce and otherwise utilize legitimate violence, beyond king, temple, and court? The answer is negative. The decay— within the theoretical structure—of the received political institutions of course is the fact, as the sage becomes the recognized government, the king and high priest in the persons of their avatars, the patriarch and the priesthood, now no longer accorded legitimate rights of violence of any kind at all. The former is represented as illegitimate, a part of an illegitimate alien government; the latter is treated as no longer a political entity at all, since the most violent act a given priest can commit is to seize the priestly rations owing to the priesthood in general by a particular farmer. Then what sorts of power does the sage alone now exercise, and how is the inherited politics revised?

When the Yerushalmi's framers speak independently and not as Mishnah exegetes, the role of the king is no longer differentiated within an overarching system of sanctions; the king is now treated in general terms and not in a specific way. There is no recognition whatsoever that the king or patriarch legitimately inflicts some sanctions, the sage others. Now what the patriarch does is simply illegitimate, and what the sage does is always and everywhere legitimate violence. The differentiation of sanctions focuses on what the sage does in one kind of case versus what he does in some other, and not on what the king does in one kind of case versus what the sage does in some other. It follows quite naturally that the role of the sage is much more richly differentiated—amplified by cases, for instance—so that the focus of political discourse, defined as it is by the legitimate exercise of power, comes to bear solely on the sage and his court. The king occupies center stage—but in parables, in which the king or prince stands for everyman, not in concrete accounts of legitimate violence, let alone in autonomous exercises on the differentiation of the authorities that exercise legitimate violence.

While, therefore, the politics of the Yerushalmi and related writings carries forward that of the Mishnah, a quite separate conception of political institutions and relationships also comes to expression. It is a political structure in which sages administer sanctions, a system in which sages make decisions; where others intervene, their sanctions—whether those of the patriarch or of the gentile—are illegitimate. Legitimate violence is executed solely by one political entity, which is the sages' court. That observation draws our attention to the question of the sanctions legitimately in the hands of sages alone. These are differentiated not in principle but only in context: what works. And the differentiation is circumstantial, expressed through description of cases, never theoretical and principled. But there should be no doubt that violence, not merely voluntary acquiescence, is at stake. Sages' power is political, not merely moral, routine and not charismatic in any sense. Thus sages are portrayed by the Talmud of the Land of Israel as exercising authority effected through concrete sanctions not only over their own circles, people who agree with them, but over the Jewish community at large.

This authority was practical and involved very specific powers. The first and most important sort of power that a rabbi (under some circumstances and in some cases) maintained he could exercise was to sort out and adjudicate rights to property and personal status affecting property. The rabbi is described as able to take chattels or real estate from one party and give them into the rightful ownership of some other. The second sort of power rabbis are supposed to have wielded was to tell people what to do, or not to do, in matters not involving property rights. Here they could administer floggings, that is, violence in its most personal form.

The Talmud alleges that rabbis could tell people outside the circles of their own disciples and estate how to conduct themselves. A rabbi is presented as able to coerce someone to do what that ordinary Jew might otherwise not wish to do, or to prevent him from doing what he wanted. That other authorities existed, and even competed with rabbinical authorities, is taken for granted. What is important to this part of our inquiry into systemic transformation is that the Yerushalmi portrays legitimate violence in a manner quite asymmetrical with the pattern set forth in the Mishnah.

The Talmud of the Land of Israel takes for granted that rabbis could define the status of persons in such ways as to affect property and marital rights and standing. It is difficult to imagine a more effective form of social authority. The Talmud treats as settled fact a range of precedents, out of which the character of the Law is defined. In those precedents, rabbis declare a woman married or free to marry; permitted as the wife of a priest to eat food in the status of leave-offering or prohibited from doing so; enjoying the support of a husband's estate or left without that support; having the right to collect a previously contracted marriage settlement or lacking that right. In all of these ways, as much as in their control of real estate, commercial, and other material and property transactions among Jews, the rabbis held they governed the Jewish community as effective political authorities. Whatever beliefs or values they proposed to instill in the people, or realize in the collective life of the community, they effected not through moral suasion or pretense of magical power. It was not hocus pocus but political power resting on the force of government authority. They could tell people what to do and force them to do it. The Talmud of the Land of Israel is remarkably reticent about the basis for rabbis' power over the Jews' political institutions: who bestowed this-worldly legitimacy and supplied the force? But the systematic provision of biblical proof texts for Mishnaic laws presents an ample myth for the Law and its enforcement: sages acted by right of their mastery of the Torah and therefore in the status of heaven. Given by God to Moses at Mount Sinai, the Law of the Torah, including the Mishnah's laws, represents the will of Heaven. But with all the faith in the world, on the basis of such an assertion about God's will, the losing party to a litigation over a piece of real estate will surely have surrendered his property to the other side only with the gravest reservations—if at all. He more likely will have complained to some other authority, if he could. Short of direct divine coercion, upon which a legal system cannot be expected to rely, there had to be more reliable means of making the system work.

What these were, however, the Talmud of the Land of Israel hardly tells us. That silence underlines the political theory of the document: the sage now acts for Heaven, in the way in which, in the Mishnah's politics, the king, high priest, and sage represented on earth a counterpart power and activity to the power and activity of Heaven. Then all parties, on earth as in heaven, carried out each its assigned and proper task. Now, it seems to us clear, the sage is the sole focus of legitimate authority on earth, and Heaven's rule is no more explicit than is the role of the king (or high priest) legitimate. The differentiated foci of the Mishnah's philosophical politics now give way to the unitary focus of the Yerushalmi's theory of the same matter. What is clear is that politics, in theory, in the Mishnah represents a diffusion of power within an articulated order and hierarchy; the focus of power is no longer cogent, but multiple and incoherent; but legitimacy, by contrast, is now single and singular, and therein lies the shift.

The Talmud of the Land of Israel is therefore clear that rabbis competed with other authorities for rule over the Jewish community. But sages alone exercised power legitimately; all other political institutions by definition were illegitimate. True, the relationship of the rabbis as judges and administrators to other Jewish community judges and administrators, who may have carried out the same tasks and exercised the same responsibilities in regard to the Jewish nation of the Land of Israel, is not clarified either in cases or as to theory. But here too the silence is indicative: it is a tacit judgment, and a devastating, eloquent one. The Talmud's picture of legitimate violence comes to concrete expression in its account of what rabbis could force people to do because of their political power and position. The sovereignty of rabbinical courts in property disputes derived from the power of the courts not only to persuade or to elicit general support, but also to call upon the power of the state to transfer ownership of real and movable property from one party to another.

Another sanction derived from the public fear of ostracism and also the active support of the people at large. Determinations of personal status by rabbinical courts depended on the power of public opinion that sages manipulated. While the courts might call upon the state to back up their rulings about property, they are not likely to have enjoyed equivalent support in matters to which the government was probably indifferent, such as whether a given woman was betrothed and so not free to marry anyone but the fiance, on the one side, or whether she was not betrothed and so free to marry anyone of her choice, on the other. Persistent meddling in such affairs can have generated only widespread protest, unless the community at large acquiesced and indeed actively supported the right of the courts to make such decisions. Nonetheless, even behind these evidences of rabbinical authority, based as they are on sanctions of moral authority, as distinct from the imperial government's ultimate threat of force, there still were elements of exchange of property or things of value.

As a matter of fact, the authorities who stood behind the Talmud of the Land of Israel preserved a vast number and wide variety of cases in which, so far as they were concerned, rabbinical courts exercised a kind of authority we may regard only as political and bureaucratic. Persons and property of Israel came under their authority. So the Talmud of the Land of Israel represents its authorities as judges of litigation and administrators of questions of personal status. Decisions are represented, moreover, as precedents, accepted in theorizing about law and uniformly authoritative for courts spread over a considerable territory. Accordingly, rabbinical judges saw themselves as part of a system and a structure, not merely local strong men or popular sages. A fully articulated system of politics and government, staffed by people who knew the Mishnah and how to apply its law to concrete cases and who had the full power to do so, is represented here. Rabbinical judges knew what to do and had full confidence in their authority to do it. The Talmud of the Land of Israel portrays rabbis' power over the estates and possessions of the Jews, including communal property and behavior.

Rabbis furthermore made decisions or gave opinions in a domain quite distinct from that of property or of property joined to determination of personal status. These decisions influenced personal behavior in private, rather than coercing it in public. They were meant to establish rules for good public order and decent behavior. Whether rabbis enjoyed the power to force people to behave in the way they wanted is not at issue. So far as the issues at hand related not to property and public policy but to individual conduct, in general it was moral, rather than civil and political, authority that rabbis claimed to exercise. But the sanctions were every bit as rich in the potential for violence as those of a more narrowly political order.

The rabbi stood on the intersecting borders of several domains: political and private, communal and individual. He served as both legal and moral authority, decider and exemplar, judge and clerk, administrator and governor, but also holy man and supernatural figure. What is important here is the representation of the rabbi— and the rabbi or sage alone, no longer also the high priest (or priesthood) and the monarch (or patriarch)—as public authority deemed to exercise supernatural power. His task was to use his supernatural power in much the same context and for the same purpose as he used his political-judicial and legal power and learning, on the one side, and his local influence and moral authority, on the other. Whatever public authority the rabbi exercised is credited, in the end, to his accurate knowledge and sincerity in living up to his own teachings, on the one side, and the peoples' willingness to accept his instructions, on the other. Nothing in the Mishnah prepares us for such an account of the supernatural politics focused on the sage. And, concomitantly, the contrast between the sages' legitimate power and the gentiles' illegitimate violence underlines the contrast between the power of the Torah and the violence of the Roman troops.

We should not confuse a theory of politics with a portrait of the political actualities of the time. The Talmud of the Land of Israel concedes that the rabbi was part of the administration of a man who stood at the margins of the rabbinical estate, one foot in, the other out. The sage was further limited in his power by popular will and consensus, by established custom, and by other sorts of Jewish local authorities. Furthermore, as the Talmud represents matters, the rabbi as clerk and bureaucrat dealt with matters of surpassing triviality, a fair portion of them of no interest to anyone but a rabbi, we should imagine. He might decide which dog a flea might bite. But would the fleas listen to him? Accordingly, the Talmud presents us with a politics that sorts out inconsequentialities. On the one side, the rabbi could make some practical decisions. On the other, he competed for authority over Israel with the patriarch and with local village heads. And, in general, no Jew decided much. From the viewpoint of the Roman Empire, moreover, the rabbi was apt to have been one among many sorts of invisible men, self-important nonentities, treating as consequential things that concerned no one but themselves, doing little, changing nothing.

These realities bear no more consequence for the political theory at hand than the everyday facts of life that shaped the politics of the initial system, the one represented by the Mishnah and related writings. Just as we can find in the Mishnah's systemic statement effected through a theory of politics not a single line that concedes legitimacy to things that have actually happened, so in the Yerushalmi's we locate not a word that takes account of the givens of the day, and that is not at all surprising. What is not to be gainsaid is the systemic transformation, represented by the reconsideration not of the details of politics but of the very category. The shift from a political to a supernatural "Israel" comes to expression in the transformation of politics.

Philosophical politics such as we find in the Mishnah, stated roughly, tells who may legitimately do what to whom. When a politics wants to know who ought *not* to be doing what to whom, we find in hand the counterpart category to the received politics. And that is an antipolitics, the systemic statement in the post-Constantinian documents of Rabbinic Judaism.

The received category set forth politics as the theory of legitimate violence, the counterpart category, politics as the theory of *illegitimate* violence. The received politics had been one of isolation and interiority, portraying Israel as *sui generis* and autocephalous in all ways. The portrait in the successor documents is of a politics of integration among the nations; a perspective of exteriority replaces the inner-facing one of the Mishnah, which recognized no government of Israel but God's. The issues of power had found definition in questions concerning who legitimately inflicts sanctions upon whom within Israel. They now shift to give an account of who illegitimately inflicts sanctions upon ("persecutes") Israel. So the points of systemic differentiation are radically revised, and the politics of the successor system becomes not a revision of the received category but a formation that in many ways mirrors the received one: once more a counterpart category. Just as, in the definition of scarce resources, Torah study has replaced land, so now weakness forms the focus in place of strength, illegitimacy in place of legitimacy. Once more the mirror image of the received category presents the perspective of the counterpart category.

The data given to us in the successor documents—when they speak on their own account and not in clarification of the Mishnah and related writings—shift in character. Now we find the answers to these questions: to whom is violence illegitimately done, and also, who may not legitimately inflict violence? With the move from the politics of legitimate to that of illegitimate power, the systemic interest now lies in defining not who legitimately does what, but rather, to whom, against whom, is power illegitimately exercised. And this movement represents not the revision of the received category, but its inversion. For thought on legitimate violence is turned on its head. A new category of empowerment is worked out alongside the old. The entity that is victim of power is at the center, rather than the entity that legitimately exercises power. That entity is now Israel *en masse,* rather than the institutions and agencies of Israel on earth—heaven above, a very considerable shift in thought on the systemic social entity. Israel as disempowered, rather than king, high priest, and sage as Israel's media of empowerment, defines the new system's politics.

In laying claim to the status of empowerment, thought on legitimate violence now asks about the illegitimacy of violence inflicted on social entities—which nonetheless are also conceived as political entities—rather than the legitimacy of violence inflicted by them. This is as much a new mode of classification, an utterly fresh category, as the odd and unpredictable economics reconsidered in the transvaluation of value. But as that remained an economics, so the inversion of the Mishnah's politics is still a politics. The reason is that the question we now seek to answer remains the same as before: Who inflicts sanctions on whom and why? On what entities do discussions of violence focus? It follows that we address a political question to an empowered entity. But the answer—the focus of attention within political thought—now centers on the violence inflicted upon Israel the nation, and differentiation now is among those who illegitimately act violently. True, when they speak of who legitimately exercises violence (in addition to Heaven, of course), sages refer to the sage. That happens to constitute a mere extension of the received system, which had assigned sages mastery of the courts, alongside the monarchy and the high priesthood. But when the successor writings tell us upon whom violence is legitimately exercised and by whom, there is a wholly new realm of thinking going on.

The Mishnah's account of practical politics and that of the Yerushalmi prove discontinuous not only in structure but also in system, for the discontinuity reveals itself in the theory of empowerment. Now gentiles are deemed not only empowered but also subject to differentiation. The earlier system had concerned itself with the internal politics of (an) Israel, with politics seen as principal taxic indicator of the social order. The later politics, by contrast, turned toward the external relationships of (an) Israel located in the disorderly world of nations. So the new politics has not only inverted the issue of violence and turned its illegitimate side upward, it also has revised the systemic vision so that attention faced outward, differentiation among the outsider vis-à-vis (an) undifferentiated Israel being the result. So the successor system's definition of what is at stake in the theory of legitimate violence that forms the centerpiece of politics therefore proves wholly other.

The burden of the systemic message assigned to the component of politics remained equally heavy in the successor system.

But the contents proved quite dissimilar. The Mishnah's political theory had focused on the inner structure and composition of Israel's social order; politics served the systemic purpose of setting forth the hierarchical taxonomy of power, just as each of the other principal parts of the Mishnah's statement of the social order represented the classification and ordering of all classes of things. When, for the Mishnah's politics, we know who within Israel legitimately inflicts sanctions upon whom within Israel, the principle of differentiation yields a clear picture of the organization of Israelite society. So the role of politics in the philosophical statement of Judaism is to represent the theoretical standing of the empowered institutions, the ones that bear the political role and responsibility. As we shall now see, the task of politics in the successor system accomplished a different sort of differentiation altogether.

The systemic message now concerned an Israel lacking all capacity to effect violence, requiring an explanation of its illegitimacy.[12] No longer an empowered nation, Israel—within the systemic writings of the late fourth and the fifth century— speculates on who is the worst among the nations, what will come of Israel, when Israel will once more take charge of its own affairs. That explains why, to deliver the systemic message, it was not only the *illegitimate* exercise of power, but differentiation among the entities, institutions and persons, that illegitimately inflict violence would require attention. Formerly sorting out who properly inflicts which sanction upon whom, now the system's political analysis concerns both the actor, now the illegitimate one, and the victim, equally illegitimate. And that inversion brings us back to our interest not in the reformation of received categories but in the formation of the counterpart ones: to what systemic purpose? The answer, for the economics of abundant and never-scarce Torah of the successor system, lies right at the surface. What about the politics of weakness?

At stake is always the social entity, for a politics—commonplace and conventional or counterpart and odd—bears the burden of definition of the social entity of the encompassing system. And here we locate the systemic message delivered by the antipolitics.

The counterpart category is one that in fact rejects as beside the point what makes a politics political: the legitimate use of violence. The data that will be sought attest to the very opposite facts. For now, as a matter of fact, all violence but God's and the sages' is illegitimate. The political entity that Israel is to form is an antipolitical one, in that it defines itself not by appeal to its legitimate exercise of sanctions, but rather by its exercising no power at all. The social entity in the politics at hand is made, therefore, to affirm the status of the victim, once again a social entity for an antipolitics indeed.

This political ideal reaches its simplest formulation in the bald statement that all God—after all, the All-Powerful—wants is the victim, done to but never doing:

### LEVITICUS RABBAH XXVII:V.1

A. God seeks what has been driven away. (Qoh. 3:15)

B. R. Huna in the name of R. Joseph said, "It is always the case that 'God seeks what has been driven away'" [favoring the victim].

C. You find when a righteous man pursues a righteous man, "God seeks what has been driven away."

D. When a wicked man pursues a wicked man, "God seeks what has been driven away."

E. All the more so when a wicked man pursues a righteous man, "God seeks what has been driven away."

F. [The same principle applies] even when you come around to a case in which a righteous man pursues a wicked man, "God seeks what has been driven away."


2. A. R. Yosé b. R. Yudan in the name of R. Yosé b. R. Nehorai says, "It is always the case that the Holy One, blessed be he, demands an accounting for the blood of those who have been pursued from the hand of the pursuer."

B. Abel was pursued by Cain, and God sought [an accounting for] the pursued: "And the Lord looked [favorably] upon Abel and his meal offering." [Gen. 4:4]

C. Noah was pursued by his generation, and God sought [an accounting for] the pursued: "You and all your household shall come into the ark." [Gen. 7:1] And it says, "For this is like the days of Noah to us, as I swore [that the waters of Noah should no more go over the earth]." [Isa. 54:9]

D. Abraham was pursued by Nimrod, "and God seeks what has been driven away": "You are the Lord, the God who chose Abram and brought him out of Ur." [Neh. 9:7]

E. Isaac was pursued by Ishmael, "and God seeks what has been driven away": "For through Isaac will seed be called for you." [Gen. 21:12]

F. Jacob was pursued by Esau, "and God seeks what has been driven away": "For the Lord has chosen Jacob, Israel for his prized possession." [Ps. 135:4]

G. Moses was pursued by Pharaoh, "and God seeks what has been driven away": "Had not Moses His chosen stood in the breach before Him.: [Ps. 106:23]

H. David was pursued by Saul, "and God seeks what has been driven away": "And he chose David, his servant." [Ps. 78:70]

I. Israel was pursued by the nations, "and God seeks what has been driven away": "And you has the Lord chosen to be a people to him." [Deut. 14:2]

J. And the rule applies also to the matter of offerings. A bull is pursued by a lion, a sheep is pursued by a wolf, a goat is pursued by a leopard.

K. Therefore the Holy One, blessed be he, has said, "Do not make offerings before me from those animals that pursue, but from those that are pursued: 'When a bull, a sheep, or a goat is born.'" (Lev. 22:27)

We can offer no better evidence that a new sense altogether has been imputed to the consideration of the legitimacy of power. No longer does politics explain the uses of power: within what sort of institutions and upon the basis of what kind of rationale, for example. The issue is now exactly the opposite: the legitimacy of powerlessness, the illegitimacy of (nearly all) power. That at stake are issues we should regard as political, not (merely) theological is underlined when Israel as such enters: it is Israel contrasted with the nations, and as the latter form political entities, so does the former. That then shows what we mean when we speak of an antipolitics, an inversion of the category to focus on not the legitimate but the illegitimate exercise of power, on not the actor but the victim.

How about Israel as victim of illegitimate power, such as formed the centerpiece of the counterpart category of politics? Illegitimate power was exercised by a member of the same family, and the illegitimacy of his power derived from his genealogical illegitimacy. Indeed, the metaphor of family made possible the differentiation in material and concrete terms between the legitimate and the illegitimate, since, after all, to begin with these formed genealogical classifications, and only by analogy and metaphor, classifications of other sorts of data altogether. So the consequence of the appeal to the genealogical metaphor for the categorization of Israel emerges when we turn from the legitimate to the illegitimate political entity.

It is, of course, Rome. The comparison of one line of a family to another line of the same family, the legitimate and the illegitimate, prepares the way for the system's project of the comprehensive interpretation of world politics. The genealogical metaphor therefore encompasses not only "Israel" but also "Rome." It makes sense of all the important social entities, for in this metaphor, "Israel" is consubstantial with other social entities, which relate to "Israel" just as "Israel" as a society relates to itself, present and past.

What is important in the metaphor of Israel as family is how that metaphor governs the conceptualization of the other political components of the sages' world. We recognize the result for the treatment of Rome: Rome is Edom, or Ishmael, or Esau—always the rejected line of the authentic ancestor. History works out the tale of siblings, of whom only one is legitimate, and history is written in the tale of the relationship of Israel and Rome. Rome as Israel's brother, counterpart, and nemesis. Rome is now what stands in the way of Israel's, and the world's, ultimate salvation. It is, of course, not a (merely) political Rome but a political and messianic Rome, participating in the sacred—that is, the familial—history of Israel, that is at issue. At stake is Rome as surrogate for Israel, Rome as obstacle to Israel. But "Rome" as family shades over into "Rome" as empire and state, comparable to "Israel" as a nation or state—and as the coming empire too. For while "Rome" stands for "Esau," the metaphorization of Rome moves into fresh ground, since Rome is differentiated from other nations, and hence the exegetical task of the new politics shifts from the differentiation of entities within Israel to the comparison and contrast of entities outside.

Accordingly, "Rome" is a family just as is "Israel," and, more to the point, "Rome" enters into "Israel's" life in an intelligible way precisely because "Rome" too is a part of that same family that is constituted by "Israel." The comparison of "Israel" and "Rome" to states, nations, peoples, empires, rests on, comes to expression in, and is generated by the genealogical metaphor. And that singles out Rome alongside Israel; now "Rome" is like "Israel" in a way in which no other state or nation is like "Israel." Rome emerges as both like and also not like "Israel," in ways in which no other nation is ever represented as "like Israel"; and, it follows, "Israel" is like "Rome" in ways in which "Israel" is not like any other people or nation.

So the counterpart category introduces illegitimate power and explains it. That initiative, within its own logic, then requires the differentiation of outsiders, who, being different from the outsider, Rome, by definition are—can be—no longer all the same. But the genealogical account takes no systemic risks[13] in simply turning the outsider into an illegitimate insider. The metaphor that joins past to present, household to household—the whole, then, to "all Israel," in fact encompasses the other noteworthy social entity and takes it into full account—a powerful, successful field theory indeed. That the theory is a distinctively political one hardly requires extended argument; Rome imposes sanctions illegitimately; Israel, legitimately. The one forms the opposite of the other; the politics of the one is the mirror of that of the other.

But the systemic focus—the exegetical task imposed by the requirement of differentiation—has shifted, and so there is a new work of differentiation. Specifically, identifying Rome as different from other outsiders of political consequence now required differentiation among the rest of those same outsiders. And that led directly to an account of the history of the empires, all of them viewed within the same frame and perspective, and of Israel's place among them. Once introduced, Rome took up a place in the unfolding of the empires—Babylonia, Media, Greece, then Rome. "Israel" takes its place in that unfolding pattern, and hence is consubstantial with Babylonia, Media, Greece, and Rome. In that context, "Rome" and "Israel" do form counterparts and opposites. Still more important, Rome is the penultimate empire on earth. Israel will constitute the ultimate one. The illegitimacy of the one politics will be replaced in due course by the legitimacy of power exercised by Israel through its anointed king. Politics now enters history: change, movement, direction, purpose. The initial system bore no teleology made explicit; the successor system is all teleology, wholly historical in medium, entirely historical in message. That systemic message pointed to the shifts in world history to elicit a pattern and place at the apex Israel itself.

The theory of Israel as *sui generis* produced a political theory in which Israel's sole legitimate ruler is God, and whoever legitimately governs does so as God's surrogate. The theory of legitimate sanctions then is recast into a religious statement of God's place in Israel's existence, but retains its political valence when we recall that the sage, the man most fully "in our image, after our likeness," governs in accord with the Law of the Torah. Here is a brief statement, framed out of the materials of Leviticus Rabbah, of the successor documents' political theory that forms also a theological creed. In it we see the definition of legitimate violence: God's alone. The theory, stated in my own words by way of summary of the doctrine of Leviticus Rabbah, is as follows: God loves Israel, so gave them the Torah, which defines their life and governs their welfare. Israel is alone in its category (*sui generis*), proved by the fact that what is a virtue to Israel is a vice to the nations; what is life-giving to Israel is poison to the gentiles.

True, Israel sins, but God forgives that sin, having punished the nation on account of it. Such a process has yet to come to an end, but it will culminate in Israel's complete regeneration. Meanwhile, Israel's assurance of God's love lies in the many expressions of special concern for even the humblest and most ordinary aspects of the national life: the food the nation eats, the sexual practices by which it procreates. These life-sustaining, life-transmitting activities draw God's special interest, as a mark of his general love for Israel. Israel then is supposed to achieve its life in conformity with the marks of God's love. Moreover, these indications also signify the character of Israel's difficulty, namely, subordination to the nations in general, but to the fourth kingdom, Rome, in particular. Both food laws and skin diseases stand for the nations. There is yet another category of sin, also collective and generative of collective punishment, and that is social. The moral character of Israel's life, the treatment of people by one another, the practice of gossip and small-scale thuggery—these too draw down divine penalty. The nation's fate therefore corresponds to its moral condition. The moral condition, however, emerges not only from the current generation. Israel's richest hope lies in the merit of the ancestors, thus in the Scriptural record of the merits attained by the founders of the nation, those who originally brought it into being and gave it life. True power lay in the renunciation of this world's understanding of legitimate violence in favor of a different kind of power altogether, that contained in the utter renunciation of violence as ever legitimate.

# 2

# TRADING VALUES

## DEFINING SCARCE RESOURCES: FROM REAL ESTATE TO TORAH STUDY, FROM "SELL ALL YOU HAVE" TO "THE CHRISTIAN EPOCH"

The word *values* bears so broad a variety of connotations as to lack all concrete meaning. For our purpose *values* means those things that people deem to constitute scarce resources. In the context of the social order, the doctrine of the rational disposition of scarce resources stands for a system's economic theory. In the setting of a religious theory of the social order, the scarcest and most valued resources may prove other than those of this-worldly wealth, but the basic rules of economics will still govern. Hence we propose to ask, What did the respective systems value in their initial formulations, and upon what did they come to place a high price later on?

Bearing a variety of inchoate meanings associated with belief, conviction, ideal, moral preference, and the like, the word to begin with bears an entirely concrete sense. Value means "that which people value, under ordinary circumstances, what they hold to be of concrete, tangible, material worth." What is "of value" conventionally is what provides a life of comfort and sustenance and material position. In commonplace language, *value* refers to those scarce resources to the rational management and increase of which economics devotes its attention: real wealth. Then when we speak of the transvaluation of value, we mean that the material and concrete things of worth were redefined—even while subjected to an economics functioning in the system as the counterpart to the initial economics of the Mishnah and of Aristotle. In the successor writings ownership of land, even in the Land of Israel, contrasts with wealth in another form altogether, and the contrast that was drawn was material and concrete, not merely symbolic and spiritual. It was material and tangible and palpable because it produced this-worldly gains—e.g., a life of security, comfort, ease—as these too found definition in the systemic context of the here and the now.

The initial statement of the Judaism of the dual Torah set forth a doctrine not only of politics but also of economics, one that identified wealth with real estate, and the second system recast the matter into supernatural terms—much as we have observed was the history of this Judaism's doctrine of politics. The second system would deem study of the Torah an abundant resource, replacing the scarce resource of real estate as the single most valued commodity. And, what is striking, that statement—Torah study instead of politics—was made in so many words, and in an explicit contrast.

Christianity, for its part, commenced with the rejection of the importance, to the kingdom of God, of economics as much as of politics, contemplating not so much the organization of the social order in accord with the precepts of Heaven, as the attainment of the kingdom of God in supernatural terms in the very near future. But as issues of social organization in practical terms confronted Christian theologians and demanded serious attention, the utter rejection of economics as a medium for systemic articulation ("sell all you have and follow me") gave way to the formation of a doctrine of what, within this world, is worthy of a high value. As the kingdom of God receded beyond the distant horizon and people expected long tenure for the dominion of Christian Rome, not only politics, but also economics, entered into the Christian theory of the social order. And that is a second way in which the two religions, Judaism and Christianity, traded places.

## DISTRIBUTIVE ECONOMICS AND THE MISHNAH'S SYSTEMIC STATEMENT

The heirs of the initial, philosophical Judaism received a system in which the subject of economics—the rational disposition of scarce resources—was utilized in order to set forth a systemic statement of fundamental importance. While making every effort to affirm the details of that statement and apply them, they in no way contributed to the theoretical work that the economics of the Mishnah can, and should, have precipitated. Consequently, their system repeated the given but made no significant use of what had been received. Instead the heirs of the Mishnah invented what we must call a counterpart category, that is to say, a category that dealt with problems of the rational utilization of scarce resources, but not with those same scarce resources defined by the philosophical system of the Mishnah. The systemic category for the aborning religious system was not an economics, but corresponded, in the new system, to the position and role of economics in the old.

The Judaic system to which the Mishnah attests is philosophical not only in method and message but in its very systemic composition. The principal components of its theory of the social order, its account of the way of life of its Israel, and its picture of the conduct of the public policy of its social entity—all of these in detail correspond in their basic definitions and indicative traits with the economics and the politics of Greco-Roman philosophy in the Aristotelian tradition. Specifically, the Mishnah's economics—in general in the theory of the rational disposition of scarce resources and of the management and increase thereof, and specifically in its definitions of wealth and ownership, production and consumption—corresponds point by point to that of Aristotle.

To be sure, sayings relevant to an economics may take shape within a religion or a philosophy without that religion's or philosophy's setting forth an economics at all, for unsystematic opinions on this and that—for instance, episodic sayings about mercy to the poor, recommendations of right action, fairness, honesty, and the like—do not by themselves add up to an economics. Indeed, one of the marks of a system's lacking an economics is the presence of merely occasional and ad hoc remarks about matters of wealth or poverty that, all together, attest to complete indifference to the systemic importance of a theory of the rational disposition of scarce resources, their preservation and increase. By contrast, when issues of the rational disposition of scarce resources are treated in a sustained and systematic, internally coherent theory that overall and in an encompassing way explains why this, not that, and defines the market in relationship to ownership of the means of production, then we have a systematic account, an economics. Not only so but, as in the case of Aristotle's economics, the economics will prove to serve the interests of the system of which it is part when it makes a statement on behalf of that larger system. Through economics, the Mishnah's system makes a critical part of its systemic statement, and this authorship found economics, and only economics, the appropriate medium for making that part of its statement. But for antiquity only two theories of economics, Aristotle's and the Mishnah's, delivered principal parts of systemic statements.

There are no other candidates for inclusion on the list of significant thinkers and system builders to whom an account of an economics mattered in a systematic way in a systemic composition.[1] While other systems made episodic reference to topics of economic interest, Plato's for instance, and any number of other figures allude to issues of wealth, Jesus for the most important example, and in his model, a great many important figures in early Christianity, none produced a well-crafted account of the wealth, the market, exchange, money, value, the definition of the unit and means of production, and other basic components of an economics, let alone a composition of all those things into a coherent statement. And—more to the point—none but Aristotle's and the Mishnah's systems undertook to make a fundamental point in its discussion of topics of economic interest. But Aristotle's and the Mishnah's systems not only did so, they did so in this-worldly terms, by appeal to well-crafted philosophical principles about the character of society and politics. That is why we characterize the Mishnah's economics as philosophical, and why, furthermore, when we understand that the Mishnah sets forth an economics in the way it does rather than in some other way, we see that economics forms an indicator of the philosophical character of the Mishnah as a system.

The general point in common between Aristotle's and the Mishnah's economics comes first: for both systems economics formed a chapter in a larger theory of the social order. The power of economics as framed by Aristotle, the only economic theorist of antiquity worthy of the name, was to develop the relationship between the economy and society as a whole.[2] And the framers of the Mishnah did precisely that when they incorporated issues of economics at a profound theoretical level into the system of society as a whole that they proposed to construct. That is why the authorship of the Mishnah will be seen as attacking the problem of people's livelihood within a system of sanctification of a holy people with a radicalism of which no later religious thinkers about utopias were capable. None has ever penetrated deeper into the material organization of human life under the aspect of God's rule. In effect, they posed, in all its breadth, the question of the critical, indeed definitive, place occupied by the economy in society under God's rule.

The points in common between Aristotle's and the Mishnah's economics in detail prove no less indicative. Both Aristotle and the Mishnah presented an anachronistic system of economics. The theory of both falls into the same classification of economic theory, that of distributive economics, familiar in the Near and Middle East from Sumerian times down to, but not including, the age of Aristotle (let alone that of the Mishnah five centuries later). But market economics had been well established prior to Aristotle's time. Let us briefly explain the difference between the two, which is a fundamental indicator in classifying economics. In market economics merchants transfer goods from place to place in response to the working of the market mechanism, which is expressed in price. In distributive economics, by contrast, traders move goods from point to point in response to political commands. In market economics, merchants make the market work by calculations of profit and loss. In distributive economics, there is no risk of loss on a transaction.[3] In market economics, money forms an arbitrary measure of value, a unit of account. In distributive economics, money gives way to barter and bears only intrinsic value, as do the goods for which it is exchanged. It is understood as "something that people accept not for its inherent value in use but because of what it will buy."[4] The idea of money requires the transaction to be completed in the exchange not of goods but of coins. The alternative is the barter transaction, in which, in theory at least, the exchange takes place when goods change hands. In distributive economics money is an instrument of direct exchange between buyers and sellers, not the basic resource in the process of production and distribution that it is in market economics. Aristotle's economics is distributive for systemic reasons, the Mishnah's replicates the received principles of the economics planned by the Temple priests and set forth in the Priestly Code of the Pentateuch, Leviticus in particular. The result—fabricated or replicated principles—was the same.

Both systems—the Mishnah's and Aristotle's—in vast detail expressed the ancient distributive economics, in their theories of fixed value and conception of the distribution of scarce resources by appeal to other than the rationality of the market. The theory of money characteristic of Aristotle (but not of Plato) and of the Mishnah, for instance, conforms to that required by distributive economics; exchange takes place through barter, not through the abstract price-setting mechanism represented by money. Consequently, the representation of the Mishnah as a philosophical Judaism derives not only from general characteristics but from very specific and indicative traits held in common with the principal figure of the Greco-Roman philosophical tradition in economics.

There was a common social foundation for the economic theory of both systems. Both Aristotle and the Mishnah's framers deemed the fundamental unit of production to be the household, and the larger social unit, the village, composed of households, marked the limits of the social entity. The Mishnah's economic tractates, such as the ones on civil law, invariably refer to the householder, making him the subject of most predicates; where issues other than economics are in play, e.g., in the political tractates such as Sanhedrin, the householder scarcely appears as a social actor. Not only so, but both Aristotle and the authorship of the Mishnah formed the conception of "true value," which maintained that something—an object, a piece of land—possessed a value extrinsic to the market and intrinsic to itself, such that, if a transaction varied from that imputed true value by (in the case of the Mishnah) 18 percent, the exchange was null. Not only so, but the sole definition of wealth for both Aristotle's and the Mishnah's economics was real estate, only land, however small. Since land does not contract or expand, of course, the conception of an increase in value through other than a steady-state exchange of real value, "true value," between parties to a transaction lay outside the theory of economics. Therefore all profit, classified as usury, was illegitimate and must be prevented.

Episodic details of these, and like, positions can have been, and surely were, entertained by a variety of system builders in the same age. Plato, for instance, had a theory of money; Jesus, a theory of the negative value of wealth and ownership; and so forth. But only for Aristotle and the Mishnah's framers do these conceptions coalesce to form an economics worthy of the name, one that moreover bears an important part of the systemic message. For in the case of the Mishnah's and Aristotle's economics the entire purpose of the system comes to expression in (among other aspects) the matter of a fully articulated economics. Aristotle's interest in economics derived from his larger program of framing a political economics for the community at large. As Polanyi states,

> Whenever Aristotle touched on a question of the economy he aimed at developing its relationship to society as a whole. The frame of reference was the community as such which exists at different levels within all functioning human groups. In terms, then, of our modern speech Aristotle's approach to human affairs was sociological. In mapping out a field of study he would relate all questions of institutional origin and function to the totality of society. Community, self-sufficiency, and justice were the focal concepts. The group as a going concern forms a community (*koinonia*) the members of which are linked by the bond of good will (*philia*). Whether *oikos* or *polis* [household or village], or else, there is a kind of *philia* specific to that *koinonia*, apart from which the group

could not remain. *Philia* expresses itself in a behavior of reciprocity . . . , that is, readiness to take on burdens in turn and share mutually. Anything that is needed to continue and maintain the community, including its self-sufficiency . . . is "natural" and intrinsically right. Autarchy may be said to be the capacity to subsist without dependence on resources from outside.[5]

We see, therefore, that for Aristotle economics formed an important building block in his larger system, and distributive economics in detail bore meanings for the larger political economy he was developing.

For Aristotle, the postulate of self-sufficiency governed all else; such trade as was required to restore self-sufficiency was natural and right.[6] The fundamental principle, with ample instantiation in the Mishnah's economics as well, is therefore natural self-sufficiency attained by the *oikos* and the *polis* made up thereof: political economy: "The institution of equivalency exchange was designed to ensure that all householders had a claim to share in the necessary staples at given rates, in exchange for such staples as they themselves happened to possess . . . barter derived from the institution of sharing of the necessities of life; the purpose of barter was to supply all householders with those necessities up to the level of sufficiency.[7] Accordingly, Aristotle's economic theory rested on the sociology of the self-sufficient community, made up of self-sufficient, if mutually dependent households.

Aristotle's is not the only economics to provide a parallel and counterpart to that of the Mishnah. In the case of the economics of the Mishnah's Judaism, we have a replay, with important variations, of the old and well-established distributive theory of economics in the Priestly Code, spelled out in the rules of the biblical books of Leviticus and Numbers, upon details of which the Mishnah's authorship drew very heavily. And in doing so, the economics of the Mishnah took its leave in important details from that of Aristotle. For in its most basic and distinctive conviction, the economics of the Mishnah's Judaism rests on the theory of the joint ownership, between God and the Israelite householder, of a designated piece of real estate. And in that system, *all* that mattered as wealth was that ownership that is shared between God and partners of a certain genus of humanity whose occupancy of that designated piece of real estate, but no other, affects the character of the dirt in question. Aristotle can never have accepted so particular, and so enchanted, a conception of wealth!

The theology of wealth, in both the Priestly Code and the Mishnah, consists in an account of what happens when ground of a certain locale is subject to the residency and ownership of persons of a certain genus of humanity. The generative conception of the theology involves a theory of the effect—the enchantment and transformation—that results from the intersection of "being Israel": land, people, individual person alike. When we find evidence that wealth has meanings other than Israelite (normally, male) ownership of a piece of real estate in the Land of Israel in particular, we shall encounter evidence of the expansion and revision of the economics set forth in the Mishnah.

In detail the economic program of the Mishnah derived from the Priestly Code and other priestly writings within the Pentateuchal mosaic. Indeed, at point after point, that authorship clearly intended merely to spin out details of the rules set forth in Scripture in general and, in economic issues such as the rational use of scarce resources, the Priestly Code in particular. The Priestly Code assigned portions of the crop to the priesthood and Levites as well as to the caste comprising the poor; it intervened in the market processes affecting real estate by insisting that land could not be permanently alienated but reverted to its "original" ownership every fifty years; it treated some produce as unmarketable even though it was entirely fit; it exacted for the Temple a share of the crop; it imposed regulations on the labor force that were not shaped by market considerations but by religious taboos, e.g., days on which work might not be performed, or might be performed only in a diminished capacity.

But the authorship of the Mishnah made its own points. The single most striking, already noted, is that the Mishnah's system severely limited its economics—and therefore the social vision and pertinence of the realm of the system as a whole!—to (1) Israelite householders, meaning (2) landowners, and among these, only the ones who (3) lived on real estate held to fall within the Land of Israel.[8] The economics of the Mishnah eliminated from its conception of the economy (1) gentiles in the Land of Israel, (2) Israelites outside the Land of Israel, and (3) Israelites in the Land of Israel who did not own land—which is to say, nearly everybody in the world. So the definition of "scarce resources" proved so particular as to call into question the viability of the economics as such and to recast economics into a (merely) systemic component. For when, in the Mishnah, we speak of the economic person, the one who owns "land," it is only land that produces a crop liable to the requirements of the sacerdotal taxes.

It follows, therefore, that ownership of "land" speaks of a very particular acreage, specifically, the territory known to the framers of the Mishnah as the Land of Israel, that alone. Land not subject to the sacerdotal taxes is not land to which the legal status and traits before us are imputed. But there is a second equally critical qualification. Land in the Land of Israel that is liable to sacerdotal taxes must be owned by an Israelite—a qualification beyond the imagination of the priestly authorship of Leviticus seven hundred years earlier. Gentiles are not expected to designate as holy portions of their crop, and if they do so, those portions of the crop that they designate as holy nonetheless are deemed secular. So we have an exceedingly specific set of conditions in hand. And what is excluded must not be missed, or we fail to grasp the odd and distinctive character of the economics of the Mishnah. Wealth for the system of the Mishnah is not ownership of land in general, for example, land held by Jews in Babylonia, Egypt, Italy, or Spain. It is ownership of land located in a very particular place. And wealth for that same system is not wealth in the hands of an undifferentiated owner. It is wealth in the domain of an Israelite owner in particular.

Wealth therefore is ownership of *Land of Israel* in two senses, both of them contained within the italicized words. It is ownership of land located in the Land *of Israel*. It is ownership of land located in the Land of Israel that is *of Israel,* belonging to an Israelite. "Israel" then forms the key to the meaning of wealth, because it modifies persons and land alike: only an Israel[ite] can possess the domain that signifies wealth; only a domain within the land called by the name of "Israel" can constitute wealth. It is in the enchanted intersection of the two Israels, (ownership of) the land, (ownership by) the people, that wealth in the system of the Mishnah finds realization. Like Aristotle's selective delimitation of the economy, the Mishnah's economics describes a tiny part of the actual economic life of the time and place and community.

Not only is the Mishnah's economics rather truncated in its definition of wealth, but the range of economic theory in its distributive mode (as distinct from the market mode) deals with only one kind of scarce resource, and that is food. True, goods and services, food and housing, were valued and understood to have value; but these are dealt with generally as components of the market, not of the distributive economics that is assumed to predominate. To identify that component of the goods and services of the market that is subjected to distributive, rather than market, economics, within the mixed economics at hand, we look at food in particular. The reason is that food alone is what is subjected to the distributive system at hand—food and, in point of fact, nothing else, certainly not capital, or even money. Manufactured goods and services—that is, shoes on the last, boards in the vise, not to mention intangibles such as medical and educational services, the services of clerks and scribes, goods in trade, commercial ventures of all kinds—none of these is subjected to the tithes and other sacerdotal offerings. The possibility of a mixed situation, in which a distributive economics leaves space for a market economics, rests on the upshot of the claim that God owns the Holy Land. It is the land that God owns, and not the factory or shop, stall and store, ship and wagon, and other instruments and means of production. Indeed, the sole unit of production for which the Mishnah legislates in rich and profound exegetical detail is the agricultural one. The distributive component of the economy, therefore, is the one responsible for the production of food, inclusive of the raising of sheep, goats, and cattle.

The key then is, What is wealth? and Where is wealth? We already know the answer to these questions in their formulation in that curious and narrow, geographical-genealogical framework of the system: wealth is (1) land (2) held by Israelites (3) in the Land of Israel. But that framework has now to be broadened considerably, since from the definition of wealth, we move to a question of considerable systemic consequence: ownership of the means of production, which amplifies the received theory of wealth. Wealth is the formation of (1) the unit and (2) means of production, the household, defined in terms of (3) command of ownership of a landed domain, however small. So wealth is located in the household, comprising, with other households, the village; the village defines the market in which all things hold together in an equal exchange of a stable population in a steady-state economy.

In this context, wealth of course is conceived as material, not figurative or metaphorical or spiritual,[9] but it also is held to be as perfect, therefore unchanging, as is real property, not subject to increase or decrease (hence, by the way, the notion of true value imputed to commodities). For if we imagine a world in which, ideally, no one rises and no one falls, and in which wealth is essentially stable, then we want to know what people understand by money, on the one hand, and how they identify riches, on the other. The answer is very simple. For the system of the Mishnah, wealth constitutes that which is of lasting value, and what lasts is real property (in the Land of Israel), that alone. Real estate (in the Land of Israel) does not increase in volume, it is not subject to the fluctuation of the market (so it was imagined), it was permanent, reliable, and, however small, always useful for something. It was perceived to form the medium of enduring value for a society made up of households engaged in agriculture. Accordingly, the definition of wealth as real and not movable, as real estate in the Land of Israel and nowhere else, real estate not as other kinds of goods, conformed to the larger systemic givens. A social system composed of units of production—households—engaged in particular in agricultural production, made a decision entirely coherent with its larger conception and character in identifying real estate as the sole measure of wealth. And, as we recall, Aristotle will not have been surprised, except, of course, by the rather peculiar definition of the sole real estate deemed of worth.

## FROM SCARCE RESOURCES IN THIS WORLD TO
## ABUNDANT RESOURCES IN HEAVEN

The transformation of economics involved the redefinition of
scarce and valued resources in so radical a manner that the concept of value, while remaining material in consequence and character, nonetheless took on a quite different sense altogether. The
counterpart category of the successor system, represented by the
authorships responsible for the final composition of the Yerushalmi, Genesis Rabbah, Leviticus Rabbah, and Pesiqta deRab Ka-
hana, concerned themselves with the same questions as did the
conventional economics, presenting an economics in function and
structure, but one that concerned things of value other than those
identified by the initial system. So indeed we deal with an economics, an economics of something other than real estate.

But it was an economics just as profoundly embedded in the
social order, just as deeply a political economics, just as pervasively
a systemic economics, as the economics of the Mishnah and of
Aristotle. Why so? Because issues such as the definition of wealth,
the means of production and the meaning of control thereof, the
disposition of wealth through distributive or other media, theory
of money, reward for labor, and the like—all these issues found
their answers in the counterpart category of economics, as much
as in the received and conventional philosophical economics. The
new "scarce resource" accomplished what the old one did, but it
was a different resource, a new currency. At stake in the category
meant to address the issues of the way of life of the social entity,
therefore, were precisely the same considerations as confront economics in its (to us) conventional and commonplace, philosophical sense. But since the definition of wealth changes, as we have
already seen, from land to Torah, much else would be transformed
on that account.

That explains why, in the formation of the counterpart category of value other than real value but in function and in social
meaning value nonetheless, we witness the transformation of a
system from philosophy to religion. We err profoundly if we sup-

pose that in contrasting land to Torah and affirming that true value lies in Torah, the framers of the successor system have formulated an essentially spiritual or otherwise immaterial conception for themselves, that is, a surrogate for economics in the conventional sense. That is not what happened. What we have is an economics that answers the questions economics answers, as we said, but that has chosen a different value from real value—real estate, as we have already seen—as its definition of that scarce resource that requires a rational policy for preservation and enhancement. Land produced a living; so did Torah. Land formed the foundation of the social entity; so did Torah.

The transvaluation of value was such that an economics concerning the rational management and increase of scarce resources worked itself out in such a way as to answer, for quite different things of value from real property or from capital such as we know as value, precisely the same questions that the received economics addressed in connection with wealth of a real character: land and its produce. Systemic transformation comes to the surface in articulated symbolic change. The utter transvaluation of value finds expression in a jarring juxtaposition, an utter shift of rationality, specifically, the substitution of Torah for real estate. We recall how in a successor document (but in none prior to the fifth century compilations) Tarfon thought wealth took the form of land, while Aqiba the form of Torah-learning. That the sense is material and concrete is explicit: land for Torah, Torah for land.

The successor system has its own definitions not only for learning, symbolized by the word *Torah,* but also for wealth, expressed in the same symbol. Accordingly, the category formation for worldview, Torah in place of philosophy, dictates, as a matter of fact, a still more striking category reformation, in which the entire matter of scarce resources is reconsidered, and a counterpart category set forth. When "Torah" substitutes for real estate, what, exactly, does the successor system know as scarce resources, and how is the counterpart category constructed?

It follows that, while in the successor system's theory of the component of the social order represented by the way of life, we find an economics, it is an economics of scarce resources defined as something other than particular real estate. Why do we insist that these questions are economic in character? It is because they deal with the rules or theory of the rational management of scarce resources, their preservation and increase, and do so in commonplace terms of philosophical economics, e.g., the control of the means of production, the definition of money and of value, the distribution of valued goods and services, whether by appeal to the market or to a theory of distributive economics, the theory of the value of labor and the like. But while the structure remained the same, the contents would differ radically, hence the transvaluation of value. It was as if a new currency were issued to replace the old, then declared of no value, capable of purchasing nothing worth having. In such an economics, there is far more than a currency reform, but rather a complete economic revolution, a new beginning, as much as a shift from socialism to capitalism. But the transvaluation, in our case, was more thoroughgoing still, since involved was the very reconsideration of the scarcity of scarce resources. Both elements then underwent transvaluation: the definition of resources of value and the rationality involved in the management of scarcity. In a word, while real estate cannot increase and by definition must always prove scarce, the value represented by Torah could expand without limit. Value could then increase indefinitely, resources that were desired and scarce could be made ever more abundant, in the transformed economics of the successor system.

✡
✠

While responding to the same questions of that same part of the social order with which the received category concerned itself, the economics that emerged in no way proves discontinuous with the received economics. Why not just another economics than the philosophical one we have considered? The reason is that so abrupt and fundamental a reworking will be seen to have taken place that the category—way of life—*while yet an economics*—nonetheless is now a wholly other economics, one completely without relationship to the inherited definition of way of life (manner of earning a living) as to both structure and system.

For at stake is not merely the spiritualization of wealth, that is to say, the re-presentation of what "wealth" *really* consists of in other-than-material terms. That would represent not an economics but a theology. For example, the familiar saying in tractate Abot, "Who is rich? One who is happy in his lot," simply does not constitute a statement of economics at all. Like sayings in the Gospels that denigrate wealth, this one tells nothing about the rational management (e.g., increase) of scarce resources. It merely tells about appropriate moral attitudes of a virtuous order: how life is worth living, not answering an economic question at all. On the other hand, the tale that contrasts wealth in the form of land and its produce with wealth in the form of Torah (whatever is meant by "Torah") does constitute a statement of economics. The reason is that the storyteller invokes precisely the category of wealth—real property—that conventional economics defines as wealth. If we have land, we have wealth, and we can support ourselves; if we have Torah, we have wealth, and we can support ourselves. Those form the two components of the contrastive equation before us. But then wealth is disenlandised and the Torah substituted for real property of all kinds. That forms not a theology, nor an economics in any conventional sense, but, rather, an antieconomics. The same will be seen to be so in politics.

Why do we insist that these kinds of stories deal with scarce resources in a concrete sense? Because in both cases cited to this point the upshot of the possession of Torah is this-worldly, concrete, tangible, and palpable. The rewards are not described as "filling treasuries in the heart," nor do they "enrich the soul," nor are they postponed to the world to come (as would be the case in a kind of capitalistic theology of investment on earth for return in heaven). The tale concerning Aqiba like the one involving Rabbi and Ardavan, insists upon precisely the same *results* of the possession of wealth of value in the form of "Torah" as characterize wealth or value in the form of real estate. The key language is this: "Go, buy us a piece of land, *so we can get a living from it* and labor in the study of Torah together." Tarfon assumes owning land buys leisure for Torah study; Aqiba does not contradict that assumption; he steps beyond it.

Then one thing forms the counterpart and opposite of the other—antieconomics and economics, respectively—but both things yield a single result: wealth to sustain leisure, which any reader of Xenophon's handbook on economics (estate management, in his context) will have found an entirely commonplace and obviously true judgment. That explains why the form that wealth in the successor system now takes—Torah rather than real estate—presents a jarring contrast, one that is, of course, the point of the story. And as a matter of fact, as we shall see in just a moment, that jarring contrast will have proved unintelligible to any authorship prior to the second stage in the formation of the canonical writings, and it explicitly contradicts the sense of matters that predominates in the first stage: the Torah is not to be made "a spade to dig with" (whatever that can have meant). In Tarfon's mind, therefore, real (in the theological sense) value is real (in the economic sense) wealth, that is, real estate, because if you own land, you can enjoy the leisure to do what you really want to do, which (as every philosopher understood) is to study (in the sages' case) the Torah together. But to Aqiba, in the tale, that is beside the point, since the real (in the theological sense) value (in the economic sense, that is, what provides a living—food to eat, for instance) is Torah (study), and that, in itself, suffices. The sense is, if we have land, we have a living, and if we have Torah, we have a living, which is no different from the living that we have from land—but which, as a matter of fact, is more secure.

103

Owning land involved control of the means of production, and so did knowing the Torah. But—more to the point—from land people derived a living, and from Torah people derived a living in *precisely* the same sense—that is to say, in the material and concrete sense—in which from land they could do so. That is alleged time and again, and at stake, then, is not the mere denigration of wealth but the transvaluation of value. Then the transvaluation consisted in (1) the disenlandisement of value, and (2) the transvaluation of (knowing or studying) the Torah, the imputation to Torah of the value formerly associated with land. And that is why it is valid to claim for Torah the status of a counterpart category: the system's economics, its theory of the way of life of the community and account of the rational disposition of those scarce resources that made everyday material existence possible and even pleasant: an economics of wealth, but of wealth differently defined, while similarly valued and utilized.

For like Aristotle, when the authorship of the Mishnah conducted discourse upon economic questions, they understood wealth in entirely this-worldly terms. The Torah formed a component in the system of hierarchical classification, not a unit of value or a measure of worth. By contrast, in the successor system portrayed by the Talmud of the Land of Israel, Genesis Rabbah, Leviticus Rabbah, and their companions, the concept of scarce resources was linked to the conception of Torah and so took on altogether fresh meanings, but in exactly the same context and producing exactly the same material consequences, e.g., having food to eat and a dwelling for shelter, with the result that we have to redefine that which serves the very category, "economics," altogether. Why is this necessary? It is because of those stunning transvaluations, already cited, of value stated explicitly and baldly in the contrast between land and Torah. When the successor documents contrast the received value with the value they recognize, then we must ask about the formation of the counterpart category and consider how to make sense of that category.

The separation of economics from land value, the transvaluation of value so that Torah replaced land as the supreme measure of value—and also, as a matter of fact, of social worth—these form (an) economics. It is, moreover, one that is fully the counterpart of the philosophical economics based on real estate as true value that Aristotle and the framers of the Mishnah constructed, each party for its own systemic purpose. If we have not reviewed the components of the economics of the Torah—the theory of means of production and who controls the operative unit of production of value, the consideration of whether we deal with a market economics or a distributive economics, the reason is that we have not had to. It is perfectly obvious that the sage controlled the means of production and fully mastered the power to govern them; the sage distributed valued resources—supernatural or material, as the case required—and the conception of a market was as alien to that economics as it was to the priestly economics revised and replicated by the Mishnah's system. Enough has been said, therefore, to establish beyond reasonable doubt the claim that in the Torah we deal with the system's counterpart category, its economics.

And yet that very fact calls into question the insistence that what we have is not (merely) another economics, with a different value, but a counterpart economics. For we claim that what we have is a systemic counterpart, not the same thing in another form: an antieconomics and the transvaluation of value, not merely the redefinition of what is to be valued. Obviously, we have reservations that have led us to insist that the systemic economics forms a counterpart to, but not a parallel and a mere replication of, another economics. A shift from valuing land to valuing liquid capital, or from valuing beads to valuing conches, for that matter, would not require the invention of the category of counterpart economics, or the rather protracted argument offered earlier concerning the movement from the subject to the predicate of the operative language of definition. Why, then, my rather odd claim that we have an economics that is transvalued, not merely redefined?

It is because economics deals with scarce resources, and the disenlandisement of economics in the successor Judaism has turned upon its head the very focus of economics: scarcity and the rational confrontation with scarcity. Rigid limits to land are set by nature; still more narrow limits apply to the Holy Land. But no limits pertain to knowledge of the Torah. So we find ourselves dealing with an economics that concerns not the rational utilization of scarce resources but the very opposite: the rational utilization of what can and ought to be the opposite of scarce. In identifying knowledge and teaching of the Torah as the ultimate value, the successor system has not simply constructed a new economics in place of an old one, finding of value something other than had earlier been valued; it has redefined economics altogether. It has done so, as a matter of fact, in a manner that is entirely familiar, by setting forth in place of an economics of scarcity an economics of abundant productivity.

Disenlandising value thus transvalues value by insisting upon its (potential) increase as the definition of what is rational economic action. The task is not preservation of power over land but increase of power over the Torah, because one can only preserve land, but one can increase one's knowledge of the Torah. So, to re-vert to the theoretical point that in context seemed so excessive, the economics of the initial system concerns the rational disposi-tion of the scarce resource that is particular real property; the rational increase of the potentially abundant resource that is Torah-learning is—serves and functions as—the economics of the successor system.

## DOES A SAGE HAVE TO WORK FOR A LIVING?

The contrast between the starting position and the end point of Rabbinic Judaism in the matter of values is best shown in a single case, the problem of the this-worldly payoff of Torah study. As we have seen, knowledge of Torah is the abundant resource through which this world's scarce resources will be attained. But that is not how the Mishnah's framers viewed matters at the outset. In the Mishnah, Torah stands for status but produces no consequences of a material order, or, as a matter of fact, even for one's caste sta-tus. It is the simple fact that studying the Torah is deemed an ac-tion to which accrues unlimited benefit. This is made explicit:

### PEAH 1:1A-E

A. These are things that have no specified measure: the quantity of produce designated as *peah;* the quantity of produce given as first fruits, the value of the appearance offering, the per-formance of righteous deeds, and time spent in study of Torah.

B. These are things the benefit of which a person enjoys in this world, while the principal remains for him in the world to come: deeds in honor of father and mother, performance of righteous deeds, and acts which bring peace between a man and his fellow.

C. But the study of Torah is as important as all of them all to-gether.

The study of Torah, or knowledge of the Torah, is equivalent to a variety of other meritorious actions, e.g., designating produce as "corner of the field" for use by the scheduled castes; bringing an offering of high cost; honoring parents. Among these comparable deeds, study of the Torah enjoys pride of place. But the rewards are not worldly, not material, not palpable. If we know the Torah, we enjoy a higher status than if we do not; but we have still to work for a living.

Knowledge of the Torah did not define the qualifications of the highest offices, for instance, a member of the priestly caste could be high priest and not have mastered the Torah:

## M. YOMA 1:6A-D

> A. If the high priest was a sage, he expounds the relevant Scriptures of the Day of Atonement, and if not, disciples of sages expound for him. If he was used to reading Scriptures, he read, and if not, they read for him.

Not only so, but the Mishnah knows nothing of using holy funds to support disciples of sages, e.g., M. Meg. 3:1: Townsfolk who sold a street of a town buy with its proceeds a synagogue, and so on. Mishnah-tractate Sheqalim, with its account of the use of public funds for the Temple, never supposes that disciples of sages associated with the Temple may be paid from the public funds represented by the *sheqel*-tax.

This underlines the simple fact that in the Mishnah it is not assumed that a disciple of a sage gets support on account of his Torah study, and it also is not assumed that the sage makes his living through Torah study, or other Torah activities. Knowledge of the Torah or the act of study enjoys no material value. For instance, an act of betrothal requires an exchange of something of value; among the examples of value the act of study or teaching of the Torah is never offered, e.g., "Lo, thou art betrothed to us in exchange for my teaching you [or your brother or your father] a teaching of the Torah" is never suggested as a possibility. So Torah-learning is not material and produces no benefits of a material character. Sages' status may derive from knowledge of Torah, but that status is not confused with the material consideration involved in who may matter to whom. In M. Qid. 4:1 sages do not form a caste. "Ten castes came up from Babylonia," but the "status" of sage has no bearing upon his caste status. Then what difference does Torah study or Torah knowledge make? It is, as we have stressed, one of taxic consequence and one of status, but with no bearing whatsoever upon one's livelihood.

Knowledge of the Torah does not change one's caste status, e.g., priest or *mamzer* or *Netin,* and that caste status does govern whom one may marry, a matter of substantial economic consequence. But it does change one's status as to precedence of another order altogether—one that is curiously unspecific at M. Horayot 3:8. Hierarchical classification for its own sake, lacking all practical consequence, characterizes the Mishnah's system, defining, after all, its purpose and its goal! Along these same lines, the premise of tractate Sanhedrin is that the sage is judge and administrator of the community; knowledge of the Torah qualifies him; but knowledge of the Torah does not provide a living or the equivalent of a living. No provision for supporting the sage as administrator, clerk, or judge is suggested in the tractate.

What about knowledge of Torah as a way of making one's living? One's merit makes the difference between poverty and wealth, or one's sinfulness. The conception that, if we study Torah, we automatically get the food we need to eat and the roof we need for shelter is not at issue here, where our concern is with being kept from evil in youth and enjoying God's blessing in old age on account of keeping the Torah—a very different thing.

The first apologia for the Mishnah, tractate Abot, takes the view that one should not make one's living through study of the Torah. That is made explicit in Torah sayings of tractate Abot, where we find explicit rejection of the theory of Torah study as a means of avoiding one's obligation to earn a living. Torah study without a craft is rejected; Torah study along with labor at a craft is defined as the ideal way of life. The following sayings make that point quite clearly:

## M. Abot 2:2 and 3:17

2:2 A. Rabban Gamaliel, a son of Rabbi Judah the Patriarch says: Fitting is learning in the Torah along with a craft, for the labor put into the two of them makes one forget sin. And all learning of the Torah which is not joined with labor is destined to be null and causes sin.

3:17 A. R. Eleazar b. Azariah says, ". . . If there is no sustenance [lit.: flour], there is no Torah-learning. If there is no Torah-learning, there is no sustenance."

Here there is no contrast between two forms of wealth, one less secure, the other more. The way of virtue lies rather in economic activity in the conventional sense, joined to intellectual or philosophical activity in sages' sense. Again, Xenophon will not have been surprised. The labor in Torah is not an economic activity and produces no solutions to this-worldly problems of getting food, shelter, or clothing. To the contrary, labor in Torah defines the purpose of human life; it is the goal, but it is not the medium for maintaining life and avoiding starvation or exposure to the elements. Do worldly benefits accrue to those who study the Torah? The prevailing view, represented by the bulk of sayings, treats Torah study as an activity that competes with economic venture and insists that Torah study take precedence, even though it is not of economic value in any commonplace sense of the term.

Torah study competes with, rather than replaces, economic activity. That is the simple position of tractate Abot, extending the conception of matters explicit in the Mishnah. If we had to make a simple statement of the situation prevailing at c. 250 C.E., sages contrast their wealth, which is spiritual and intellectual, with material wealth; they do not deem the one to form the counterpart of the other, but only as the opposite.

And that brings us to consider the re-presentation of wealth in the successor documents. A system that forbids the use of the Torah as a spade with which to dig, as a means of making one's living, will have found proof for its position in the numerous allegations in wisdom literature that the value of wisdom, understood of course as the Torah is beyond price: "Happy is the man who finds wisdom . . . for the gain from it is better than gain from silver, and its profit better than gold; she is more precious than jewels, and nothing you desire can compare with her." (Prov. 3:13–15). That and numerous parallels were not understood to mean that if people devoted themselves to the study of the Torah and the teaching thereof, they would not have to work any more. Nor do the praises of wisdom specifically contrast Torah-learning with landownership. But in the successor writings, that is precisely what is commonplace. And the conclusion is drawn that one may derive one's living from study of the Torah: then it becomes a spade with which to dig, as much as a real spade served to dig in the earth to make the ground yield a living.

## "SELL ALL YOU HAVE AND FOLLOW ME": THE CHRISTIAN ECONOMY OF SALVATION

When Christianity emerged, other popular movements were also taking shape; taken together, the members of those other groups at times greatly outnumbered Christians. Among those movements, the ones called Gnostic exerted the strongest influence on the church, and provided so serious a challenge that Christian theology spelled itself out as an alternative to Gnosticism. The debate between Christians and Gnostics enables us clearly to see the articulation of Christian values.

The words *Gnostic* and *Gnosticism* derive from the Greek term *gnosis*, which means "knowledge." The knowledge designated by the religious usage of the term was not simply a matter of data or information. Gnostics claimed that they enjoyed insight into the divine realm itself. The origins of Gnosticism have been hotly debated in the history of scholarship. It has been seen, to give some examples, as just an elite, intellectual phase within Christianity, or as a typically Hellenistic tendency, or as the transformation of Jewish apocalyptic speculation into a new key. All of those suggestions have merit, but it is not possible to fix upon a single origin of Gnosticism. It is a very widespread phenomenon of the Hellenistic world, and it thrived in an environment of syncretism, in which the contributions of many different religions were brought together into new configurations. Gnosticism is one of those syncretistic configurations.

### PAUL'S DEBATE CONCERNING KNOWLEDGE (GNOSIS)

In his correspondence with Christians in Corinth (c. 55–56 C.E.), Paul provides an early indication of the roots of Gnosticism. The group that he addresses within the community in Corinth is not Gnostic in the formal sense, because no claim is made to supersede all prior forms of Christianity, but they do claim a particular form of knowledge. The issue in play is the difficult question of food sacrificed to idols. Some of Paul's readers know, and Paul acknowledges, that "there is no idol in the world, and there is no God but one" (1 Cor. 8:4, see also vv. 5–6). In other words, people in the community could purchase meat sold in the marketplace, where it might have been slaughtered as a notional sacrifice to some god or another. The position of James, which is confirmed by the apostles in the book of Acts, is that all Christians—including non-Jewish Christians—are required to abstain from meat that has been sacrificed to idols (Acts 15:13–29). That was part of the minimal purity required of all. Paul agrees with the opinion that knowledge can overrule that apostolic decree. Indeed, this difference with James is one of the principal indications that Paul's circle had an identity all its own.

At the same time, Paul wishes to qualify any direct, unqualified appeal to such knowledge as the basis of community discipline (1 Cor. 8:1-3):

> Concerning meat sacrificed to idols: we know that we all have knowledge. Knowledge puffs up, while love builds up. If anyone thinks to have known something, one has not yet known as it is necessary to know. But if anyone loves God, that person has been known by God.

As Paul crafts his argument, there is both an immediate result and a profound implication of what he says. As applied to the immediate question of meat sacrificed to idols, Paul wants to control the insight that idols are a myth with concern for one's neighbor. If one's neighbor believes in idols, then seeing a person with knowledge eating an idol's meat might well confirm that false belief. Better not to eat meat at all, concludes Paul, than to do that (1 Cor. 8:7–13). In the ethical realm, therefore, Paul sees love as overruling knowledge.

That leads us on to the profound implication of Paul's teaching, which is a fundamental value of Christianity in every age. Paul not only insists that knowledge should be tempered by love; he also maintains that love is the *measure* of knowledge. He knows, from the teaching of Jesus, that love of God and love of neighbor are the fulfillment of the Law (see Rom. 13:8–10). On that basis, Paul proceeds to the heart of his new principle: loving God arouses God's love, and then one is in a reciprocal relationship of familiarity with God. That is the basis on which he can say explicitly (in 1 Cor. 8:3, quoted above in context), "if anyone loves God, that person has been known by God." The principle is so simple and succinct that a reader can easily miss what Paul has done here: knowledge is now not insight at all, not a matter of personal perception, but a function of one's familiarity with God. Paul replaces knowledge as mastery over theological fact with knowledge as a consequence of a loving relationship with God.

It may seem somewhat ironic that Paul, the greatest Christian intellectual in the period of the New Testament, should have been responsible for this insight. His letters are a finely balanced combination of theological creativity and powerful rhetoric, all in the service of a distinctive understanding of what the church is and should be. But Paul was able to achieve the insight that knowledge needs to be qualified by love precisely because he had an analytic ability that most other teachers lacked. In addition, what Paul faced in Corinth was what he called a puffed up or arrogant claim of knowledge. It is no coincidence that the problem arose in that recently developed commercial city. Located on a vital shipping route (offering portage overland between two major seaports), Corinth was subject to influences from all over the Hellenistic world.[10] That made it an ideal setting for the kind of religious syncretism that an appeal to *gnosis* thrived on.

By the first century C.E., the gods of Greece and Rome had long been viewed with skepticism. Gods imported from other cultures, such as Isis from Egypt or Attis and Cybele from Asia Minor, found a following among many, but such new cults appeared to be more a matter of fashion than of conviction. On the other hand, the religious philosophies that stressed the importance of knowledge continued to hold sway: there was a general agreement that reasoning could bring knowledge of the divine. The type of reasoning varied widely. Aristotelians looked at the connection between the divine and the actual in terms of causation, while Platonists saw a divine ideal reflected in what we can see. Stoicism became a very popular movement, in its claim that a single reason lies behind both the natural and the social worlds.

In addition to the philosophical reason of Aristotelians, Platonists, Stoics, and many other groups, the classical world by the time of the New Testament also had recourse to a different sort of inspiration. Oracles had long been featured at Delphi, and belief in the possibilities of direct communication with the divine survived skepticism concerning the gods themselves (Apollo, in the case of Delphi). More general communication with the divine realm was offered in the Mystery cults: an initiate might join in the release of Persephone from the underworld, or in the rebirth of the dismembered Dionysus. Knowledge of such initiation—which typically involved elaborate and expensive procedures and sacrifices— amounted to direct, unmediated communication with the divine.

Paul is combating just such an understanding of knowledge in the passage from 1 Corinthians that we have already considered. Unless love is clearly perceived as the social dimension of God's spirit within his community, Paul argues that there is no genuine knowledge, which is God's knowing of his own children. For the same reason, Paul will later argue in the most famous chapter of the same letter, "And if I have prophecy and I know all mysteries and all knowledge and if I have all faith so as to move mountains, but I have not love, I am nothing" (1 Cor. 13:2).

## THE EMERGENCE OF GNOSTICISM

The quest for knowledge by itself, even knowledge of the divine, is not the same thing as Gnosticism. Gnosticism rather represents a further development, a development that successfully competed with Christianity, even as it adopted (and transformed) elements of Christian teaching. The emergence of Gnosticism reflects the appeal of dualism within the period. Dualism refers to any bifurcation of experience into two distinct realms. Gnostics typically made a radical distinction between the present, material world and the ineffable nature of God. This world is subject to decay and the rule of evil forces; only release from it can bring the spiritual awakening and freedom of *gnosis*. Although appeals to the power of *gnosis* such as we have seen disputed by Paul in 1 Corinthians were commonly made by the first century, Gnosticism proper with its dualistic emphasis had not yet fully emerged.

Attempts have been made in the past to explain the emergence of Gnosticism on the basis of the apocalyptic literature of Judaism. Apocalypses such as the books of Daniel and *4 Ezra* represent a clear separation between those who are to be saved in a final judgment and those who are to be punished. Similarly, one of the documents found at Qumran, *The War of the Sons of Light and the Sons of Darkness,* provides a clear example of dualism.[11] The whole of Gnosticism cannot be explained simply as an inheritance of apocalyptic thought, but its ethical dualism, the hard distinction between the saved and the doomed, does emerge just after the period of the most intense production of apocalypses.

Works such as *4 Ezra* and *2 Baruch* are examples of apocalyptic dualism, and they are joined on the Christian side by the Revelation of John. All were produced after the destruction of the Temple in Jerusalem, which was an incentive to explain how recent history could possibly fit within the overall plan of God. To this list, we should also add *The Testaments of the Twelve Patriarchs.* The work is a composite Judaic and Christian document, reflecting an interest in adding new dimensions of meaning to previously existing text. That is also a characteristic of Gnosticism, which emerged fully during the second century. It is something of an irony that the Roman campaigns in Judaea occasioned a literature that itself helped to push Greco-Roman religion in a dualistic direction.

A good example of a Gnostic text from the second century is *The Gospel of Truth,* which begins:[12]

> The gospel of truth is a joy for those who have received from the Father of truth the gift of knowing him, through the power of the Word that came forth from the fullness—the one who is in the thought and the mind of the Father, that is, the one who is ad-

dressed as the Savior, that being the name of the work he is to perform for the redemption of those who were ignorant of the Father, while the name of the gospel is the proclamation of hope, being discovery for those who search for him.

What is useful about that initial statement is that it is a very simplified summary of major precepts and assumptions of Gnosticism. "Knowledge" here comes only as a gift of the Father, and is mediated by the "Word," a designation for Jesus taken from the first chapter of John's Gospel. But that Word comes forth from "the fullness," emanations outward from the Father. The complexity of the divine world around the Father is often emphasized in Gnostic texts, and developed to a bewildering degree of detail. The fascination with schemes representing the generation of the world is probably an inheritance from Greek and Roman mythology and philosophy. The mastery of that detail is held to mean that one has successfully become one who knows, a Gnostic.

A firm distinction is made in *The Gospel of Truth* between those who are spiritual, capable of receiving illumination, and those who are material, ignorant of what is being offered (see *Gospel of Truth* 28–31). Failure to attain *gnosis,* then, is a mark of one's incapacity to be rescued from the conditions of this world. The assumption throughout is that the material world is a pit of ignorance and decay, from which the Gnostic must be extricated. That explains what is otherwise a puzzling feature of Gnosticism: the wide variance between ascetical self-denial and the encouragement of libertine behavior. In both cases, freedom from what is material was being claimed and put into practice.

Charges against Gnostics of libertinism should not be pressed literally. The same sort of accusations—of such crimes as incest, cannibalism, and debauchery—were brought against Christians during the same period.[13] Both Gnostics and Christians fell under suspicion of beings practitioners of nontraditional religions (superstitions), which would not support the interests of the empire. Also in both cases, the emphasis on esoteric doctrine opened the way for the charge that secrecy was intended to conceal something shameful. Christianity and Gnosticism also challenged the sensibilities of the Greco-Roman religious philosophies that we have mentioned. During the second century, both of them had discovered the idiom of philosophy itself in order to develop and convey their claims. Particularly, each crafted a distinctive view of the divine "Word" (*logos*) which conveys the truth of God to humanity. For most Christians, that Logos was Jesus Christ, understood as the human teacher who at last fully incarnated what philosophers and prophets had been searching for and had partially seen.

## THE RESPONSE OF CATHOLIC CHRISTIANITY

Justin Martyr was the theologian who articulated that doctrine most clearly from the perspective of Christianity, on the basis of the Gospel according to John. In 151 C.E. he addressed his *Apology* to the emperor, Antoninus Pius himself. Such was his confidence that the "true philosophy" represented by Christ, attested in the Hebrew Scriptures, would triumph among the other options available at the time. Justin himself had been trained within some of those traditions, and by his Samaritan birth he could claim to represent something of the wisdom of the east. Somewhere between 162 and 168, however, Justin was martyred in Rome, a victim of the increasing hostility to Christianity under the reign of Marcus Aurelius.[14] Justin argued that the light of reason in people is put there by God, and is to be equated with the Word of God incarnate in Jesus. His belief in the salvation of people as they actually are is attested by his attachment to millenarianism, the conviction that Christ would return to reign with his saints for a thousand years. That conviction, derived from Revelation 20, was fervently maintained by catholic Christians during the second century, in opposition to the abstract view of salvation that Gnostics preferred.

As we saw in the passage from *The Gospel of Truth,* the Gnostic perspective on the *logos* was very different. It had to do first of all with an emanation from the Father in the fullness of the divine realm, and had less to do with Jesus personally and historically. Indeed, some Gnostics did not find it necessary to use Christian traditions at all in order to articulate their position, and even those that did adopt Christian materials transformed them in the interests of abstraction.

The emerging difference between Christians and Gnostics over the question of Christology was inevitable, in that the issue of dualism separated them. Some Gnostics, such as Marcion,[15] believed that the God of the Hebrew Bible was a false pretender, and that the Christian canon should be reduced to the nub of those portions of Luke and Paul that portray Christianity as superseding Judaism. It must be stressed that not all Gnostics were Christians, and not all rejected the God of Israel as firmly as Marcion did, but the tendency of the Gnostic movements in all their variety was in a dualistic direction.

In his response to the claims of Gnosticism, Clement of Alexandria, who was active in the catechetical school in that great city during the latter part of the second century, stands out as a leader among Christians. Alexandria was a center for Gnosticism as well as Christianity, and the two groups contended over a similar constituency. Clement's strategy was to insist that the Gospel offered its own *gnosis* in that form of Jesus Christ himself, whom Clement portrayed as "the Paedagogue." That term in Greek had a particular meaning. It did not refer to a schoolmaster, but to someone who leads children to school. So Clement's choice of words conceives of Jesus as a companion on the way to learning. He frames our habits according to divine wisdom, brings us to the point where we can decide to act according to Jesus' Word (for Jesus is himself the Logos), and even offers us the prospect of control over our passions.[16]

117

The role of Christ as the Paedagogue is a daring conception. Clement deliberately avoids the more exalted terminology of divine emanation, which had been developed by that time within Gnostic circles. Instead, Clement stresses the offer of mediation to all that is involved in Christ. By choosing an example from a rather low social status, Clement also hit upon a resonance with the social experience of his own constituency. But that choice had another—and more profound—implication. The Paedagogue who leads the children to school is less exalted than the teacher in the academy, but he also knows those children in ways that the teacher does not. Clement understands Jesus to be involved in the formation of passions, as well as of reason.

Reason is certainly at the center of Clement's view of education. It is the point from which one might decide to learn from the Logos. But that decision takes place in a particular social and individual context. Socially, there are habits of behavior and speech that the Paedagogue instills; they are the habits that make the personal decision to learn possible and even likely. Individually, the power of the Logos is such that even human passions may fall within its influence. Clement is quite clear that passions are more recalcitrant than reason, and that inadvertent disobedience is inevitable, but he is also insistent in the claim that emotions as well as intellect are reformed in the light of the Logos.

Clement's developmental model expresses the anthropology of early Christianity in a way that distinguishes it from Gnosticism. He aggressively reclaims the realm of human passion as part of the potential and actual rule of Christ. Where Gnosticism focuses on the issue of intellectual illumination alone, to the exclusion of the realm of moral and emotional engagement, Christianity during the second century came to insist upon a more integrative understanding of salvation.

Far to the west of Alexandria, in Lyons (in modern France), a contemporary of Clement found a language to describe this more unified vision of salvation. Irenaeus, bishop of Lyons, countered Gnostic understandings of the gospel with what was called by his time a "catholic" faith. Faith as catholic is "through the whole" (*kath holou*[17]) of the church. It is faith such as you would find it in Alexandria, Lyons, Rome, Ephesus, Corinth, Antioch, or wherever. That construction of Christianity is designed to avoid any particular requirement (such as one of the schemes of Gnosticism) being made upon Christians as such.

Irenaeus's attempt to join in establishing a generic or catholic Christianity called attention to four aspects of faith that have remained constant in classic definitions of Christianity. First, faith was to be expressed by means of the Scriptures as received from Israel; there was no question of eliminating the Hebrew Bible. Second, faith was grounded in the preaching of the apostles, as instanced in their own writings and the creeds. Third, communities were to practice their faith by means of the sacraments that were universally recognized at that time, baptism and eucharist. Fourth, the loyalty of the church to these principles was to be assured by the authority of bishops and priests, understood as successors of the apostles. Taken together, these were the constituents of "the great and glorious body of Christ." They made the church a divine institution: "Where the Spirit of God is, there is the Church and all grace, and the Spirit is truth."[18]

Although Irenaeus's conception was designed to be inclusive, it also was at odds with emerging Gnosticism. The issue was not only the authority of the Hebrew Bible. Gnostics also cherished writings that were not apostolic, sacraments that were not universal, leaders who were set up privately. The sort of tensions involved might be compared to the relations between adherents of one of the "New Age" movements and, say, Presbyterianism. Although formal exclusion is not in question, neither is one group truly comfortable with the other.

119

Irenaeus's concern to establish this fourfold definition of the church is consonant with one of his most vivid observations. Just as there are four quarters of the heavens, four principal winds that circle the world, and four cherubim before the throne of God, he says, so there are four Gospels. Indeed, the number four corresponds to the four universal (or catholic) covenants between God and humanity: those of Noah, Abraham, Moses, and Christ.[19] The Gospels belong to the order of the very basics of life, and—what is equally important to appreciate—the basics of life belong to the Gospels. The power of God is not to be abstracted from the terms and conditions of the world in which we live. In insisting upon that, teachers such as Clement and Irenaeus opposed the popular dualism that was a principal appeal of the Gnostics. Instead, catholic Christians insisted on the incarnation as the key to the revelation of God's truth to humanity.

The incarnational emphasis of catholic Christianity is accurately conveyed by its creed, which is still in use under the title of the Apostles' Creed:

> I believe in (1) God the Father almighty, maker of heaven and earth, and in (2) Jesus Christ, his only son, our Lord, who was conceived by the Holy Spirit, born of the virgin Mary, suffered under Pontius Pilate, was crucified, dead, and buried. He descended into hell; the third day he rose from the dead, and ascended into heaven, and sits at the right hand of God the father almighty. I believe in (3) the Holy Spirit, the holy catholic Church, the communion of saints, the forgiveness of sins, the resurrection of the body, and the life everlasting. Amen.

The division of the creed into three sections—corresponding to Father, Son, and Spirit—is evident. That marks the commitment of catholic Christianity to the Trinity as a means of conceiving God. Indeed, that conception correlates with the kind of incarnational faith that is expressed in the creed.

The incarnation refers principally to Jesus as the embodiment of God, from the time of the prologue of John's Gospel (1:1–18). In the creed, however, that view of the incarnation is developed further. The longest, middle section shows that the ancient practice of Christian catechesis is at the heart of the creed, and that section is a fine summary of the Gospels (compare Peter's speech in Acts 10:34–43). Its level of detail articulates a rigorous alternative to the tendency of Gnosticism toward abstraction. But the statement about Jesus does not stand on its own. His status as Son is rooted in the Father's creation of the heavens and the earth. The creed begins with an embrace of the God of Israel as creator and with an equally emphatic (if indirect) rejection of dualism.

The last paragraph of the creed, devoted to the Holy Spirit, also recollects the catechesis of Christians that climaxed with baptism and reception of the Spirit. That basic understanding is rooted in the catechesis of Peter (again, see Acts 10:34–43, and the sequel in vv. 44–48). But here the common reception of the Spirit is used to assert the communal nature of life in the Spirit. To be baptized is to share the Spirit with the catholic Church: that is where communion with God and forgiveness are to be found.

Finally, the creed closes on a deeply personal and existential note: "The resurrection of the body" refers not to Jesus' resurrection (which has already been mentioned in the preceding paragraph of the creed), but to the ultimate destiny of all who believe in him. The creed does not spell out its understanding of how God raised Jesus and is to raise us from the dead, but it is unequivocal that we are all to be raised as ourselves, as embodied personality. There is no trace here of joining an undifferentiated divine entity, or of some part of us (a soul, an essence) surviving in a disembodied way.

At the same time, the creed was probably composed with a full awareness of Paul's discussion of the issue of the resurrection in 1 Corinthians 15. When Paul thinks of a person, he conceives of a body as composed of flesh, physical substance that varies from one created thing to another (for example, people, animals, birds, and fish; 1 Cor. 15:35–39). But in addition to being physical bodies, people are also what Paul calls a "psychic body," that is bodies with souls (1 Cor. 15:44). (Unfortunately, the phrase is wrongly translated in many modern versions, but its dependence on the noun for "soul" [*psukhe*] is obvious. The adjective does not mean "physical" as we use that word.) In other words, people as bodies are not just lumps of flesh, but they are self-aware. That self-awareness is precisely what makes them "psychic body."

Now in addition to being physical body and psychic body, Paul says we are (or can be, within the power of resurrection) "spiritual body" (1 Cor. 15:44). That is, we can relate thoughts and feelings *to one another and to God*. The explanation of how spirit may be the medium of God's communication is developed earlier in 1 Corinthians (2:10–11). Paul develops his position by quoting a passage from Isaiah 64:4 (in 2:9), which speaks of things beyond human understanding that God has readied for those who love him, and Paul then goes on to say (2:10–11):

> God has revealed them to us through the spirit; for the spirit searches all things, even the depths of God. For who knows a

person's affairs except the person's spirit within? So also no one
has known God's affairs except the spirit of God.

As Paul sees human relations, one person can know what another thinks and feels only on the basis of their shared "spirit."
"Spirit" is the name for what links one person with another, and
by means of that link we can also know what God thinks and feels.
The spirit at issue, Paul goes on to say, is not "the spirit of the
world," but "the spirit of God" (1 Cor. 2:12): the medium of ordinary, human exchange becomes in baptism the vehicle of divine
revelation.

Paul's analysis in 1 Corinthians 2 is part of a complete anthropology, which is spelled out further in 1 Corinthians 15. Jesus,
on the basis of the resurrection, is the last Adam, a life-giving spirit
just as the first Adam was a living being or soul (the two words are
the same in Greek, *psukhe*; see 1 Cor. 15:45). Jesus is the basis on
which we can realize our identities as God's children, the brothers and sisters of Christ, and know the power of the resurrection.
In so saying, Paul defines a distinctive Christology as well as a
characteristic spirituality.

By the second century, Paul had emerged posthumously victorious from his struggles with Peter and James, to some extent because a non-Jewish constituency now predominated within the
church. Likewise, the Pauline anthropology of a resurrection of
the body closes the creed with a vigorous assertion that who we
are now matters in terms of what we shall be raised as by God.

In its assertion of the continuity of the body before and after
the resurrection, non-Gnostic Christianity came increasingly to
stress the actual (that is, material) identity of what God raised in
the case of Jesus and would raise in the case of believers. Resurrection was not merely of the body, the identity that figures in the
medium of flesh, but of the flesh itself. The Latin version of the
creed actually refers to the resurrection of the flesh at its close.[20]
Catholic Christianity emerged as orthodox at the moment it became credal, and regularized faith in terms of certain opinions
(*doxai*) that were held to be right (*ortho-*). That emergence came in
the context of opposition to Gnostic versions of Christianity, and

the result was the greater attachment to literal, material theologies of the resurrection from the second century onward. Christianity had attached itself to a profound validation of flesh as a possible vehicle of the divine. From its incarnational beginnings, the Church had affirmed that God had entered the realm of humanity in the case of Jesus Christ. The corresponding result for those who followed Jesus was, logically, that they could become "participants of the divine nature." That phrase is not a late development within Christianity, but a direct citation from the New Testament (2 Pet. 1:4). But what was not specified by the incarnational theology of the New Testament was that flesh was to be the method of participation. From the second century, that became the common understanding.

By the time that Constantine embraced Christianity, a logical question confronted the church. If Jesus as God's child permitted believers to become children of God, fellow heirs with Christ, did that mean that Jesus shared the same basic nature of God? Was he like God (*homoiousios*) or of one nature with God (*homoousios*)?[21] To say that he was of one nature with God the Father implied that, even in the flesh, God had been made accessible to humanity. There the partisans of *homoiousios* balked, and held that, insofar as he became human, Jesus was less than the Father. The partisans of *homoousios* retaliated with the understanding of the Christian life such that all disciples were to attain to the perfection of the enfleshed Christ, who was during the whole of his life of one nature with God the Father.

123

The partisans of *homoousios* were ultimately victorious, beginning with the council that Constantine convened at Nicea in 325. His commitment to discovering a single orthodox truth in regard to the question is typical of the increasingly institutional quality that the church took on in the age of Constantine. At the same time, Christian preachers became increasingly wary of the entrapments of power and property, even as they acquired more legitimacy.

The stringency of orthodox Christianity by this stage is famous. Asceticism and the renunciation of property were commonly extolled as Christian virtues. A common practice put baptism off until near one's death, in order to reduce the probability of sin after baptism. After all, one was to be perfected by that initiation into Christ; any sin afterward would amount to a complete fall from grace. In all of those manifestations, however, what Christianity of the fourth century represents is not a rejection of the flesh, but a commitment to the prospect of its becoming divine. Some of the same attitudes of radical skepticism towards the world that had been developed by the Gnostics were also embraced by many Christians, but in the interests of a different motivation.

# 3

# Trading Teleologies

## From an Ahistorical Teleology to Messianic Judaism: From the End of Days to the Enduring Kingdom of This World

R abbinic Judaism commenced with a teleology requiring little service from the Messiah theme and ended up appealing to the coming of the sage-Messiah as the generative myth in sustaining the entire system. Christianity commenced its history as a messianic religion par excellence, representing Jesus as Christ and the new age as the age of the end time, but in the fourth century emerged with a message that the end of days and the Second Coming was to be differently conceived. Christ then stood for many things, but his role as Messiah in any historical sense for the here and now scarcely took priority. That is what we mean by "trading teleologies"—a teleology without eschatology for one defined by eschatology, an eschatological teleology set aside in favor of an expectation of cosmic and individual transformation.

In the first and second centuries Rabbinic Judaism, through the Mishnah, gave little sustained attention to the large questions of history, inclusive of the end of history and the coming of the Messiah. These questions are in two aspects. First, as we shall see in this chapter, the Mishnah's teleology—its account of the purpose and end of matters—made its statement without heavy stress

on the end of time and the conclusion of history, such as a doctrine of eschatology produces. Therefore the Mishnah's is a teleology without eschatology, an ahistorical teleology. By 400, by
contrast, the documents of Rabbinic Judaism set forth a fully articulated Messiah doctrine, which was deeply embedded within
the deepest structures of that Judaism. Those documents maintained that if only the people will realize the vision of the sages, the
Messiah will come. This explicit messianization of the system's
teleology sharply contrasts with the state of affairs in the earlier
period. For its part, Christianity began its life with the conviction
that Jesus is Christ, the Messiah. Messianism formed a critical
component of the whole, with the concomitant conviction that the
end of time was at hand, a fully realized eschatology therefore
forming Christianity's teleology. But by the fourth century, people
recognized that the kingdom of God would not arrive quite so
promptly as had been anticipated, and the imminent arrival of
Christ no longer framed Christianity's teleological formation.

But that is not the only consideration; there is also the matter
of the meaning and end of history, the theology of history, which
both religions would have to sort out in response to Scripture's
emphatic insistence on history as a medium for divine revelation.
So, second, in the next chapter we shall address the larger questions of the conception of history that animated the two religions
in their formative centuries. The Mishnah, as we shall see, set forth
a Judaism lacking all historical perspectives, a Judaism that treated
events in a way other than that characteristic of historical thinking. History treats events as singular and one-time, arranged in a
harmonious and linear pattern, leading to the explanation of the
everyday out of the resources of a purposeful sequence of causative
moments. The Mishnah, as we shall see, treated events as not singular but exemplary, not linear but embedded in structures and
patterns of the timeless social order. The successor documents
took up major historical events and examined them carefully, seeking their indicative traits. But this historical perspective did not
yield narrative, linear, unitary, purposive history, such as historical
thinking generates. Rather, Israel's history served to yield paradigms; explaining the present in light of the past for Rabbinic Ju-

daism led to the enduring presence of the past, matched by the stately retreat of the present into the chambers of the past.

In the case of Christianity, the idiom in which teleology was at first worked out was thoroughly eschatological. Jesus' preaching of the kingdom of God involved a nuanced conception, but his emphasis on the kingdom as bringing a definitive transformation is evident. The coming of the kingdom, for which his disciples were to pray, meant the "end" of things as they are; their prayer was "eschatological" in that proper sense.

But Jesus' conception was not apocalyptic. An apocalypse, in the manner of the book of Daniel and the Revelation of John in the Bible, exhibits certain characteristic traits. An eschatology, a teaching of the end of things, is typically present, but it is far more detailed in an apocalypse than in the teaching of Jesus. Events up to and including the end are described in symbolic language, so that the claim is made that understanding the apocalypse means knowing how and when the definitive judgment of God will be completed. The privilege of the "apocalypse" (from the Greek *apokalupsis,* meaning "revelation") is given in the form of a vision. The seer of that vision, who is usually identified as some famous person from the past, is then provided with an interpretation of the meaning of the vision by angelic mediation.

127

The reader or hearer of an apocalypse, then, is put in a position to understand the events of the past and the present on the basis of the future. The vision and the interpretation are received from Heaven, and their truth is attested by a famous figure from the past. And because that figure is from the past, events can be described accurately from the time of Daniel in ancient Babylonia (say) until the desecration of the Temple in 167 B.C.E. That "prediction" of what had already happened supported the promise that what followed in the vision would also prove to be accurate.

Apocalyptic expectation, in the nature of the case, requires to be updated. The victory of the Maccabees during the period in which the book of Daniel was written did not bring with it the definitive victory of Israel, "the saints of the Most High" described in chapter 7 of Daniel. The Maccabean regime proved to be transient, and the restored Temple, much extended by Herod the Great, was destroyed again in the year 70 C.E. Such was the strength of apocalyptic expectation, however, that it remained undefeated by that catastrophe.

Two works in particular demonstrate that apocalyptic expectation continued in both Judaism and Christianity after the disaster of 70 C.E. The work called *4 Ezra* (2 Esdr. in the Apocrypha) was first produced c. 100 C.E. Under the authority of Ezra, the scribe of the Torah who brought the Scriptures back from Babylon to Jerusalem, an account of the universal judgment of humanity, on the basis of their relationship toward the Torah, is graphically depicted. Messianic expectation features in the apocalypse, but the emphasis falls unmistakably on the accountability of all people before God in God's final judgment. Near the same time, the Revelation of John was produced. Its focus is more on the relationship between those who are to be saved of Israel and those who are to be saved of the nations (the gentiles). Revelation 7 envisions just 144,000 people of Israel (from all time, 12,000 from each of the twelve tribes) as "sealed" by an angelic symbol to show that they belong to God. That number is juxtaposed to a numberless throng "from every nation and all tribes, peoples, and languages, standing in front of the throne and before the Lamb" (Rev. 7:9). Here, the perfected number of Israel (12 times 12,000) is incorporated within the limitless reach of the kingdom of God.

Both *4 Ezra* and the Revelation of John demonstrate that apocalyptic eschatology thrived within Judaism and Christianity. Both of them also demonstrate that the issue of the Messiah was ancillary to the focus upon ultimate judgment: each envisages only a temporary messianic era, followed by God's further intervention. In *4 Ezra* (7:28), the messianic era is to last 400 years, while it endures 1,000 years in the Revelation (20:4–6). The latter figure is what gives rise to the concern with the millennium in the apocalyptic vein of Christianity, which continues to this day. But in both cases, that of *4 Ezra* and that of the Revelation, what is striking is that the expectation of the Messiah is not the definitive hope that is envisaged. He is only a part (however important, in the case of Christianity) of the unfolding events. At precisely the moment that Judaism under the guidance of the Rabbinic ethos moved into the idiom of an ahistorical teleology, Christianity embraced apocalyptic speculation, even at a popular level. The Revelation of John (c. 100 C.E.) and *The Shepherd of Hermas* (c. 150 C.E.) attest the extent to which final judgment became a keen expectation within the early church. Among the theologians who supported millenarian hope during the second century, Justin and Irenaeus are to be numbered. The challenge that Christianity increasingly faced was to correlate its deep passion for apocalypticism with its even more profound commitment to the incarnation. If this world is to be swept away in the coming judgment by the Son of Man, what about those parts of the world that have in fact already been incorporated into Christ? In other words, how can the continuing presence of God in the world be reconciled with the radical disruption of that world that is characteristic of apocalyptic expectation? That crucial question was answered by the development of a distinctly Christian teleology between the second and the fourth centuries, as will be discussed below.

Scripture, the written Torah, left no doubt that history, made up of singular events in a straight line from beginning to end point, headed toward a goal and conclusion, bound up with the figure of the Messiah. But the Judaic system put forth by the Mishnah treated historical events in a systematic way, to be classified and subjected to appropriate rules, not as one-time, unique signposts on the path from start to the end time, or eschaton. For the Mishnah, these events did not constitute those one-time, unique, linear sequences that formed the raw material for historical study and interpretation; rather, they contributed to the discovery of timeless patterns, removed from all historical context. Lacking a conception of the movement of time toward an inexorable goal, the Mishnah's teleology found slight use for the Messiah theme. The Messiah played no considerable part in the Mishnah's teleology, which put forth a teleology without an eschatology at all. "Messiah" bore a taxic purpose within the Mishnah's system of hierarchical classification, indicating which priest, or which general, took precedence over some other. But in the fourth century documents, the Messiah becomes a palpable presence, and eschatology defines the framework for Judaism's systemic teleology.

129

Rabbinic Judaism was "messianized," its teleology "eschatolo-gized."[1]

The Messiah theme, by contrast, emerged as paramount in the earliest writings of Christianity, with the Gospels explicitly iden-tifying Jesus as Christ, the Messiah. The identification of Jesus as *the* Messiah, agent of divine judgment at the end of time, had be-come universal in Christian circles by the close of the period of the New Testament. But how was the end of time to be viewed? Was it strictly discontinuous with present experience or had it already begun? What status as compared to God did Jesus have, such that he could exercise a divine function? Responses to such questions by writers such as Irenaeus, Eusebius, and the Cappadocian fa-thers, saw radical developments in the nature of Christianity as a philosophy. During the second century, theologians such as Justin Martyr began to articulate Christianity as the most satis-factory philosophy. Because of their success, faith was increasingly expressed in philosophical terms, and integrated within a com-prehensive view of the world. The manifestation of God within this world (rather than at its end) came increasingly to be empha-sized. We can see this shift in Christianity in that the first-century sources' Christology stressed the messiahship of Jesus, in prefer-ence to other readings of Christ. The fourth-century Christologies stressed ontological over historical questions, philosophical readings of Christ over eschatological ones, putting aside the conviction of God's kingdom on earth in favor of a different dominion—the Christian emperors'—and a different role for Christ from that of the Messiah who brings all things to an end.

## THE MISHNAH'S TELEOLOGY WITHOUT ESCHATOLOGY

When constructing a systematic account of its Judaism, the philoso-phers of the Mishnah did not make use of the Messiah myth in the construction of a teleology for their system. They found it possi-ble to present a statement of goals for their projected life of Israel that was entirely separate from appeals to history and eschatology. Since they certainly knew, and even alluded to, long-standing and widely held convictions on eschatological subjects, beginning with those in Scripture, the framers thereby testified that, knowing the larger repertoire, they made choices different from others before and after them. Their document accurately and ubiquitously expresses these choices, both affirmative and negative.

Now that fact is surprising, because the character of the Israelite Scriptures, with their emphasis on historical narrative as a mode of theological explanation, leads us to expect all Judaisms to evolve as deeply messianic religions. With all prescribed actions pointed toward the coming of the Messiah at the end of time, and all interest focused on answering the historical-salvific questions ("how long?"), Judaism from late antiquity to the present day presents no surprises. Its liturgy evokes historical events to prefigure salvation; prayers of petition repeatedly turn to the speedy coming of the Messiah; and the experience of worship invariably leaves the devotee expectant and hopeful. Just as Rabbinic Judaism is a deeply messianic religion, secular extensions of Judaism have commonly proposed secularized versions of the focus on history and have shown interest in the purpose and denouement of events. Teleology again appears as an eschatology embodied in messianic symbols.

131

Yet, for a brief moment, the Mishnah presented a kind of Judaism in which history did not define the main framework by which the issue of teleology took a form other than the familiar eschatological one, and in which historical events were absorbed, through their trivialization in taxonomic structures, into an ahistorical system. In the kind of Judaism in this document, Messiahs played a part. But these "anointed men" had no historical role. They undertook a task quite different from that assigned to Jesus by the framers of the Gospels. They were merely a species of priest, falling into one classification rather than another.

The Mishnah finds little of consequence to say about the Messiah as savior of Israel, one particular person at one time, but manages to set forth its system's teleology without appeal to eschatology in any form. That is not the function served by the Messiah theme at all. Rather, for the Mishnah, "Messiah" is a category of priest or general—an anointed priest, a general anointed for war. The term also refers to the savior at the end of time, only once in the entire document. That is because the Messiah theme proved marginal to the system's program. What happens if we ask the Mishnah to answer the questions at hand: What of the Messiah? When will he come? To whom, in Israel, will he come? And what must, or can, we do while we wait to hasten his coming? The answers do not emerge from the Mishnah. But they do find elaborate responses in the Talmud of the Land of Israel. If we now reframe these questions and divest them of their mythic cloak, we ask about the Mishnah's theory of the history and destiny of Israel and the purpose of the Mishnah's own system in relationship to Israel's present and end: the implicit teleology of the philosophical law at hand.

Answering these questions out of the resources of the Mishnah is not possible. The Mishnah presents no large view of history. It contains no reflection whatever on the nature and meaning of the destruction of the Temple in 70, an event that surfaces only in connection with some changes in the Law explained as resulting from the end of the cult. The Mishnah pays no attention to the matter of the end time. The word "salvation" is rare, "sanctification" commonplace. More strikingly, the framers of the Mishnah are virtually silent on the teleology of the system; they never tell us why we should do what the Mishnah tells us, let alone explain what will happen if we do. Incidents in the Mishnah are preserved either as narrative settings for the statement of the Law, or, occasionally, as precedents. Historical events are classified and turned into entries on lists. But incidents in any case come few and far between. True, events do make an impact. But it always is for the Mishnah's own purpose and within its own taxonomic system and rule-seeking mode of thought. To be sure, the framers of the Mishnah may also have had a theory of the Messiah and of the meaning of Israel's history and destiny. But they kept it hidden, and their document manages to provide an immense account of Israel's life without explicitly telling us about such matters.

The Mishnah sets forth the decline of generations, in which the destruction of the Temple and the deaths of great sages mark the movement of time and impart to an age the general rules that govern life therein. In the Mishnah the Messiah does not stand at the forefront of the framers' consciousness. The issues encapsulated in the myth and person of the Messiah are scarcely addressed. The framers of the Mishnah do not resort to speculation about the Messiah as a historical-supernatural figure. So far as that kind of speculation provides the vehicle for reflection on salvific issues, or in mythic terms, narratives on the meaning of history and the destiny of Israel, we cannot say that the Mishnah's philosophers take up those encompassing categories of being: Where are we heading? What can we do about it? That does not mean questions found urgent in the aftermath of the destruction of the Temple and the disaster of Bar Kokhba failed to attract the attention of the Mishnah's sages. But they treated history in a different way, offering their own answers to its questions. To these answers we now turn.

When it comes to history and the end of time, the Mishnah absorbs into its encompassing system all events, small and large. With them the sages accomplish what they accomplish in everything else: a vast labor of taxonomy, an immense construction of the order and rules governing the classification of everything on earth and in heaven. The disruptive character of history—one-time events of ineluctable significance—scarcely impresses the philosophers. They find no difficulty in showing that what appears unique and beyond classification has in fact happened before and so falls within the range of trustworthy rules and known procedures. Once history's components, one-time events, lose their distinctiveness, then history as a didactic intellectual construct, as a source of lessons and rules, also loses all pertinence.

## THE MESSIAH THEME IN ABOT

If the end of time and the coming of the Messiah do not serve to explain, for the Mishnah's system, why people should do what the Mishnah says, then what alternative teleology does the Mishnah's first apologetic, Abot, provide? Only when we appreciate the clear answers given in that document, brought to closure at c. 250, shall we grasp how remarkable is the shift, which took place in later documents of the Rabbinic canon, to a messianic framing of the issues of the Torah's ultimate purpose and value. Let us see how the framers of Abot, in the aftermath of the creation of the Mishnah, explain the purpose and goal of the Mishnah: an ahistorical, nonmessianic teleology.

The first document generated by the Mishnah's heirs took up the work of completing the Mishnah's system by answering questions of purpose and meaning. Whatever teleology the Mishnah as such would ever acquire would derive from Abot, which presents statements to express the ethos and ethic of the Mishnah, and so provides a kind of theory. Abot agreed with the other sixty-two tractates: history proved no more important here than it had been before. With scarcely a word about history and no account of events at all, Abot manages to provide an ample account of how the Torah—written and oral, thus in later eyes, Scripture and Mishnah—came down to its own day. Accordingly, the passage of time as such plays no role in the explanation of the origins of the document, nor is the Mishnah presented as eschatological.

Occurrences of great weight ("history") are never invoked. How then does the tractate tell the story of Torah, narrate the history of God's revelation to Israel, encompassing both Scripture and Mishnah? The answer is that Abot's framers manage to do their work of explanation without telling a story or invoking history at all. They pursue a different way of answering the same question, by exploiting a nonhistorical mode of thought and method of legitimation. And that is the main point: teleology serves the purpose of legitimation, and hence is accomplished in ways other than explaining how things originated or assuming that historical fact explains anything.

In the Mishnah, time is differentiated entirely in other than national-historical categories. For, as in Abot, "this world" is when one is alive, "the world to come" is when a person dies. True, we find also "this world" and "the time of the Messiah." But detailed differentiation among the ages of "this world" or "this age" hardly generates problems in Mishnaic thought. Indeed, no such differentiation appears. Accordingly, the developments briefly outlined here constitute a significant shift in the course of intellectual events, to which the sources at hand—the Mishnah and the Talmud of the Land of Israel—amply testify. In c. 200 C.E. events posed a problem of classification and generalization. In c. 400 c.e., events were singular and demanded interpretation because, in all their particularity, they bore messages just as they had in prophetic thought. In the reconsideration of the singularity of events and the systematic effort at interpreting them and the lessons to be drawn from them, the sages of the Talmud of the Land of Israel regained for their theological thought the powerful resources of history, the single most powerful arena for, and principal medium of, Judaic theology then as now.

## THE ADVENT OF THE MESSIAH:
## THE TALMUD OF THE LAND OF ISRAEL

By this point in our examination of the system of Rabbinic Judaism—its account not of how things are but of how they work—we cannot find surprising the simple fact that the Messiah theme, trivial in the Mishnah, moves to the forefront in the Yerushalmi. That correlates with the same document's keen interest in history and its patterns. If the Mishnah provided a teleology without eschatology, the framers of the Yerushalmi and related Midrash-compilations could not conceive of any but an utterly eschatological goal for themselves. Historical events entered into the construction of a teleology for the Yerushalmi's system of Judaism as a whole. What the Law demanded reflected the consequences of wrongful action on the part of Israel. So, again, Israel's own deeds defined the events of history. Rome's role, like Assyria's and Babylonia's, depended upon Israel's provoking divine wrath as it was executed by the great empires. This mode of thought comes to simple expression in what follows.

### YERUSHALMI ERUBIN 3:9

IV. B. R. Ba, R. Hiyya in the name of R. Yohanan: "'Do not gaze at me because I am swarthy, because the sun has scorched me. My mother's sons were angry with me, they made me keeper of the vineyards; but, my own vineyard, we have not kept!'"

[Song 1:6]. What made me guard the vineyards? It is because of not keeping my own vineyard.

C. What made me keep two festival days in Syria? It is because we did not keep the proper festival day in the Holy Land.

D. "We imagined that we would receive a reward for the two days, but we received a reward only for one of them.

E. "Who made it necessary that we should have to separate two pieces of dough-offering from grain grown in Syria? It is because we did not separate a single piece of dough-offering in the Land of Israel."

Israel had to learn the lesson of its history to also take command of its own destiny.

But this notion of determining one's own destiny should not be misunderstood. The framers of the Talmud of the Land of Israel were not telling the Jews to please God by doing commandments in order that they should thereby gain control of their own destiny. To the contrary, the paradox of the Yerushalmi's system lies in the fact that Israel can free itself of control by other nations only by humbly agreeing to accept God's rule. The nations—Rome, in the present instance—rest on one side of the balance, while God rests on the other. Israel must then choose between them. There is no such thing for Israel as freedom from both God and the nations, total autonomy and independence. There is only a choice of masters, a ruler on earth or a ruler in heaven.

With propositions such as these, the framers of the Mishnah will certainly have concurred. And why not? For the fundamental affirmations of the Mishnah about the centrality of Israel's perfection in stasis—sanctification—readily prove congruent to the attitudes at hand. Once the Messiah's coming had become dependent on Israel's condition and not on Israel's actions in historical time, then the Mishnah's system will have imposed its fundamental and definitive character on the Messiah myth. An eschatological teleology framed through that myth then would prove wholly appropriate to the method of the larger system of the Mishnah. That is true for a simple, striking reason. The Messiah theme is made to repeat, in its terms, the doctrine of virtuous attitudes and emotions that prevail throughout; the condition of the coming of the Messiah is Israel's humility, its submission to the tides and currents of history. What, after all, makes a Messiah a false Messiah? In this Talmud, it is not his claim to save Israel, but his claim to save Israel without the help of God. The meaning of the true Messiah is Israel's total submission, through the Messiah's gentle rule, to God's yoke and service. So God is not to be manipulated through Israel's humoring of Heaven in rite and cult.

The notion of keeping the commandments so as to please Heaven and get God to do what Israel wants is totally incongruent to the text at hand. Keeping the commandments as a mark of submission, loyalty, humility before God is the Rabbinic system of salvation. So Israel does not "save itself." Israel never controls its own destiny, either on earth or in heaven. The only choice is whether to cast one's fate into the hands of cruel, deceitful men, or to trust in the living God of mercy and love. The stress on the fact that Israel's arrogance alienates God and Israel's humility and submission win God's favor cannot surprise us; this is the very point of the doctrine of emotions that defines Rabbinic Judaism's ethics.

✡

137

✝

The issue of the Messiah and the meaning of Israel's history framed through the Messiah myth convey in their terms precisely the same position that we find everywhere else in all other symbolic components of the Rabbinic system and canon. The heart of the matter, then, is Israel's subservience to God's will, as expressed in the Torah and embodied in the teachings and lives of the great sages. When Israel fully accepts God's rule, then the Messiah will come. Until Israel subjects itself to God's rule, the Jews will be subjugated to pagan domination. Since the condition of Israel governs, Israel itself holds the key to its own redemption. But this it can achieve only by throwing away the key!

Israel acts to redeem itself through the opposite of self-determination, namely, by subjugating itself to God. Israel's power lies in its negation of power. Its destiny lies in giving up all pretense at deciding its own destiny, so weakness is the ultimate strength, forbearance the final act of self-assertion, passive resignation the sure step toward liberation. (The parallel is the crucified Christ.) Israel's freedom is engraved on the tablets of the commandments of God:

to be free is freely to obey. That is not the meaning associated with these words in the minds of others who, like the sages of the Rabbinical canon, declared their view of what Israel must do to secure the coming of the Messiah. The passage, praising Israel for its humility, completes the circle begun with the description of Bar Kokhba as arrogant and boastful. Gentile kings are boastful; Israelite kings are humble. So, in all, the Messiah myth deals with a very concrete and limited consideration of the national life and character. The theory of Israel's history and destiny as it was expressed within that myth interprets matters in terms of a single criterion. What others within the Israelite world had done or in the future would do with the conviction that, at the end of time, God would send a (or the) Messiah to "save" Israel, it was a single idea for the sages of the Mishnah and the Talmuds and collections of scriptural exegesis. And that conception stands at the center of their system; it shapes and is shaped by their system. In context, the Messiah expresses the system's meaning and so makes it work.

The appearance of a messianic eschatology fully consonant with the larger characteristic of the Rabbinic system—with its stress on the viewpoints and proof-texts of Scripture, its interest in what was happening to Israel, its focus on the national-historical dimension of the life of the group—indicates that the encompassing Rabbinic system stands essentially autonomous of the prior Mishnaic system. True, what had gone before was absorbed and fully assimilated, but the Rabbinic system first appearing in the Talmud of the Land of Israel is different in the aggregate from the Mishnaic system. It represents more, however, than a negative response to its predecessor. The Rabbinic system of the two Talmuds took over the fundamental convictions of the Mishnaic worldview about the importance of Israel's constructing for itself a life beyond time.

The Rabbinic system then transformed the Messiah myth in its totality into an essentially ahistorical force. If people wanted to reach the end of time, they had to rise above time—that is, history—and stand off at the side of great movements of political and military character. That is the message of the Messiah myth as it reaches full exposure in the Rabbinic system of the two Talmuds.

At its foundation it is precisely the message of teleology without eschatology expressed by the Mishnah and its associated documents. Accordingly, we cannot claim that the Rabbinic or Talmudic system in this regard constitutes a reaction against the Mishnaic one. We must conclude, quite to the contrary, that in the Talmuds and their associated documents we see the restatement in classical-mythic form of the ontological convictions that had informed the minds of the second-century philosophers. The new medium contained the old and enduring message: Israel must turn away from time and change, submit to whatever happens, so as to win for itself the only government worth having, that is, God's rule, accomplished through God's anointed agent, the Messiah.

In the Talmud's theory of salvation the framers provided Israel with an account of how to overcome the unsatisfactory circumstances of an unredeemed present, so as to accomplish the movement from here to the much-desired future. When the Talmud's authorities present statements on the promise of the Law for those who keep it, therefore, they provide glimpses of the goal of the system as a whole. These invoked the primacy of the rabbi and the legitimating power of the Torah, and in those two components of the system we find the principles of the messianic doctrine. And these bring us back to the argument with Christ triumphant, as the Christians perceived him.

## MESSIAH IN CONTEXT: THE CHRISTIAN CHALLENGE

Here is a case in which the view that the two religions traded places helps us to understand an important change in the character of one of them. The context in which the Talmud of the Land of Israel and related Midrash-compilations restated the received Messiah theme, defining the Messiah as a humble sage, finds its definition in the triumph of Christianity. The government's adoption of Christianity as the state religion was taken to validate the Christian claim that Jesus was, and is, Christ. Indeed, every page of Eusebius's writings bears the message that the conversion of Constantine proves the Christhood of Jesus: his messianic standing. History—the affairs of nations and monarchs—

yields laws of society, proves God's will, and matters now speak for themselves. For Judaism the dramatic shift in the fortunes of the competing biblical faith raised a simple and unpleasant possibility: perhaps Israel had been wrong after all. Since the Jews as a whole, and sages among them, anticipated the coming of the Messiah promised by the prophets, the issue could be fairly joined. If history proves propositions, as the prophets and apocalyptic visionaries had maintained, then how could Jews deny the Christians' claim that the conversion of the emperor, then of the empire, demonstrated the true state of affairs in heaven as much as on earth?

John Chrysostom, who represents Christianity on the messianic issue, typifies Christian theologians' concern that converts should not establish or retain connections with synagogues. The burden of his case was that since Christ had now been proved to be the Messiah, Christians no longer could associate themselves with Judaic rites. Judaism had lost, Christianity had won, and people had to choose the one and give up the other. At stake for Chrysostom, whose sermons on Judaism, preached in 386–87, provide for our purpose the statement of Christianity on the messianic issue, was Christians' participation in synagogue rites and Judaic practices. He invoked the Jews' failure in the fiasco of the proposed rebuilding of the Temple in Jerusalem only a quarter of a century earlier. He drew upon the failure of that project to demonstrate that Judaic rites no longer held any power. He further cited that incident to prove that Israel's salvation lay wholly in the past, in the time of the return to Zion, and never in the future. So the happenings of the day demonstrated proofs of the faith. The struggle between sages and theologians concerned the meaning of important contemporary happenings, and the same happenings, read in light of the same Scripture, provoked discussion of the same issues: a confrontation.

The messianic crisis confronting the Christian theologians hardly matches that facing the Judaic sages. The one dealt with problems of triumph, the other, despair; the one had to interpret a new day, the other to explain disaster. Scripture explicitly promised that Israel would receive salvation from God's anointed Messiah at the end of time. The teleology of Israelite faith, in the biblical account, focused upon eschatology and, within eschatology, on the salvific, therefore the messianic, dimension. On the other hand, the Mishnah had for its part taken up a view of its own on the issue of teleology, presenting an ahistorical and essentially nonmessianic teleology. Sages' response to the messianic crisis had to mediate two distinct and contradictory positions. Sages explained what the messianic hope now entailed, and how to identify the Messiah, who would be a sage. They further included the messianic issue in their larger historical theory. So we cannot address the question at hand as if the Christians defined the agenda. True, to Israel all they had to say was, "Why not?" But sages responded with a far-reaching doctrine of their own, deeming the question, in its Christian formulation, trivial.

But the issue confronting both Judaic sages and Christian theologians was one and the same: precisely what difference the Messiah makes. To state matters as they would be worked out by both parties in the light of the events of the day, What do we have to do because the Messiah has come (Christian) or because we want the Messiah to come (Judaic)? That question encompasses two sides of a single issue. On the issue of the messiahship of Jesus all other matters depended. It follows that one party believed precisely the opposite of the other on an issue shared in identical definition by both. For Christians, the sole issue—belief or unbelief—carried a clear implication for the audience subject to address. When debate would go forward, it would center on the wavering of Christians and the unbelief of Jews. Our exemplary figure, Chrysostom, framed matters in those terms, drawing upon the events of his own day for ample instantiation of the matter. The Christian formulation thus focused all argument on the vindication of Jesus as Christ. When Christians found attractive aspects of Judaic rite and belief, the Christian theologians invoked the fundamental issue: is Jesus Christ? If so, then Judaism falls. If not, then Christianity fails. No question, therefore, drew the two sets of intellectuals into more direct conflict; none bore so immediate and fundamental consequences. Christians did not have to keep the Torah—that was a principal message of Chrysostom in context.

141

The Christian challenge is what stimulated sages' thought to focus upon the Messiah theme. The Mishnaic system had come to full expression without an elaborated doctrine of the Messiah, or even an eschatological theory of the purpose and goal of matters. The Mishnah had put forth (in tractate Abot) a teleology without an eschatological dimension at all. By the closing of the Talmud of the Land of Israel, by contrast, the purpose and end of everything centered on the coming of the Messiah, in sages' terms and definition, to be sure. That is surprising in light of the character of the Mishnah's system, to which the Talmud of the Land of Israel attached itself as a commentary.

In order to understand sages' development of the Messiah theme in the Talmud of the Land of Israel, therefore, we have to backtrack and consider how the theme had made its appearance in the Mishnah. Only in comparison to its earlier expression and use does the Talmud's formulation of the matter enter the proper context for interpretation. Critical issues of teleology had been worked out through messianic eschatology in other, earlier Judaic systems. Later ones as well would invoke the Messiah theme. These systems, including the Christian one, resorted to the myth of the Messiah as savior and redeemer of Israel, a supernatural figure engaged in political-historical tasks as king of the Jews, even a God-man facing the crucial historical questions of Israel's life and then resolving them—Christ as king of the world, of the ages, even of death itself.

## IDENTIFYING THE MESSIAH AND HASTENING HIS ADVENT

In the Talmud of the Land of Israel we find a fully exposed doctrine not only of a Messiah (e.g., a kind of priest or general), but of *the* Messiah, the one man who will save Israel: who he is, how we will know him, what we must do to bring him. It follows that the Talmud of the Land of Israel presents clear evidence that the Messiah myth had found its place within that larger Torah myth that characterized Judaism in its later formative literature. A clear effort to identify the person of the Messiah and to confront the claim that a specific, named individual had been, or would be, the Messiah—these come to the fore. This means that the issue had reached the center of lively discourse, at least in some Rabbinic circles. The disposition of the issue proves distinctive to sages: the Messiah will be a sage, the Messiah will come when Israel has attained that condition of sanctification marked by that profound humility and complete acceptance of God's will that signify sanctification.

These two conditions say the same thing twice: sages' Judaism will identify the Messiah and teach how to bring him nearer. In these allegations we find no point of intersection with issues important to Chrysostom, even though the Talmud of the Land of Israel reached closure at the same time as Chrysostom's preaching. For Chrysostom dealt with the Messiah theme in terms pertinent to his larger system, and sages did the same. But the issue was fairly joined. In Chrysostom's terms, it was: Jesus is Christ, as was proved by the events of the recent past. In sages' terms it was: the Messiah will be a sage, coming when Israel fully accepts, in all humility, God's sole rule. The first stage in the position of each hardly matches that in the outline of the other. But the second does: Jesus is Christ, therefore Israel will have no other Messiah. The Messiah will come, in the form of a sage, and therefore no one who now claims to be the Messiah is in fact the savior.

143

Issues are joined in a confrontation of ideas. There is a clear fit between one side's framing of the Messiah theme and the other party's framing of the same theme. And we cannot forget that larger context in which the theme worked itself out: the Messiah joined to the doctrine of history and of Israel, fore and aft, forms a large and integrated picture. If Jesus is Christ, then history has come to its fulfillment and Israel is no longer God's people. The sages' counterpart system: the Messiah has not yet come, history as the sequence of empires has in store yet one more age, the age of Israel, and Israel remains the family, the children of Abraham, Isaac, and Jacob. So Christianity, so Judaism: both confronted precisely the same issues defined in exactly the same way.

In the Talmud of the Land of Israel two historical contexts framed discussion of the Messiah, the destruction of the Temple, as with Chrysostom's framing of the issue, and the messianic claim of Bar Kokhba. Rome played a role in both, and the authors of the materials gathered in the Talmud made a place for Rome in the history of Israel. This they did in conformity to their larger theory of who is Israel, specifically by assigning to Rome a place in the family. As to the destruction of the Temple, we find a statement that the Messiah was born on the day that the Temple was destroyed. The Talmud's doctrine of the Messiah therefore finds its place in its encompassing doctrine of history. What is fresh in the Talmud is the perception of Rome as an autonomous actor, as an entity with a point of origin (just as Israel has a point of origin) and a tradition of wisdom (just as Israel has such a tradition). So as Rome is Esau, so Esau is part of the family—a point to which we shall return—and therefore plays a role in history. And—yet another point of considerable importance—since Rome does play a role in history, Rome also finds a position in the eschatological drama. This sense of poised opposites, Israel and Rome, comes to expression in two ways. First, Israel's own history calls into being its counterpart, the antihistory of Rome. Without Israel, there would be no Rome—a wonderful consolation to the defeated nation. For if Israel's sin created Rome's power, then Israel's repentance would bring Rome's downfall. Here is the way in which the Talmud presents the match:

The concept of two histories, balanced opposite one another, comes to particular expression, within the Talmud of the Land of Israel, in the balance of Israelite sage and Roman emperor. Just as Israel and Rome, God and no-gods, compete (with a foreordained conclusion), so do sage and emperor. In this age, it appears that the emperor has the power. God's Temple, by contrast to the great churches of the age, lies in ruins. But just as sages can overcome the emperor through their inherent supernatural power, so too will Israel and Israel's God in the coming age control the course of events. In the doctrine at hand, we see the true balance: sage as against emperor. In the age of the Christian emperors, the polemic acquires power.

The sage, in his small-claims court, weighs in the balance against the emperor in Constantinople—a rather considerable claim. So two stunning innovations appear: first, the notion of emperor and sage in mortal struggle; second, the idea of an age of idolatry and an age beyond idolatry. The world had to move into a new orbit indeed for Rome to enter into the historical context formerly defined wholly by what happened to Israel. How does all this relate to the messianic crisis at hand? The doctrine of sages, directly pertinent to the issue of the coming of the Messiah, holds that Israel can free itself of control by other nations only by humbly agreeing to accept God's rule. The nations—Rome, in the present instance—rest on one side of the balance, while God rests on the other. Israel must then choose between them. There is no such thing for Israel as freedom from both God and the nations, total autonomy and independence. There is only a choice of masters, a ruler on earth or a ruler in heaven.

Once the figure of the Messiah has come on stage, there arises discussion on who, among the living, the Messiah might be. The identification of the Messiah begins with the person of David himself: "If the Messiah-King comes from among the living, his name will be David. If he comes from among the dead, it will be King David himself." (Yerushalmi Ber. 2:3 V P) A variety of evidence announced the advent of the Messiah as a figure in the larger system of formative Judaism. The rabbinization of David constitutes one kind of evidence. Serious discussion, within the framework of the accepted documents of Mishnaic exegesis and the Law, concerning the identification and claim of diverse figures asserted to be messiahs, presents still more telling proof.

145

## YERUSHALMI BERAKHOT 2:4

    A. Once a Jew was plowing and his ox snorted once before him. An Arab who was passing and heard the sound said to him, "Jew, loosen your ox and loosen the plow and stop plowing. For today your Temple was destroyed."

    B. The ox snorted again. He [the Arab] said to him, "Jew, bind your ox and bind your plow, for today the Messiah-King was born."

C. He said to him, "What is his name?"

D. "Menahem."

E. He said to him, "And what is his father's name?"

F. The Arab said to him, "Hezekiah."

G. He said to him, "Where is he from?"

H. He said to him, "From the royal capital of Bethlehem in Judaea."

I. The Jew went and sold his ox and sold his plow. And he became a peddler of infant's felt-cloths [diapers]. And he went from place to place until he came to that very city. All of the women bought from him. But Menahem's mother did not buy from him.

J. He heard the women saying, "Menahem's mother, Menahem's mother, come buy for your child."

K. She said, "We want to bring him up to hate Israel. For on the day he was born, the Temple was destroyed."

L. They said to her, "We are sure that on this day it was destroyed, and on this day of the year it will be rebuilt."

M. She said to the peddler, "We have no money."

N. He said to her, "It is of no matter to us. Come and buy for him and pay me when we return."

O. A while later he returned to that city. He said to her, "How is the infant doing?"

P. She said to him, "Since the time you saw him a spirit came and carried him away from me."

Q. Said R. Bun, "Why do we learn this from [a story about] an Arab? Do we not have explicit scriptural evidence for it? 'Lebanon with its majestic trees will fall.' [Isa. 10:34] And what follows this? 'There shall come forth a shoot from the stump of Jesse.' [Isa. 11:1] [Right after an allusion to the destruction of the Temple the prophet speaks of the messianic age.]"

This is a set-piece story, adduced to prove that the Messiah was born on the day the Temple was destroyed. The Messiah was born when the Temple was destroyed; hence, God prepared for Israel a better fate than had appeared.

Now we should not conclude that the Talmud at hand has simply moved beyond the Mishnah's orbit. The opposite is the case. What the framers of the document have done is to assemble materials in which the eschatological, therefore messianic, teleology is absorbed within the ahistorical, therefore sagacious one. The Messiah turned into a sage is no longer the Messiah embodied in the figure of the arrogant Bar Kokhba (in the Talmud's representation of the figure). The reversion to the prophetic notion of learning history's lessons carried in its wake a reengagement with the Messiah myth. But the reengagement does not represent a change in the unfolding system. Why not? Because the climax comes in an explicit statement that the conduct required by the Torah will bring the coming Messiah. That explanation of the holy way of life focuses on the end of time and the advent of the Messiah—both of which therefore depend on the sanctification of Israel. So sanctification takes priority; salvation depends on it. The framers of the Mishnah had found it possible to construct a complete and encompassing teleology for their system with scarcely a single word about the Messiah's coming at that time when the system would be perfectly achieved.

The Yerushalmi, heir to the Mishnah, accomplished the remessianization of the system of Rabbinic Judaism. The reversion to the prophetic notion of learning the lessons of history carried in its wake reengagement with the Messiah myth. The climax of the matter comes in an explicit statement that the practice of conduct required by the Torah will bring about the coming of the Messiah. That explanation of the purpose of the holy way of life, focused now upon the end of time and the advent of the Messiah, must strike us as surprising. For the framers of the Mishnah had found it possible to construct a complete and encompassing teleology for their system with scarcely a single word about the Messiah's coming when the system would be perfectly achieved. So with their interest in explaining events and accounting for history, the third- and fourth-century sages represented in the units of discourse at hand invoked what their predecessors had at best found of peripheral consequence to their system. The following contains the most striking expression of the viewpoint at hand:

### YERUSHALMI TAANIT 1:1

J. "The oracle concerning Dumah. One is calling to us from Seir, 'Watchman, what of the night? Watchman, what of the night?'" (Isa. 21:11)

K. The Israelites said to Isaiah, "O our Rabbi, Isaiah, what will come for us out of this night?"

L. He said to them, "Wait for me, until we can present the question."

M. Once he had asked the question, he came back to them.

N. They said to him, "Watchman, what of the night? What did the Guardian of the ages tell you?"

O. He said to them, "The watchman says" 'Morning comes; and also the night. If you will inquire, inquire; come back again.'" (Isa. 21:12)

P. They said to him, "Also the night?"

Q. He said to them, "It is not what you are thinking. But there will be morning for the righteous, and night for the wicked, morning for Israel, and night for idolaters."

R. They said to him, "When?"

S. He said to them, "Whenever you want, He too wants [it to be]—if you want it, he wants it."

T. They said to him, "What is standing in the way?"

U. He said to them, "Repentance: 'Come back again.'" (Isa. 21:12)

V. R. Aha in the name of R. Tanhum b. R. Hiyya, "If Israel repents for one day, forthwith the son of David will come.

W. "What is the Scriptural basis? 'O that today you would hearken to his voice!'" (Ps. 95:7)

X. Said R. Levi, "If Israel would keep a single Sabbath in the proper way, forthwith the son of David will come.

Y. "What is the Scriptural basis for this view? 'Moses said, Eat it today, for today is a Sabbath to the Lord; today you will not find it in the field.' (Exod. 16:25)

Z. "And it says, 'For thus said the Lord God, the Holy One of Israel. In returning and rest you shall be saved; in quietness and in trust shall be your strength.' And you would not.'" (Isa. 30:15)

The discussion of the power of repentance would hardly have surprised a Mishnah sage. What is new is at V–Z, the explicit linkage of keeping the Law with achieving the end of time and the coming of the Messiah. That motif stands separate from the notions of righteousness and repentance, which surely do not require it. So the condition of "all Israel," a social category in historical time, comes under consideration, and not only the status of individual Israelites in life and in death. The latter had formed the arena for Abot's account of the Mishnah's meaning. Now history as an operative category, drawing in its wake Israel as a social entity, comes once more on the scene. But, except for the Mishnah's sages, it had never left the stage.

We must not lose sight of the importance of this passage, with its emphasis on repentance, on the one side, and the power of Israel to reform itself, on the other. The Messiah will come any day that Israel makes it possible. If all Israel will keep a single Sabbath in the proper (Rabbinic) way, the Messiah will come. If all Israel will repent for one day, the Messiah will come. "Whenever you want . . . ," the Messiah will come.

Any account of the Messiah doctrine of the Talmud of the Land of Israel must lay appropriate stress on that conviction: Israel makes its own history and therefore shapes its own destiny. This lesson, sages maintained, derives from the very condition of Israel even then, its suffering and its despair. How so? History taught moral lessons. Historical events entered into the construction of a teleology for the Talmud of the Land of Israel's system of Judaism as a whole. What the Law demanded reflected the consequences of wrongful action on the part of Israel. So, again, Israel's own deeds defined the events of history. Rome's role, like Assyria's and Babylonia's, depended on Israel's provoking divine wrath as it was executed by the great powers on earth.

## MESSIANIC JUDAISM: THE SAVIOR-SAGE

Looking backward from the end of the fourth century to the end of the first, the framers of the Talmud surely perceived what two hundred years earlier, with the closure of the Mishnah, need not have appeared obvious and unavoidable, namely, the definitive end, for here and now at any rate, of the old order of cultic sanctification. After a hundred years there may have been some doubt. After two centuries more with the fiasco of Julian near at hand, there can have been little hope left. The Mishnah had designed a world in which the Temple stood at the center, a society in which the priests presided at the top, and a way of life in which the dominant issue was the sanctification of Israelite life. Whether the full realization of that world, society, and way of life was thought to come sooner or later, the system had been meant only initially as a utopia, but in the end, as a plan and constitution for a material society here in the Land of Israel.

Two hundred years had now passed from the closure of the Mishnah to the completion of the Talmud of the Land of Israel. Much had changed. Roman power had receded from part of the world. Pagan rule had given way to the sovereignty of Christian emperors. The old order was cracking; the new order was not yet established. But, from the perspective of Israel, the waiting went on. The interim from Temple to Temple was not differentiated. Whether conditions were less favorable or more favorable hardly made a difference. History stretched backward, to a point of disaster, and forward, to an unseen and incalculable time beyond the near horizon. Short of supernatural events, salvation was not in sight. Israel for its part lived under its own government, framed within the rules of sanctification, and constituted a holy society.

But when would salvation come, and how could people even now hasten its day? These issues, in the nature of things, proved more pressing as the decades rolled by, becoming first one century, then another, while none knew how many more, and how much more, must still be endured. So the unredeemed state of Israel and the world, the uncertain fate of the individual—these framed and defined the context in which all forms of Judaism necessarily took shape. The question of salvation presented each with a single ineluctable agenda. But it is not merely an axiom generated by our hindsight that makes it necessary to interpret all of a system's answers in the light of the single question of salvation. In the case of the Judaism to which the Talmud of the Land of Israel attests, the matter is explicitly stated.

For the important fact is that the Talmud of the Land of Israel expressly links salvation to keeping the Law, and, in the opposite way, so did Chrysostom. We recall that he held that not keeping the Law showed that the Messiah had come and Israel's hope was finally defeated. Sages maintained that keeping the Law now signified keeping the faith: the act of hope. This means that the issues of the Law were drawn upward into the highest realm of Israelite consciousness. Keeping the Law in the right way is represented as not merely right or expedient. It is the way to bring the Messiah, the son of David.

The Mishnah's system, whole and complete, had remained reticent on the entire Messiah theme. By contrast, our Talmud finds ample place for a rich collection of statements on the messianic theme. What this means is that, between the conclusion of the Mishnah and the closure of the Talmud, room had been found for the messianic hope, expressed in images not revised to conform to the definitive and distinctive traits of the Talmud itself. We do not have to argue that the stunning success of Christ (in the Christians' views) made the issue urgent for Jews. The issue had never lost its urgency, except in the tiny circle of philosophers who, in the system of the Mishnah, reduced the matter to a minor detail of taxonomy. And yet, in that exercise, the Mishnah's sages confronted a considerable social problem, one that faced the fourth-century authorities as well.

151

The messianic hope in concrete political terms also required neutralization, so that peoples' hopes would not be raised prematurely, with consequent, incalculable damage to the defeated nation. That was true in the second century, in the aftermath of Bar Kokhba's war, and in the fourth century, for obvious reasons, as well. This "rabbinization" of the Messiah theme meant, first of all, that rabbis insisted the Messiah would come in a process extending over a long period of time, thus not imposing a caesura upon the existence of the nation and disrupting its ordinary life. Accordingly, the Talmud of the Land of Israel treats the messianic hope as something gradual, to be worked toward, not a sudden cataclysmic event. That conception was fully in accord with the notion that the everyday deeds of people formed a pattern continuous with the salvific history of Israel.

From the viewpoint of Eusebius and Chrysostom alike, the matter had come suddenly, miraculously. Sages saw things differently. We may regard the emphasis upon the slow but steady advent of the Messiah's day as entirely consonant with the notion that the Messiah will come when Israel's condition warrants it. The improvement in standards of observing the Torah, therefore, to be effected by the nation's obedience to the clerks will serve as a guidepost on the road to redemption. The moral condition of the nation ultimately guarantees salvation. God will respond to Israel's regeneration, planning all the while to save the saved, that is, those who save themselves.

What is most interesting about the picture in the Talmud of the Land of Israel is that the hope for the Messiah's coming is further joined to the moral condition of each individual Israelite. Hence the messianic fulfillment was made to depend on the repentance of Israel. The entire drama, envisioned by others in earlier types of Judaism as a world-historical event, was reworked in context into a moment in the life of the individual and the people of Israel collectively. The coming of the Messiah depended not on historical action but on moral regeneration. So from a force that moved Israelites to take up weapons on the battlefield, the messianic hope and yearning was transformed into motives for spiritual regeneration and ethical behavior. The energies released in the messianic fervor were then linked to rabbinical government, through which Israel would form the godly society. When we reflect that the message, "If you want it, He too wants it to be," comes in a generation confronting a dreadful disappointment, its full weight and meaning become clear.

The advent of the Messiah will not be heralded by the actions of a pagan or of a Christian king. Whoever relies upon the salvation of a gentile is going to be disappointed. Israel's salvation depends wholly upon Israel itself. Two things follow. First, the Jews were made to take up the burden of guilt for their own sorry situation. But, second, they also gained not only responsibility for, but also power over, their fate. They could do something about salvation, just as their sins had brought about their tragedy. This old, familiar message, in no way particular to the Talmud's bureaucrats, took on specificity and concreteness in the context of the Talmud, which offered a rather detailed program for reform and regeneration. The message to a disappointed generation, attracted to the kin-faith, with its now-triumphant messianic fulfillment, and fearful of its own fate in an age of violent attacks upon the synagogue buildings and faithful alike, was stern. But it also promised strength to the weak and hope to the despairing. No one could be asked to believe that the Messiah would come very soon. The events of the day testified otherwise. So the counsel of the Talmud's sages was patience and consequential deeds. People could not hasten things, but they could do something. The duty of Israel, in the meantime, was to accept the sovereignty of heavenly government.

The heavenly government, revealed in the Torah, was embodied in this world by the figure of the sage. The meaning of the salvific doctrine just outlined becomes fully clear when we uncover the simple fact that the rule of Heaven and the learning and authority of the rabbi on earth turned out to be identified with one another. It follows that salvation for Israel depended on adherence to the sage and acceptance of his discipline. God's will in heaven and the sage's words on earth—both constituted Torah. And Israel would be saved through Torah, so the sage was the savior—especially the humble one. The humblest of them all would be the sage-Messiah, victor over time and circumstance, savior of Israel. The sages of the Mishnah surely will have agreed, even though they would not have said—and did not say—things in quite this way. The structure of Rabbinic Judaism corresponds to its system; as things were, so they functioned. And so would they endure through all time to come.

## THE CHRISTIAN TELEOLOGY OF TRANSCENDENCE

The Rabbinic teleology that had emerged by the fourth century was profoundly transcendent in its emphasis. The Torah in heaven and in the figure of the sage was not dependent on this world, nor could they even be correlated with the conditions of this world. That emphatic declaration of independence, the conviction that what determines our existence is outside the world, is what is meant when a position is described as claiming transcendence.

Within the theology of the primitive and the early church, no teacher was more insistent upon divine transcendence than Jesus. His conception of the kingdom of God involved the claim that God could be seen to be transforming the world definitively, and outside the realm of any established authority, whether in Israel or in Rome. We may compare and contrast the transcendence asserted by Jesus in the first century with the similarly emphatic transcendence claimed by the Rabbinic sages from the fourth century onward.

In the cases of both Jesus and the Rabbinic sages, little or no sympathy with the government of the day is expressed. When Jesus is remembered to tell his followers to turn the other cheek, to offer two garments when one is demanded, and to go the extra mile (see Matt. 5:39–41), he is not talking about normal human relationships. Smiting, confiscation, and compulsory service are rather the trademarks of the military jurisdiction of Rome. Jesus' teaching involves accepting an injustice one can do nothing about, much as he advises the payment of tax to Caesar in Caesar's own coin (see Matt. 22:15–22; Mark 12:13–17; Luke 20:20–26).

Jesus' simple acceptance of a government that he could not change became the basis on which Hellenists such as Paul, who were more enthusiastic about the institutions of Rome, could claim that obeying the authorities honored God (see Rom. 13:1–7). But Jesus' own position was far from Paul's: Jesus insisted that what you rendered Caesar (from Caesar's own) and what your rendered God (from God's own) were two quite different orders of value and practice. To this extent, the Talmudic denial of any claim to justice on the part of those in authority resonates with the position of Jesus better than Paul's defense of the rightful authority of government. Nearness in chronology obviously does not guarantee agreement in principle.

Where Jesus and the sages part company, however, is in their very different assertions of what the divine power is that transcends the injustice of this world. For Jesus, God transcends and transforms the world as the kingdom of God. God makes God manifest to people who know how to see God in the world, and their joining in fellowship celebrates the coming of the kingdom they pray for. For the sages, God transcends and transforms the world as Torah. That heavenly government stands supreme in its own realm, until obedience ultimately and in God's own time includes our world in that realm.

Jesus and the sages are symmetrical in their insistence on transcendence, but their difference in the assertion of how (or with what) precisely God transcends our world is profound in its consequences. Jesus' social position involved an alienation, not only from the Roman government, but also from the authorities of the Temple. The extent of his alienation is attested by the Crucifixion itself, an execution that joined Rome and Jerusalem in the mutual interest of dispatching with someone who posed a threat to the public institution that was the seal their supremacy. It is consistent with Jesus' social position that his teaching of the kingdom involves the assertion that God will make a new social entity, the fellowship of forgiven Israel, out of those who respond positively to the message of the kingdom. The focus of his activity was therefore Israel as a whole, not Jerusalem in particular; in fact, he came to assert that the kingdom had been delocalized from the Temple as a result of Caiaphas's arrangements there (see Preface, pp. xv–xviii).

The sages' alienation from the Roman government was, if anything, even more extreme than Jesus'. After all, they knew official hostility to their religious identity in a way Jesus did not (although his followers were to have a cognate experience from the second century onward, as we have seen). But the sages benefited from the philosophical structure of the Torah, which was their inheritance from the Mishnah. That was not a physical place, but it was a stable, defined locus of transcendence, which they could assert as a matter of traditional authority.

The social distinction between Jesus and the sages agrees with their differing constructions of how transcendence makes the world

different, and whole in that difference. Jesus' kingdom is a matter
of perceiving what is present but hidden, and permitting that yeast
to leaven the whole world (see Matt. 13:33; Luke 13:20–21). The
sages' Torah is a "government above" (see Sanhedrin 6:9.III in the
Talmud Yerushalmi, cited above), complete in all its essentials even
on earth—but for obedience. Because what transforms the world
is different in the two systems, there is also a difference in how the
world is transformed. Finally, and perhaps most strikingly, the directions in which the world is transformed are differently mapped.
To start from what you perceive and then to move through social
consolidation and on to transcendence is the direction of Jesus,
while the sages start with the social inheritance of the Torah and
proceed to obedience and transcendence on that basis.

While it is quite possible, as we have just now seen, to compare
and contrast Jesus with the sages of the fourth century and later,
there an obvious anachronism is involved in that exercise. From
a historical point of view, what intervenes between them in the
case of Judaism is the Mishnah, a product (for the most part) of
the second century. And what intervenes between them in the case
of Christianity is the rise of popular apocalypticism, especially after
the year 70 C.E., and its transition into a more philosophical mode.

In general terms, we have already discussed the growth of
apocalypticism earlier in the present chapter. But the quality of
apocalyptic expectation changed radically after it became a primary idiom of Christianity. The principal reason for that change
has been described by scholars as eschatological disappointment:
because the anticipated return of Christ did not occur as predicted,
other forms of hope replaced the old confidence in apocalyptic
speculation. Jaroslav Pelikan has vigorously shown the weakness
of such a position:

> Any such description is based on too simplistic a view of the role
> of apocalyptic in the teaching of Jesus and in the early church.
> Nor is it corroborated by later texts, for one looks in vain for
> proof of a bitter disappointment over the postponement of the
> parousia [that is, Christ's second coming] or of a shattering of the
> early Christian communities by the delay of the Lord's return.

What the texts do suggest is a shift within the polarity of already/ not yet and a great variety of solutions to the exegetical and theological difficulties caused by such a shift.[2]

Pelikan goes on to describe *The Shepherd of Hermas* in reference to popular apocalypticism, and the works of Origen in their polemic against literal millenarianism. What came out of that mix, in Pelikan's account, was an emphasis on the "supernatural order," as influential in human affairs.[3] The eschatological Christianity of the first two centuries became a Christianity centered on supernatural being, on what is known as ontology (from the Greek term *onta*, which refers to that which actually exists).

The level of generality in Pelikan's analysis prevents it from being inaccurate, but his account is not very helpful. He offers no insight into how the acutely eschatological theology of the first two centuries became the emphatically ontological theology of the third and fourth centuries. The answer to the question is to be found within an analysis of the way in which sources such as *The Shepherd of Hermas* and Origen frame the entire question of transcendence in relation to life as we know it.

## THE SHEPHERD OF HERMAS AND THE THEOLOGY OF SURVIVAL

Pelikan is representative of scholarship in his description of the apocalypticism of *The Shepherd of Hermas:*

> The author (or authors) of the *Shepherd* used the format of an apocalyptic summons to call the readers to repentance. The vividness of its eschatological language is exceeded only by the decisiveness of its plea. The Lord had not yet returned, and therefore the work of judgment was not yet complete; but it would soon be finished, and then the consummation would come.[4]

As Pelikan points out, the use of the word *apocalyptic* here does not refer to the hard and fast distinction between this world and the world to come. Rather, a process started within the world is pointed toward its eschatological completion. In fact, the line of demarcation between the present and the future is less sharply drawn in Hermas than it is, say, in the Revelation of John.

In the first vision of Hermas (chapter 1), an angelic lady appears to him and accuses him of sin (specifically, of impure thoughts about a woman, whom the angelic lady resembles). Her analysis of the rewards that attend righteousness, and therefore of the punishments that await evil, is succinct: "For the righteous man has righteous designs. As long as his designs are righteous, his repute stands fast in heaven, and he finds the Lord ready to assist him in all his doings. But they who have evil designs in their hearts bring upon themselves death and captivity, especially those who obtain this world for themselves, and glory in their wealth, and do not lay hold of the good things that are to come." The apocalyptic perspective of the angelic promise and threat is evident in the wording of the citation. "The good things that are to come" refers to the heavenly treasure that was commonly held by Christians to be stored for them until the day of judgment (see 1 Pet. 1:3–5).

Although the apocalyptic assumptions of *The Shepherd of Hermas* are evident, and amply support the scholarly reading of the document that has become a matter of consensus, it is equally apparent that there is another sort of assumption at work. Hermas is assured that the righteous find God ready to assist them in all their doings—the promise, that is, is for support in the present, not only in the final judgment that is to come. Similarly, the fate of the wicked is "death and captivity," and not a purely eschatological threat.

The social setting of *The Shepherd of Hermas* makes the promise and the threat all the more striking. On the basis of earlier materials, Hermas finally composed *The Shepherd* around the year 150 C.E., just when intellectuals reached a crescendo in their attacks on Christians. Fronto, tutor of the emperors Antoninus and Marcus Aurelius (and consul under Hadrian), charged that Christians worshiped an ass's head, sacrificed children, and encouraged promiscuity during worship.[5] Under such circumstances, to imagine oneself as assisted and punished by God takes on a particular meaning.

The righteous who "finds the Lord ready to assist him in all his doings" discovers support, then and there, in the midst of suspicion, but not so much prosperity that he becomes one of those who "obtain this world for themselves, and glory in their wealth." Just as the church attempted to walk a fine line between the Roman hostility that would destroy its life and the accommodation to Rome that would destroy its soul, so Hermas is called to a life of just getting along with divine support. In that position, he is to escape both the wrath of God and death at the hands of Caesar.

The Shepherd of Hermas is often written off as a product of "no great intelligence."[6] That evaluation is framed in intellectual and literary terms, in comparison with the vigorous theology of other Christian works of the second century (Justin's above all). But The Shepherd should be evaluated within the social function that it evidently performed in Rome, and performed to such good effect that it was actively discussed whether the work belonged within the New Testament.[7] The Shepherd elaborates and develops the recommendation for the social posture of disciples already evident in the Gospel according to Mark, which was also composed in Rome.

Mark's ending has long caused perplexity, because the Gospel closes with the women at the tomb, having been told of the resurrection of Jesus, departing in silence, "for they were afraid" (16:8). Longer endings were later added to Mark, to make it accord better with the other Gospels, but the emphatic silence of the women was clearly intended as the final image of the original work. Such silence is only perplexing, however, when Mark is read outside the context of the recent and vicious persecution that had been instituted by Nero (discussed in chapter 1). Within that setting, Mark is recommending a rational policy: discipleship with a low profile.[8] The women are to know what they know, but not to spread their knowledge abroad.

The position of Christians in Rome by the time of Hermas is less fraught with immediate danger, but still precarious. Hermas describes himself as a freed slave who had acquired family and property. His precarious situation, then, is defined as in between the unstable policy of Rome and the absolute requirements of God. The only acceptable position is to be assisted by God in one's living (on the one hand), but (on the other hand) also not to permit even this divine assistance to turn into a love of wealth. The

Markan motif of low-profile discipleship becomes in *The Shepherd of Hermas* a complete program of how to realize that aim in a hostile environment.

Hermas lays out his chief concern as the problem of sin. Given that, as he is told, the righteous are only as righteous as their *intentions,* Hermas panics, "If this sin is recorded against me, how shall I be saved?" (*Shepherd* I.2.1). In another vision, the grounds of his fear are only confirmed. A great and old woman appears, seated on a throne of snow-white wool. That description echoes the appearance of God himself in the vision of Daniel 7:9, and Hermas is eventually told that the venerable matron is the church (*Shepherd* II.4.1). It is she who underscores what Hermas has already learned (*Shepherd* I.2.4): "For it is an evil and mad purpose against a revered spirit and one already approved, if a man desire an evil deed, and especially if it be Hermas the temperate, who abstains from every evil desire and is full of all simplicity and great innocence." The authority of the church, then, only reinforces the desperate predicament of all who are like Hermas. Because the issue is one's intentions and desires, not only one's actions, the problem seems here to be set up as intractable. And in that the issue is the lack of complete control over what he thinks, Hermas' predicament seems to be universal.

The Shepherd of Hermas here identifies, with the greatest precision of any extant document from the early church, how the problem of sin was seen to threaten the integrity of the faith overall. As compared to the social issue of how to conduct oneself as a disciple in an inhospitable environment, the deeper paradox of being held responsible for whatever one might think and feel was a far more fundamental problem. After all, that concern could feed the response of a dualistic Gnosticism, which would make the nature of one's desire a symptom of whether one was spiritual in one's constitution. A counsel of despair is an obvious response to the command to control one's desire. If Hermas must determine his desires in order to be saved, the most rational course might be to admit that he is not saved, and cannot be.

The Shepherd of Hermas resolves the dilemma in what the angelic representation of the church goes on to say. God's anger for evil intents is confirmed, but the grounds of his anger are now said to be other than the issue of intentions (*Shepherd* I.3.1): "But it is not for this that God is angry with you, but in order that you should convert your family, which has sinned against the Lord, and against you, their parents." The answer to the dilemma of human intention is given: it is the mercy of divine restraint. Although God would justly be angered by the failure of good intent among the righteous, he is compassionate enough to provide a remedy. If at least they will see to the nurture of their families, he will not be angry.

The symmetry of God's willingness to accept the nurture of one's family in the place of intentional perfection is simply stated. In the social realm, one can act with greater conscious control than in the purely personal realm (*Shepherd* I.3.2): "For as the smith, by hammering his work, overcomes the task that he desires, so also the daily righteous word overcomes all wickedness." *The Shepherd* comes to a confidence in reasoned behavior, as influenced by the "Word" (Logos) of God, which corresponds to Clement of Alexandria's theology of Christ as the *paidagogos* (discussed in chapter 2). Clement's own theology was inventive, and a continuation of the identification between Jesus and the Word of God made in the fourth Gospel and by Justin Martyr. Particularly, we saw that Clement insisted that the Word was influential even over one's passions. But Clement's thought, *The Shepherd* shows us, is also representative of popular Christian belief. The "daily righteous word" of God, God's accessibility through reason and speech and deliberate action, was widely understood to "overcome all wickedness," whether in the world or in one's heart.

The family is a vital sphere of Christian action in *The Shepherd of Hermas,* because it is the one place where it is assumed Hermas exerts influence. "The affairs of daily life" in the world are assumed to corrupt families, and Hermas is instructed to correct his own family, especially his children (*Shepherd* I.3.1–2). Later, the same principle will include Hermas's wife within his family, and it will be extended to the church at large (*Shepherd* II.2).

The placement of the family at the center of action marks a signal development in Christian theology. The position attributed to Jesus in the primitive church envisaged the renunciation of family for the sake of the gospel (see Matt. 19:27-30; Mark 10:28–31; Luke 18:28-30). That position was modulated within primitive Christianity as represented within the New Testament: the relationships of family were portrayed as providing an opportunity for enacting the love one had learned in Christ (see 1 Pet. 2:18–3:7). By the time of *The Shepherd of Hermas,* however, a deeper transformation in the evaluation of family had occurred. It was now the sphere of first recourse in working out one's constitutional inability to offer God the perfection God required. Here, in fact, is the source of the vital concern for family within classical Christianity. It is not merely a "value" or a place of affection; family is where salvation is ordinarily worked out. The imperative to Christian leaders sums up the ethical perspective on salvation that is developed in *The Shepherd of Hermas* (II.2.7): "You, therefore, who do righteousness, remain steadfast and do not be double-minded, that your way might be with the angels." By this point in the book, it has already been shown that an individual can not avoid being double-minded to some extent: aspects of the imagination simply evade complete control. But one can be dedicated to the rational, deliberate task of nurturing one's family and the family of the church: that is what God demands by way of repentance.

A remarkable tension has been evident within Christianity from the time of its classical formulations during the course of the second century. On the one hand, family and sexual relations have been viewed as pertaining to a condition of flesh that is to be overcome; on the other hand, such relationships have been held up as the normative field within which salvation may be worked out. *The Shepherd of Hermas,* precisely because it is a relatively unsophisticated document, represents the tension quite clearly (II.2.3): "But make these words known to all your children and to your wife, who shall in future be to you as a sister. For she does not refrain her tongue, with which she sins; but when she has heard these words she will refrain it, and will obtain mercy." Sexual relations are blandly put aside, when they are typified as incestuous (relations with a "sister"). By contrast, inappropriate speech is given labored attention. Christianity constructed for itself the image of the perfect woman—obedient, celibate, and silent—because it located the struggle for salvation within social and human terms. Making flesh the vessel of spirit inevitably meant that the flesh was neither embraced nor denied as it is, but changed. Wives become "sisters" as certainly as people become angelic in the resurrection (see Matt. 22:30; Mark 12:25; Luke 20:36). The perspective of Jesus had emphasized that transformation, but without insisting that people in their flesh would become like angels. In its struggle with Gnosticism during the second century (as we saw in chapter 2), the faith that came to be known as orthodox embraced the flesh as an ultimate concern in a way that had not been the case earlier.

### ORIGEN'S PHILOSOPHY OF TRANSCENDENCE

The impact of that new emphasis involved a programmatic involvement with asceticism within the church. That orientation had earlier been characteristic of Gnosticism, but the claiming of flesh as belonging to the realm of salvation resulted in a comparable Christian asceticism. No theologian of the church wrestled more effectively and passionately with the consequences of the new orientation than Origen of Alexandria. Born in 185, Origen knew the consequences that faith could have in the Roman world: his father died in the persecution of Severus in 202. Origen accepted the sort of renunciation demanded of apostles in the Gospels, putting aside his possessions to develop what Eusebius calls the philosophical life demanded by Jesus (see Eusebius, *History of the Church*, 6.3). His learning resulted in his appointment to the catechetical school in Alexandria, following the great examples of Pantaenus and Clement. Origen later moved to Caesarea in Palestine, as a result of a bitter dispute with Demetrius, the bishop of Alexandria. Indeed, Origen remained a controversial figure after his death (and until this day), to a large extent because he wrestled more profoundly than most thinkers with the consequences of divinizing flesh. The dispute surrounding Origen specifically included his sexuality. According to Eusebius, as part of his acceptance of evangelical precepts of renunciation, Origen took literally the reference in Matthew to people making eunuchs of themselves for the sake of the kingdom of heaven (Matt. 19:12). Accordingly, he emasculated himself (*History of the Church,* 6.8). As Eusebius immediately goes on to say, Demetrius later capitalized on the story by using it to discredit Origen. Scholarship has been divided over the question of whether Origen in fact castrated himself.

The scholarly debate about Origen's genitals is less interesting than the fact that there has been such a debate. If Origen did castrate himself, the argument has been (since the time of Eusebius!), it must have been because his interpretation of Scripture was literal at that stage of his life. If he did not, Demetrius must have invented the story. Castration is the extreme and negative form of the celibacy required of Hermas; the physical cutting crosses the line between renunciation and mutilation. Whether the act is taken to have been performed on Origen's body or only in Demetrius's mind, no one defends it. Most scholars would probably not agree with Irenaeus that flesh may become the vehicle of spirit, and yet cutting it is commonly held to deface something of value. That high valuation of the physical flesh, axiomatic within Western culture, is an inheritance of orthodoxy (as described in chapter 2). The story about Origen violates that axiom.

In fact, Origen himself argued against any literal interpretation of Matthew 19:12, insisting that it did not refer to self-mutilation.[9] His interpretation has been used to suggest that Origen did castrate himself, and later saw the error of the act, as well as to argue that he never would have done such a thing. The matter is not likely ever to be settled, but what Origen did settle to his own satisfaction was the fraught issue of the relationship between flesh and spirit, the tension between which produced the plausibility of the claim that a great Christian teacher might castrate himself.

In his treatment of the resurrection, Origen shows himself a brilliant exegete and a profound theologian. He sees clearly that, in 1 Corinthians 15, Paul insists that the resurrection from the dead must be bodily. And Origen provides the logical grounding of Paul's claim: "if it is necessary, as it certainly is, for us to live in bodies, we ought to live in no other bodies but our own" (*On First Principles,* 10.1). But Origen equally insists upon Paul's assertion that "flesh and blood can not inherit the kingdom of God" (1 Cor. 15:50). There must be a radical transition from flesh to spirit, as

God fashions a body that can dwell in the heavens (*On First Principles,* 10.3).

For all that the transition from flesh to spirit is radical, Origen is also clear that personal continuity is involved. To put the matter positively, one is clothed bodily with one's *own* body, as we have already seen. To put the matter negatively, sins borne by the body of flesh may be thought of as visited upon the body that is raised from the dead (*On First Principles,* 10.8): "Just as the saints will receive back the very bodies in which they have lived in holiness and purity during their stay in this life, but bright and glorious as a result of the resurrection, so, too, the wicked, who in this life have loved the darkness of error and the night of ignorance, will after the resurrection be clothed with murky and black bodies, in order that this very gloom of ignorance, which in the present world has taken possession of the inner parts of their mind, may in the world to come be revealed through the garment of their outward body." Although Origen is quite consciously engaging in speculation at this point, he firmly rejects the notion that the flesh is involved in the resurrection, even when biblical promises appear to envisage earthly joys (*On First Principles,* 11.2).

His reasons for rejecting such a millenarian view are both exegetical and theological. Paul is the ground of the apostolic authority he invokes, in his reading of 1 Corinthians 15. He uses that perspective to consider the Scriptures generally (*On First Principles,* 11.3). But Origen deepens his argument from interpretation with a profoundly theological argument. He maintains that the most urgent longing is the desire "to learn the design of those things which we perceive to have been made by God." This longing is as basic to our minds as the eye is to the body: constitutionally, we long for the vision of God (*On First Principles,* 11.4). The logic of that desire is that the resurrection is spiritual, cognate with the Spirit of God itself.

The manner in which Origen develops his own thought is complex, involving a notion of education in paradise prior to one's entry into the realm of heaven proper (*On First Principles,* 11.5–7). But two factors remain plain and simple. First, the vision of God is the moving element through the entire discussion. Second, Origen clearly represents and develops a construction of the Christian faith in which eschatology has been swallowed up in an emphasis upon transcendence. The only time that truly matters is that time until one's personal death, which determines one's experience in paradise and in the resurrection. "Heaven" now occupies the central position once occupied by the kingdom of God.

# 4

# MARCHING IN PLACE: THE JUDAIC DEPARTURE FROM HISTORY AND THE CHRISTIAN INVENTION OF HISTORY

## FROM HISTORICAL PATTERN TO PARADIGM (JUDAISM); FROM PARADIGM RECAPITULATED TO HISTORY INVENTED (CHRISTIANITY)

Neither Christianity nor Judaism in the formative age engaged in historical thinking as we know it. Historical thinking requires three procedures: (1) criticism of the allegations as to past events set forth by received writings; (2) selection of consequential events; (3) organization of the selected events into patterns meant to demonstrate reasoned propositions out of secular facts, that is, the this-worldly explanation of the present out of the resources of the past. Imposed paradigms from heaven do not pertain; we can find our own way. The premises of historical thinking about time and especially past time, with us to this day, are then self-evident. The past is clearly differentiated from the present. An accurate knowledge of precisely what happened long ago bears self-evident meaning for the understanding of the present. For events critically narrated produce intelligible patterns, not chaos. The passage of time is read as linear, cumulative, and purposive; secular rationality substitutes for the teleology of revealed religion.

History's distinction between past and present is not the only indicator of historical modes of organizing experience. A further trait of historical thinking is the linearity of events, a sense for the teleology of matters, however the goal may find its definition. Past was then but leads to now. The past is not now but it guides us into the acute present tense, and onward to the future. For what just *may* happen is not to be predicted; linearity presupposes predictability, regularity, and order, and therefore contradicts the unpredictability of the world. Historical study correlates this to that, ideas to events, always seeking a reasonable explanation for what has come about. History then forms a subset of the quest for order—a persuasive one, one that enjoys the standing of self-evidence.

The premise of history in the modern understanding is that events critically reconstructed and properly selected and ordered yield an order that follows a rule. That governing premise accounts for the importance of critical history, which out of singular and one-time happenings will derive those social rules, those laws to describe the orderly character of human events that explain how things are now and what will come about. Historical thinking about the past, with its premises concerning the certainty of ordering events into meaningful patterns—the rationality of what was then to be called, and endowed with authority as, history, and above all the absolute separation between present and past time—presented a quite unprecedented mode of thinking about the course of human events. The language of organizing the past, "History proves . . ." then substituted for "God reveals."

All modern scholarship concurs that the Hebrew Scriptures from Genesis through Kings, as well as the prophetic books, present a historical account of Israel's past. These books conform in their premises to the rules of historical thinking. The Hebrew Scriptures were put together to impose upon the past a meaningful pattern so as to answer an urgent question. But those same Scriptures made their way into the West through the media of Judaism and Christianity, and both heirs recast the historical writings in an altogether different, ahistorical structure.

The Hebrew Scriptures of ancient Israel set forth Israel's life as history, with a beginning, middle, and end; a purpose and a coherence; a teleological system. All accounts agree that Scriptures distinguished past from present and present from future, and composed a sustained narrative, made up of one-time, irreversible events. All maintain that, in Scripture's historical portrait, Israel's present condition appealed for explanation to Israel's past, perceived as a coherent sequence of weighty events, each unique, all formed into a great chain of meaning. But that is not how the Hebrew Scriptures were read by Judaism and Christianity for most of the history of Western civilization. The idea of history, with its rigid distinction between past and present and its careful sifting of connections from the one to the other, came quite late onto the scene of intellectual life.

Both Judaism and Christianity for most of their histories have read the Hebrew Scriptures in an other-than-historical framework. They found in Scripture's words paradigms of an enduring present, by which all things must take their measure; they possessed no conception whatsoever of the pastness of the past. In due course, we shall consider an explanation for how and why, in Judaism, paradigmatic thinking replaced the historical kind. But first, let us explore the full and detailed character of the paradigmatic approach to the explanation of Israel's condition, viewed (to state the negative side of matters) atemporally, ahistorically, episodically, and not through sustained narrative—or its personal counterpart, biography—composed of connected, one-time and unique, irreversible events, in the manner of history.

All that has been said demonstrates that, while Rabbinic Judaism rests upon the Hebrew Scriptures of ancient Israel, this Judaism in no way merely recapitulates the main points of Scripture, let alone its modes of thought. It represents a profound re-presentation of those points, effected through a different way of thinking altogether. If Scripture sets forth the past in a manner we

169

must call historical, Rabbinic Judaism in no way pursues the path of historical organization of the past. A critical chapter in the system of Rabbinic Judaism records how the historical premises of Scripture—with its authorized history, from Genesis through Kings, with a beginning and middle and end—are recast in other terms entirely. Historical events are treated as not singular and not linear but as exemplary and paradigmatic.

Christianity, for its part, took over the Scriptures' linear, unitary history and identified Jesus as the climax and conclusion thereof. While, therefore, Christianity in such documents as the Epistle to the Hebrews took over and made its own the linear perspective of scriptural history, at the outset Christianity conceived history to have come to an end. Christians lived on the other side of time. With the advent of the Christian empire, however, the prospect of a long future history emerged. At that point Christianity had to invent history to accommodate its vision—and it did just that.

In both cases, we see, the initial statement of thinking about history endured but underwent important revision. Here we see not so much a trading of places as a marching in place, each religion following its own course within itself, continuous with its original conception. The two originate in Scripture and, from that perspective, start in the same place; but each went in its own direction, and the lines of progress proved not parallel; indeed, they did not even intersect. Rabbinic Judaism began with an ahistorical statement of its system and later on took over scriptural history only in order to recapitulate its systemic statement. Christianity began with the appropriation of scriptural history for its systemic statement, later on reverting to that conception of time as a sequence of unique events, coming from somewhere and pointing toward a fore-ordained point at the end of time, that had characterized Scripture.

Here, therefore, we cannot maintain that the one at the end took up the position of the other at the outset. Rather, each religious system reversed its march, but only within the limits and terms set by that system itself. That is what we mean by marching in place. Christianity had treated history as paradigm and came to adopt a linear conception of events. But, as we shall see, the upshot was to restate in fresh language the position adopted at the outset: history reaches its climax and conclusion in Christ. What changed was the definition of history's end. Rabbinic Judaism had formed its system within an eternity beyond changing time. Confronted by events of a cataclysmic dimension, Rabbinic Judaism would recast its systemic statement but preserve the systemic message. Here too, the result was to recapitulate the initial conception that events are not unique, not linear, and not aimed at a foreordained end but rather are organized into a large-scale structure. But the structure now would articulately accommodate events that in ordinary thought were understood as unique, linear, and purposeful. So, as with Christianity, the recapitulation of the problem of history involved an extension and amplification of the initial position, rather than its reversal.

## THE AHISTORICAL SYSTEM OF THE MISHNAH

Examining the Mishnah on its own terms, we do well to speak of structure rather than of system; for the Mishnah, by its own word, finds nothing to say about time and change, history and the teleology of history defined by eschatology, with its implication of movement from here to there; for the Mishnah, all things were to be formed into a hierarchical classification, for, in the fantasy of the Mishnah's framers, nothing much happened; the issue of intellect was ordering the chaotic, not confronting the permanence of change such as the concept of history entailed.

✡
171
✠

By "history" we mean the way that happenings identified as consequential—that is to say, as events—are so organized and narrated as to teach lessons, reveal patterns, tell what people must do and why, and indicate what will happen tomorrow. The Pentateuchal and prophetic writings of Scripture lay heavy stress on history in the sense just now given. By contrast, the framers of the Mishnah present a kind of historical thinking quite different from the one they, along with all Israel, had inherited in Scripture. The legacy of prophecy, apocalypse, and mythic history handed on by the writers of the books of the Old Testament exhibits a single and quite familiar conception of history seen whole. Events bear meaning: God's message and judgment. Therefore, what happens is singular, an event to be noted, and points toward lessons to be drawn about where things are heading and why.

If things do not happen at random, they also do not form indifferent patterns of merely secular, social facts. What happens is important because of the meaning contained therein. That meaning is to be discovered and revealed through the narrative of what has happened. So for all forms of Judaism until the Mishnah, the writing of history serves as a form of prophecy. Just as prophecy takes up the interpretation of historical events, so historians retell these events in the frame of prophetic theses. And out of the two—historiography as a mode of mythic reflection, prophecy as a means of mythic construction—emerges a picture of future history, that is, of what is going to happen. That picture, framed in terms of visions and supernatural symbols, in the end focuses, as much as do prophecy and history writing, upon the here and now.

History consists of a sequence of one-time events, each singular, all meaningful. These events move from a beginning somewhere to an end at a foreordained goal. History moves toward eschatology, the end of history. As we saw in the last chapter, the teleology of Israel's life finds its definition in eschatological fulfillment. Eschatology therefore constitutes not a choice within teleology, but the definition of teleology. History done in this way then sits enthroned as the queen of theological science. Events do not conform to patterns; they form patterns. What happens matters because events bear meaning, constitute history. Now, as is clear, such a conception of mythic and apocalyptic history comes to realization in the writing of history in the prophetic pattern or in the apocalyptic framework, both of them mythic modes of organizing events. We have every right to expect such a view of matters to lead people to write books of a certain sort, rather than of some other. In the case of Judaism, obviously, we should expect people to write history books that teach lessons or apocalyptic books that through pregnant imagery predict the future and record the direction and end of time. And in antiquity that kind of writing proves commonplace among all kinds of groups and characteristic of all sorts of Judaisms but one.

The Mishnah contains no sustained narrative whatsoever, a very few tales, and no large-scale conception of history. It organizes its system in nonhistorical and socially unspecific terms, lacking all precedent in prior systems of Judaism or in prior kinds of Judaic literature. Instead of narrative, it gives description of how things are done, that is, descriptive laws in the timeless present tense; it locates its system in space, not in time, the space being the time-less Land of Israel, holy and separate from all other lands—when occupied by the people beyond time, that Israel that is holy and (as we noted earlier) imparts holiness to the land by its presence upon it. The social rules of that Israel upon its land then form the ob-ject of the Mishnah's description. Instead of reflection on the meaning and end of history, it constructs a world in which history plays little or no part. Instead of narratives full of didactic mean-ing, it provides lists of events so as to expose the traits that they share and thus the rules to which they conform. The definitive components of a historical-eschatological system of Judaism— description of events as one time happenings, analysis of the mean-ing and end of events, and interpretation of the end and future of singular events—none of these commonplace constituents of all other systems of Judaism (including nascent Christianity) of an-cient times finds a place in the Mishnah's system of Judaism.

✿
173
✞

Disorderly historical events entered the system of the Mishnah and found their place within the larger framework of the Mish-nah's orderly world. So to claim that the Mishnah's framers merely ignored what was happening would be incorrect. They worked out their own way of dealing with significant happenings that we should classify as historical events, the disruptive power of which they not only conceded but freely recognized. Further, to begin with, the Mishnah's authors did not intend to compose a history book or a work of prophecy or apocalypse. Even if they had wanted to narrate the course of events, they could hardly have done so through the medium of the Mishnah. Yet the Mishnah presents its philosophy in full awareness of the issues of historical calamity confronting the Jewish nation. So far as the philosophy of the doc-ument confronts the totality of Israel's existence, the Mishnah by definition also presents a philosophy of history.

But the Mishnah finds no precedent in prior Israelite writings for its mode of dealing with things that happen. The Mishnah's way of identifying happenings as consequential and describing them, its way of analyzing those events it chooses as bearing meaning, its interpretation of the future to which significant events point—all those in context were unique. Yet to say that the Mishnah's system is ahistorical could not be more wrong. The Mishnah presents a different kind of history. More to the point, it revises the inherited conception of history and reshapes that conception to fit into its own system. When we consider the power of the biblical myth, the force of its eschatological and messianic interpretation of history, the effect of apocalypse, we must find astonishing the capacity of the Mishnah's framers to think in a different way about the same things. As teleology constructed outside the eschatological mode of thought in the setting of the biblical world of ancient Israel, the Mishnah's formulation proves amazing, since Scripture framed teleology in historical terms, and therefore invoked the conception of eschatology as the medium for thought about the goal and purpose of matters. By contrast the sages in the Mishnah set forth a teleology entirely outside the framework of historical-eschatological thinking.

The framers of the Mishnah explicitly refer to very few events, treating those they do mention within a focus quite separate from what happened—the unfolding of the events themselves. They rarely create or use narratives. More probative still, historical events do not supply organizing categories or taxonomic classifications. We find no tractate devoted to the destruction of the Temple, no complete chapter detailing the events of Bar Kokhba, nor even a sustained celebration of the events of the sages' own historical life. When things that have happened are mentioned, it is neither in order to narrate, nor to interpret and draw lessons from, the event. It is either to illustrate a point of law or to pose a problem of the Law—always *en passant,* never in a pointed way.

So when sages refer to what has happened, this is casual and tangential to the main thrust of discourse. Famous events, of enduring meaning—such as the return to Zion from Babylonia during the sixth century B.C.E. and onward to the time of Ezra and

Nehemiah—gain entry into the Mishnah's discourse only because of the genealogical division of Israelite society into castes among the immigrants (M. Qiddushin 4:1). Where the Mishnah provides little tales or narratives, moreover, they more often treat how things in the cult are done in general than what, in particular, happened on some one day. It is sufficient to refer casually to well-known incidents. Narrative, in the Mishnah's limited rhetorical repertoire, is reserved for the narrow framework of what priests and others do on recurrent occasions and around the Temple. In all, that staple of history, stories about dramatic events and important deeds, in the minds of the Mishnah's jurisprudents provide little nourishment. Events, if they appear at all, are treated as trivial. They may be well known, but are consequential in some way other than is revealed in the detailed account of what actually happened.

Sages' treatment of events determines what in the Mishnah is important about what happens. Since the greatest event in the century and a half from c. 50 C.E. to c. 200, in which the Mishnah's materials came into being, was the destruction of the Temple in 70 C.E., we must expect the Mishnah's treatment of that incident to illustrate the document's larger theory of history: what is important and unimportant about what happens. The treatment of the destruction occurs in two ways.

First, the destruction of the Temple constitutes a noteworthy fact in the history of the Law. Why? Because various laws about rite and cult had to undergo revision on account of the destruction. Second, although the sages surely mourned for the destruction and the loss of Israel's principal mode of worship, and certainly recorded the event of the ninth of Ab in the year 70 C.E., they did so in their characteristic way: they listed the event as an item in a catalog of things that are like one another and so demand the same response. But then the destruction no longer appears as a unique event. It is absorbed into a pattern of like disasters, all exhibiting similar taxonomic traits, events to which the people, now well schooled in tragedy, knows full well the appropriate response. So it is in demonstrating regularity that sages reveal their way of coping. Then the uniqueness of the event fades away, and its mundane character is emphasized. The power of taxonomy in imposing order upon chaos once more does its healing work. The consequence was reassurance that historical events obeyed discoverable laws. Israel's ongoing life would override disruptive, one-time happenings. So catalogs of events, as much as lists of species of melons, served as brilliant apologetic by providing reassurance that nothing lies beyond the range and power of ordering system and stabilizing pattern.

Along these same lines, the entire history of the cult, so critical in the larger system created by the Mishnah's lawyers, produced a patterned, therefore sensible and intelligible, picture. Everything that happened turned out to be susceptible of classification, once the taxonomic traits were specified. A monothetic exercise, sorting out periods and their characteristics, took the place of narrative, to explain things in its own way: first this, and then that, and, in consequence, the other. So on the neutral turf of holy ground, as much as in the trembling earth of the Temple Mount, everything was absorbed into one thing, all classified in its proper place and by its appropriate rule. Indeed, so far as the lawyers proposed to write history at all, they wrote it into their picture of the long tale of the way in which Israel served God: the places in which the sacrificial labor was carried on, the people who did it, the places in which the priests ate the meat left over for their portion after God's portion was set aside and burned up. This "historical" account forthwith generated precisely that problem of locating the regular and orderly, which the philosophers loved to investigate: the intersection of conflicting principles by equally correct taxonomic rules.

The Mishnah absorbs into its encompassing system all events, small and large. With what happens the sages accomplish what they do with everything else: a vast labor of taxonomy, an immense construction of the order and rules governing the classification of everything on earth and in heaven. The disruptive character of history—one-time events of ineluctable significance—scarcely impresses the philosophers. They find no difficulty in showing that what appears unique and beyond classification has in fact happened before and so falls within the range of trustworthy rules and known procedures. Once history's components, one-time events, lose their distinctiveness, then history as a didactic intellectual construct, as a source of lessons and rules, also loses all pertinence. So lessons and rules come from sorting things out and classifying them, that is, from the procedures and modes of thought of the philosopher seeking regularity. To this labor of taxonomy, the historian's way of selecting data and arranging them into patterns of meaning to teach lessons, proves inconsequential. One-time events are not what matters. The world is composed of nature and supernature. The repetitious laws that count are those to be discovered in heaven and, in heaven's creation and counterpart, on earth. Keep those laws, and things will work out. Break them, and the result is predictable: calamity of whatever sort will supervene in accordance with the rules. But just because it is predictable, a catastrophic happening testifies to what has always been and must always be, in accordance with reliable rules and within categories already discovered and well explained. That is why the lawyer-philosophers of the mid-second century produced the Mishnah— to explain how things are. Within the framework of well-classified rules, there could be messiahs, but no single Messiah. Theirs was a teleology without eschatology.

History as an account of a meaningful pattern of events, making sense of the past and giving guidance about the future, begins with the necessary conviction that events matter, one after another. The Mishnah's framers, however, present us with no elaborate theory of events, a fact fully consonant with their systematic points of insistence and encompassing concern. Events do not matter one by one. The philosopher-lawyers exhibited no theory of history either. Their conception of Israel's destiny in no way called upon historical categories of either narrative or didactic explanation to describe and account for the future. The small importance attributed to the figure of the Messiah as a historical-eschatological figure, such as we noted in chapter 3, therefore, fully accords with the larger traits of the system as a whole. If what is important in Israel's existence is sanctification, an ongoing process, and not salvation, understood as a one-time event at the end, then no one will find reason to narrate history. The Judaism that was to emerge from late antiquity was richly eschatological, obsessed with the Messiah and his coming, and engaged by the history of Israel and the nations. Judaism at the end did indeed provide an ample account and explanation of Israel's history and destiny.

## HISTORY RECAPITULATED AS PARADIGM:
## GENESIS RABBAH AND ISRAEL'S HISTORY

In Genesis Rabbah, a document generally regarded as belonging to the century after Constantine, a commentary to the Book of Genesis made up of episodic comments on verses and their themes, the Judaic sages who framed the document thus presented a profound and cogent theory of the history of Israel, the Jewish people. The Israelite sages invoked the recurring and therefore cyclical patterns of time, finding in their own day meaning imparted by patterns revealed long ago. The framers of Genesis Rabbah intended to find those principles of society and of history that would permit them to make sense of the ongoing history of Israel. They took for granted that Scripture speaks to the life and condition of Israel, the Jewish people. God repeatedly says exactly that to Abraham and to Jacob. The entire narrative of Genesis is so formed as to point toward the sacred history of Israel, the Jewish people: its slavery and redemption; its coming Temple in Jerusalem; its exile and salvation at the end of time. In the reading of the authors at hand, therefore, the powerful message of Genesis proclaims that the world's creation commenced a single, straight line of events, leading in the end to the salvation of Israel and through Israel all humanity. That message—that history heads toward Israel's salvation—sages derived from the Book of Genesis and contributed to in their own day. Therefore in their reading of Scripture a given story will bear a deeper truth about what it means to be Israel, on the one side, and what in the end of days will happen to Israel, on the other. But their reading makes no explicit reference to what, if anything, had changed in the age of Constantine. Still, we do find repeated references to the four kingdoms—Babylonia, Media, Greece, and Rome—and beyond the fourth will come Israel, fifth and last. So sages' message, in their theology of history, was that the present anguish prefigured the coming vindication of God's people.

The Judaic sages worked out a view of history consisting in a rereading of the Book of Genesis in light of the entire history of Israel, read under the aspect of eternity. The Book of Genesis then provided a complete, profoundly typological interpretation of everything that had happened as well as a reliable picture of what, following the rules of history laid down in Genesis, was going to happen in the future. Typological in what sense? The events of Genesis served as types, prefiguring what would happen to Israel in its future history. Just as the Christians read stories of the (to them) Old Testament as types of the life of Christ, so the sages understood the tales of Genesis in a similarly typological manner. For neither party can history have retained that singular and one-dimensional, linear quality that it had had in Scripture itself.

Sages had inherited two conflicting ways of sorting out events and declaring some of them to add up to history, to meaning. From the biblical prophets they learned that God made God's will known through what happened, using pagan empires to carry out a plan. So some events formed a pattern and proved a proposition. They inherited, also from Scripture, a congruent scheme for dealing with history. This scheme involved differentiating one period from another, one empire from another, assigning to each a symbol, e.g., an animal, and imputing to each animal traits characteristic of the empire, and the age, symbolized by it. This apocalyptic approach to history did not contradict the basic principles of the prophetic view of events, but expressed that view in somewhat different, more concrete terms, specifically, terms defined by the Book of Genesis.

179

In looking to the past to explain the present, the Judaic sages turned to the story of the beginnings of creation, humanity, and Israel, that is, to the Book of Genesis. This was on the supposition that if we can discern beginnings, we can understand the end. The Israelite sages took up the beginnings that marked the original pattern for ongoing history. Sages could not imagine, after all, that what had happened in their own day marked the goal and climax of historical time. Rome formed an episode, not the end. But then, sages had to state what they thought constituted the real history of the world and of Israel.

Accordingly, sages read Genesis as the history of the world with emphasis on Israel. So the lives portrayed, the domestic quarrels and petty conflicts with the neighbors, all serve to yield insight into what was to be. Why so? Because the deeds of the patriarchs taught lessons on how the children were to act and, it further followed, the lives of the patriarchs signaled the history of Israel. Israel constituted one extended family, and the metaphor of the family, serving the nation as it did, imparted to the stories of Genesis the character of a family record. History become genealogy that conveyed the message of salvation. These propositions really laid down the same judgment, one for the individual and the family, the other for the community and the nation, since there was no differentiating. Every detail of the narrative therefore served to prefigure what was to be, and Israel found itself, time and again, in the revealed facts of the history of the creation of the world, the decline of humanity down to the time of Noah, and, finally, its ascent to Abraham, Isaac, and Israel.

What are the laws of history, and, more important, how do they apply to the crisis at hand? The principal message of the story of the beginnings, as sages read Genesis, is that the world depends on Abraham, Isaac, and Jacob; Israel, for its part, is today the family of the patriarchs and matriarchs. That conception of matters constitutes the sages' doctrine of history: the family forms the basic and irreducible historical unit. Israel is not so much a nation as a family, and the heritage of the patriarchs and matriarchs sustains that family from the beginning even to the end. So the sages' doctrine of history transforms history into genealogy. The consequence, for sages, will take the form of the symbolization through family relationships of the conflict between (Christian) Rome and eternal Israel. The rivalry of the brothers Esau and Jacob then contains the history of the fourth century—from sages' viewpoint a perfectly logical mode of historical reflection. That, in detail, expresses the main point of the system of historical thought yielded by Genesis Rabbah.

Genesis now is read as both a literal statement and an effort to prefigure the history of Israel's suffering and redemption. Ishmael, standing now for Christian Rome, claims God's blessing, but Isaac gets it, as Jacob will take it from Esau. Details, as much as the main point, yielded laws of history. Salvation is going to derive from the inherited status and merit of the matriarchs and patriarchs.

Everything that the matriarchs and patriarchs did brought a reward to their descendants. The enormous emphasis on the way in which Abraham's deeds prefigured the history of Israel, both in the wilderness, and in the Land of Israel, and, finally, in the age to come, provokes us to wonder who held that there were children of Abraham besides Israel. When we recall how Christian exegetes imparted to the Old Testament the lessons of the New, we realize that sages constructed an equally epochal and encompassing reading of Scripture. They now understood the meaning of what happened then, and, therefore, they also grasped from what had happened then the sense and direction of events of their own day. So history yielded patterns, and patterns proved points, and the points at hand indicated the direction of Israel. The substance of historical doctrine remains social in its focus. Sages present their theory of the meaning of history within a larger theory of the identification of Israel. Specifically, they see Israel as an extended family, children of one original ancestral couple, Abraham and Sarah. Whatever happens, then, constitutes family history, which is why the inheritance from the ancestors protects their children even now, in the fourth century.

In this reading Israel's history takes place under the aspect of eternity. Events do not take place one time only. Events, to make a difference and so to matter, constitute paradigms and generate patterns. Salvation is all the same; its particularization is all that history records. So we can move in interrupted flow from Abraham to Esther to David. The lessons of history therefore do not derive from sequences of unique moments but from patterns that generate recurring and reliable rules. Accordingly, sages read the present in light of the past, rather than following the way of reading the past in light of the present. Given their present, they had little choice.

The heritage of the patriarchs and matriarchs sustains, and the failures exact a cost, for the history of the nation and the ongoing life of the family form a single entity in history. That is a point we should not miss.

### GENESIS RABBAH LIV:IV

1. A. "Abraham set seven ewe-lambs of the flock apart" (Gen. 21:28):

   B. Said the Holy One, blessed be he, to him, "You have given him seven ewe-lambs. By your life I shall postpone the joy of your descendants for seven generations.

   C. "You have given him seven ewe-lambs. By your life matching them his descendants [the Philistines] will kill seven righteous men among your descendants, and these are they: Hofni, Phineas, Samson, Saul and his three sons.

   D. "You have given him seven ewe-lambs. By your life, matching them the seven sanctuaries of your descendants will be destroyed, namely, the tent of meeting, the altars at Gilgal, Nob, Gibeon, Shiloh, and the two eternal houses of the sanctuary.

   E. "You have given him seven ewe-lambs. [By your life, matching them] my ark will spend seven months in the fields of the Philistines."

No. 1 reverts to the theme of indignation at Abraham's coming to an agreement with Abimelech, forcefully imposing the theme of the later history of Israel upon the story at hand. A much more exemplary case derives from the binding of Isaac, the point from which the heritage of Abraham flows. The aptness of the incident derives from its domestic character: relationship of mother, father, and only child. What Abraham and Isaac were prepared to sacrifice (and Sarah to lose) won for them and their descendants—as the story itself makes explicit—an ongoing treasury of unearned grace, original virtue, so to speak, in place of original sin. So the children of Abraham and Isaac through history will derive salvation from the original act of binding Isaac to the altar. The reference to the third day at Genesis 22:2 then invokes the entire panoply of Israel's history. The relevance of the composition emerges at the end. Prior to the concluding segment, the passage forms a kind of litany and falls into the category of a liturgy. Still, the recurrent hermeneutics that teaches that the stories of the patriarchs prefigure the history of Israel certainly makes its appearance.

Sages found a place for Rome in Israel's history only by assigning to Rome a place in the family. Their larger theory of the social identity of Israel left them no choice. But it also permitted them to assign to Rome an appropriately significant place in world history, while preserving for Israel the climactic role. Whatever future history finds adumbration in the life of Jacob derives from the struggle with Esau. Israel and Rome—these two contend for the world. Still, Isaac plays his part in the matter. Rome does have a legitimate claim, and that claim demands recognition—an amazing, if grudging, concession on the part of sages that Christian Rome at least is Esau.

### GENESIS RABBAH LXVII:IV

1. A. When Esau heard the words of his father, he cried out with an exceedingly great and bitter cry [and said to his father, 'Bless me, even me also, O my father!']." (Gen. 27:34)

   B. Said R. Hanina, "Whoever says that the Holy One, blessed be he, is lax, may his intestines become lax. While he is patient, he does collect what is coming to him.

   C. "Jacob made Esau cry out one cry, and where was he penalized? It was in the castle of Shushan: 'And he cried with a loud and bitter cry.'" (Esther 4:1)

183

2. A. "But he said, 'Your brother came with guile and he has taken away your blessing.'" (Gen. 33:35)

   B. R. Yohanan said, "[He came] with the wisdom of his knowledge of the Torah."

So Rome really is Israel's brother. No pagan empire ever enjoyed an equivalent place; no pagan era ever found identification with an event in Israel's family history. The passage presents a stunning concession and an astounding claim. The history of the two brothers forms a set of counterpoints, the rise of one standing for the decline of the other. There can be no more powerful claim for Israel: the ultimate end, Israel's final glory, will permanently mark the subjugation of Esau. Israel then will follow, the fifth and final monarchy. The point of No. 1 is to link the present passage to the history of Israel's redemption later on. In this case, however, the matter concerns Israel's paying recompense for causing anguish to

Esau. No. 2 introduces Jacob's knowledge of Torah in place of Esau's view of Jacob as full of guile.

The redemption in the past prefigures what is to come. The *zekhut* that protects Israel in the present derives from the heritage of the past. So history is one and seamless, as the life of a family goes on through time. Do people wonder, with the triumph of Christianity in politics, what is to become of Israel? In rereading the story of Israel's beginnings, sifting and resifting the events in the life of the patriarchs and matriarchs, sages found the answer to the question. What will happen is what has happened. History recapitulates the life of the family. And to a family, the politics of empire makes slight difference. Israel therefore will endure in hope. The critical component of the system—as distinct from its structure—is its capacity to translate all things into a single proposition.

## THE PRESENCE OF THE PAST

184

The sages represent the Torah as portraying the past in complete indifference to considerations of temporal order:

> "And the Lord spoke to Moses in the wilderness of Sinai in the first month of the second year after they had come out of the land of Egypt, saying, ['Let the people of Israel keep the passover at its appointed time. On the fourteenth day of this month, in the evening, you shall keep it at its appointed time; according to all its statutes and all its ordinances you shall keep it.']" (Num. 9:1-14)
>
> Scripture teaches you that *considerations of temporal order do not apply to the sequence of scriptural stories.* For at the beginning of the present book Scripture states, "The Lord spoke to Moses in the wilderness of Sinai in the tent of meeting on the first day of the *second* month in the second year after they had come out of the land of Egypt." (Num. 1:1)
>
> And here Scripture refers to "the *first* month," so serving to teach you that *considerations of temporal order do not apply to the sequence of scriptural stories.*

Sifré to Numbers LXIV:I:1

At first glance, this allegation concerning the Torah's way of organizing the past is jarring. But upon reflection, we realize that history's premise—the self-evidence of the linearity of events, so that, first came this, then came that, and this "stands behind" or explains or causes that—contradicts the everyday experience of humanity, in which chaos governs, while from history's perspective, order should reign. Sometimes "this" yields "that," as it should, but sometimes it does not.

Ordinary life does not yield events that relate to one another like pearls on a necklace: first this, then that, then the other thing, in proper procession. Life is unpredictable; if this happens, we cannot securely assume that that must occur in sequence, in order—at least, not in the experience of humanity. That is proven by the irregularity of events, the unpredictability, by all and any rules, of what, if this happens, will follow next. Knowing "this," we never can securely claim to predict "that" as well. But if the past is not organized in the historical way, then how? Clearly, a different way of ordering the past provides the framework for the statement of the Rabbinic document before us. To understand that different way, we have to step back and consider the various ways by which we tell time, for history's linearity and order represent only one way.

That other way of ordering the past, as we have seen in Genesis Rabbah, treats what has happened as present, and what happens as a recapitulation of the past. Events are therefore transformed into paradigms. Paradigms describe the structure of being: how (some) things are, whether now or then, here or there, large or small—without regard to scale and therefore in complete indifference to the specificities of context. Paradigms derive from imagination, not from perceived reality. They impose upon the world their own structure and order, selecting among things that happen those few moments that are eventful and meaningful. Paradigms form a different conception of time from the historical, define a different conception of relationship from the linear. To call the religious way of reading Scripture ahistorical is both accurate and monumentally beside the point; it is only to say what it is not, not what it is. We claim it is paradigmatic thinking, in place of linear thinking, and here we shall set forth precisely what that way of thinking is, so far as the Judaism of the dual Torah exemplifies paradigmatic thinking: how history and time give way to a different order of being altogether.

The Rabbinic mode of organizing the past makes its statement through a different, quite ahistorical medium, one that explicitly rejects distinctions among past, present, and future, and treats the past as a powerful presence, but the present as a chapter of the past, and the future as a negotiation not of time but of principle. A paradigm governs, all events conforming to its atemporal rule. Consequently, the two conflicting conceptions of social explanation—the historical, the paradigmatic—appeal to two different ways of conceiving of, and evaluating, time. Historical time measures one thing and paradigmatic time, another, though both refer to the same facts of nature and of the social order. Paradigmatic time—having no "earlier" or "later"—corresponds to nature's time, not history's time.

A paradigm forms a way of keeping time that invokes its own differentiating indicators, its own counterparts to the indicators of nature's time. Nature defines time as that span that is marked off by one spell of night and day; or by one sequence of positions and phases of the moon; or by one cycle of the sun around the earth (in the pre-Copernican paradigm). History further defines nature's time by the marking of a solar year in reference to an important human event, e.g., a reign, a battle, the completion of a building. So history's time intersects with, and is superimposed upon, nature's time. And cyclical time forms a modification of history's time, appealing for its divisions of the aggregates of time to the analogy, in human life, to nature's time: the natural sequence of events in a human life viewed as counterpart to the natural sequence of events in solar and lunar time.

Paradigms are set forth neither by nature (by definition) nor by natural history (what happens on its own here on earth); by neither the cosmos (sun and moon) or the natural history of humanity (the life cycle and analogies drawn therefrom). In the setting of Judaism and Christianity, paradigms are set forth in revelation;

they explain the Creator's sense of order and regularity, which is neither imposed upon, nor derived from, nature's time, nor to be discovered through history's time. And that is why to paradigmatic time, history is wildly incongruous, and considerations of linearity, temporality, and historical order are beyond all comprehension. God has set forth the paradigms that measure time by indicators of an other-than-natural character: supernatural time, which is beyond all conception of time.

The paradigm takes its measures in terms not of historical movements or recurrent cycles but rather atemporal units of experience, those same aggregates of time such as nature makes available through the movement of the sun and moon and the passing of the seasons, on the one hand, and through the life of the human being on the other. A model or pattern or paradigm will set forth an account of the life of the social entity (village, kingdom, people, territory) in terms of differentiated events—wars, reigns, for one example, building a given building and destroying it, for another—yet entirely out of phase with sequences of time.

A paradigm imposed upon time does not call upon the day or month or year to accomplish its task. It will simply set aside nature's time altogether, regarding years and months as bearing a significance other than the temporal one (sequence, span of time, aggregates of time) that history, inclusive of cyclical time's history, posits. Time paradigmatic then views humanity's time as formed into aggregates out of all phase with nature's time, measured in aggregates not coherent with those of the solar year and the lunar month. The aggregates of humanity's time are dictated by humanity's life, as much as the aggregates of nature's time are defined by the course of nature. Nature's time serves not to correlate with humanity's patterns (no longer, humanity's time), but rather to mark off units of time to be correlated with the paradigm's aggregates.

For Rabbinic Judaism the Torah, the written part of the Torah in particular, defined a set of paradigms that served without regard to circumstance, context, or, for that matter, dimension and scale of happening. A very small number of models emerged from Scripture, captured in the sets (1) Eden and Adam, (2) Sinai and the Torah, (3) the land and Israel, and (4) the Temple and its building, destruction, rebuilding. These paradigms served severally and jointly, e.g., Eden and Adam on its own but also superimposed upon the land and Israel; Sinai and the Torah on its own but also superimposed upon the Land and Israel; and the Temple, embodying natural creation and its intersection with national and social history. Each paradigm could stand entirely on its own or be superimposed upon any and all of the other paradigms. In many ways, then, we have the symbolic equivalent of a set of two- and three- or even four-dimensional grids. A given pattern forms a grid on its own, one set of lines being set forth in terms of, e.g., Eden, timeless perfection, in contrast with the other set of lines: Adam, temporal disobedience. But upon that grid, a comparable grid can be superimposed, the Land and Israel being an obvious one; and upon the two, yet a third and fourth, Sinai and Torah, Temple and the confluence of nature and history.

In Rabbinic Judaism the natural way of telling time precipitated celebration of nature. True, those same events were associated with moments of Israel's experience as well: the Exodus above all. The language of prayer, e.g., the Sabbath's classification as a memorial to creation and also a remembrance of the Exodus from Egypt, leaves no doubt about the dual character of the annotation of time. But the Exodus, memorialized hither and yon through the solar seasons and the Sabbath alike, constituted no more a specific, never-to-be-repeated, one-time historical event, part of a sustained narrative of such events, than any other moment in Israel's time, inclusive of the building and the destruction of the Temple. Quite to the contrary, linking creation and Exodus classified both in a single category; the character of that category—historical or paradigmatic—is not difficult to define; the Exodus is treated as consubstantial with creation, a paradigm, not a one-time event.

It follows that this Judaism's Israel kept time in two ways, and the one particular to Israel (in the way in which the natural calendar was not particular to Israel) through its formulation as a model instead of a singular event, was made to accord with the natural calendar, not vice versa. That is to say, just as the natural calendar recorded time that was the opposite of historical, because it was not linear and singular and teleological but reversible and repetitive, so Israel kept time with reference to events, whether past or present, that also were not singular, linear, or teleological. These were, rather, reconstitutive in the forever of here and now—not a return to a perfect time but a recapitulation of a model forever present. Israel could treat as comparable the creation of the world and the Exodus from Egypt (as the liturgy commonly does, e.g., in connection with the Sabbath) because Israel's paradigm (not "history") and nature's time corresponded in character, were consubstantial and not mutually contradictory.

The upshot, then, we state with heavy emphasis: *The rhythms of the sun and moon are celebrated in the very forum in which the land, Israel's Eden, yields its celebration to the Creator.* The rhythmic quality of the paradigm then compares with the rhythmic quality of natural time: not cyclical, but also not linear. Nature's way of telling time and the Torah's way meet in the Temple: its events are nature's, its story a tale of nature too. Past and present flow together and join in future time too because, as in nature, what is past is what is now and what will be. The paradigms, specified in a moment, form counterparts to the significations of nature's time.

✡
189
✝

These events of Israel's life (we cannot now refer to Israel's "history")—or, rather, the models or patterns that they yielded—served as the criteria for selection, among happenings of any time, past, present, or future, of the things that mattered out of the things that did not matter: a way of keeping track, a mode of marking time. The model or paradigm that set forth the measure of meaning then applied whether to events of vast consequence or to the trivialities of everyday concern alone. Sense was where sense was found by the measure of the paradigm; everything else lost consequence. Connections were then to be made between this and that, and the other thing did not count. Conclusions then were to be drawn between the connection of this and that, and no consequences were to be imputed to the thing that did not count.

That is not an ideal way of discovering or positing order amid chaos; much was left, if not unaccounted for, then not counted to begin with. We cannot take for granted that the range of events chosen for paradigms struck everyone concerned as urgent or even deserving of high priority, and we also must assume that other

Israelites, besides those responsible for writing and preserving the books surveyed here, will have identified other paradigms altogether. But—for those who accorded to these books authority and self-evidence—the paradigm encompassing the things that did conform to the pattern and did replicate its structure excluded what it did not explain. So it left the sense that while chaos characterized the realm beyond consciousness, the things of which people took cognizance also made sense—a self-fulfilling system of enormously compelling logic. For the system could explain what it regarded as important, and also dismiss what it regarded as inconsequential or meaningless, therefore defining the data that fit and dismissing those that did not.

At stake in the paradigm is discerning order and regularity not everywhere but in some few sets of happenings. These are, specifically, the sets that organize the past, together with contemporary experience, in an encompassing and coherent way. The scale revised both upward and downward the range of concern: These are not all happenings, but they are the ones that matter—and they matter very much. Realizing or replicating the paradigm, they uniquely constitute events and that is why, by definition, these are the only events that matter. Paradigmatic thinking about past, present, and future ignores issues of linear order and temporal sequence because it recognizes another logic all together, besides the one of priority and posteriority and causation formulated in historical terms. That mode of thinking, as its name states, appeals to the logic of models or patterns that serve without regard to time and circumstance, on the one side, or scale on the other. The sense for order unfolds, first of all, through that logic of selection that dictates what matters and what does not. And, out of the things that matter, that same logic defines the connections of things, so forming a system of description, analysis, and explanation that consists in the making of connections between this and that, but not the other thing, and the drawing of conclusions from those ineluctable, self-evident connections.

Nature's time is the sole way of marking time, and Israel's paradigm conforms to nature's time and proves enduringly congruent with it. Israel conforming to nature yields not cyclical history but a reality formed by appeal to the paradigm of cult and Temple, just as God had defined that pattern and paradigm to Moses in the Torah. Genesis begins with nature's time and systematically explains how the resources of nature came to Israel's service to God. History's time yielded an Israel against and despite history; nature's time, as the Torah tells it, yielded an Israel fully harmonious with nature. At stake in the paradigm then is creation: how come? So long as the Judaism set forth by sages in the Mishnah, Tosefta, Talmuds, and Midrash-compilations governed, Israel formed itself in response to the eternities of nature's time, bringing into conformity the ephemerals of the here and now. That answers the questions, why here? Why now? So what? When and where this Judaism lost its power of self-evidence, there history intervened. Philosophy and theology, including normative law, gave way to narrative, and the lines of structure and order took a new turning.

## THE CHRISTIAN INVENTION OF GLOBAL HISTORY

Christianity in its primitive phase of development was a movement, or a collection of movements, within Judaism. That was both its perception of itself and the way it was generally seen by outsiders. The claim of the first followers of Jesus was that they were the true Israel, and they took for granted the normative status of the Scriptures of Israel.[1] In the Introduction, we saw how the Epistle to the Hebrews reads the Scriptures of Israel as the foreshadowed truth of what Jesus, the great high priest, fully reveals. What came before Jesus were types of the truth, while Jesus himself is the substance of truth.

The power of the contribution of the Epistle to the Hebrews resides in its use of the idea and method of types in order to explain how Jesus was related to the Scriptures of Israel. Within the catechesis of primitive Christianity, it had already been a matter of consensus that there was a stable analogy between Christ and the Scriptures. Sometimes, as we saw in the Introduction, within the stories of the feedings of the five thousand and the four thousand in the synoptic Gospels (Matt. 14:13–21; Mark 6:32–44; Luke 9:10b–17; and Matt. 15:32–39; Mark 8:1–10), that analogy could be worked out in symbolic terms that were quite complicated. Hebrews, therefore, was not influential because its reading of Christ's significance was totally unique. Rather, its development of typology explained how there could be a constant analogy between Christ and Scripture on the basis of a single way of reading the text and experiencing Jesus.

In that Jesus is the key to understanding the Scripture, Scripture may also be used to illuminate the significance of Jesus. That is the method of Hebrews, and its execution became classic because its method was taken up and elaborated in later centuries. Hebrews' focus was on Jesus Christ as "yesterday and today the same, and forever" (Heb. 13:8).

A similar indifference to what we would call history was expressed by Paul: "So we from now on regard no one according to the flesh; although we once regarded Christ according to the flesh, we no longer regard him in that way" (2 Cor. 5:16). In his judicious commentary, Victor Paul Furnish paraphrases Paul's concern as "to emphasize that for the Christian no worldly standards have any proper role in the evaluation of other persons (v. 16a), since they certainly play no role in one's evaluation of Christ (v. 16b)."[2]

Paul's conviction that, somehow, Christ was to be the standard of everything we might know and do was developed in Hebrews by means of its theory and method of typology. The genius of Hebrews was that it could explain and explore the insight that Paul (however brilliantly) could only assert and insist upon. Types provided the link between Jesus and the Scriptures of Israel, while insisting upon the prior importance of the Son to any ancillary testimony to the will and purposes of God.

The relative sophistication of Hebrews, however, in no way implies that its stance is more historical than Paul's, or than that of primitive Christianity as a whole. In chapter 5, Jesus is referred to under the figure of Melchizedek in the Book of Psalms, and then immediate reference is made to his passion (Heb. 5:7):

> In the days of his flesh, he offered prayers and supplications, with a strong cry and tears, to the one who was able to save him from death, and he was heard for his piety.

A connection between this statement and the synoptic description of Jesus in Gethsemane (Matt. 26:36–46; Mark 14:32–42; Luke 22:39–46) has frequently been observed. But in the synoptic passage, no "loud cry" is at issue; Hebrews is enhancing the scene in the interests of its Christology of the significance of Jesus' suffering (see Heb. 5:8). The eternal significance of Jesus means that some things must have been so "in the days of his flesh." Just as Hebrews articulates Jesus' eternal status in the mind of primitive Christianity and early Christianity, so it articulates the corollary motif: what is eternally true about Jesus must in some way have been reflected in the course of his physical life.

In many ways, of course, assertions of what must have been the case during Jesus' life will give the appearance of what we call history. The first two chapters of Luke, for example, provide what seem superficially to be circumstantial reports concerning Jesus' birth. But at many points, the Lukan chapters contradict the opening chapters of Matthew. For example, when Jesus' family is fleeing to Egypt in Matthew (2:13–15), they are circumcising the child and bringing him to Jerusalem to present him at the Temple in Luke (2:21–24). In addition, of course, Luke has the characters speak in psalmic arias, which are still used as part of Christian worship, and which probably originated in that setting. The point about such material is not that it is a simple matter of legend. Rather, circumstantial material speaks of the truth of Jesus' sonship in the flesh just as clearly as symbolic material points to the truth of his eternal status. Both types of assertion, embedded in the synoptic Gospels, are articulated clearly and to telling effect in the Epistle to the Hebrews.

193

For the purposes of our discussion, what is crucial to appreciate is the difference between a circumstantial statement and a historical statement. What shows the truth about Jesus in Hebrews and in the Gospels is not any ordered sequence of consequential events but the revelation of divine purpose and salvation within human affairs. That is, typology involves a view of past events that sees them as consequential but not as essentially sequential. Time is not a vital consideration because what determines one's faith is atemporal: the types of Israel, Jesus in the flesh, and the eternal Christ. Those three fundamental categories of existence are coordinated with one another, but they do not necessitate a sequence of development from year to year. Moreover, they do not involve any claim of causal connection from event to event.

In its assertion of consequence without necessary sequence, typology as developed in Hebrews and in early Christianity remains an ahistorical perspective. Nonetheless, it increasingly involved an emphasis on Jesus in what Hebrews called "the days of his flesh," and it insisted upon the significance of salvation for people who continued to live in the flesh. The struggle with Gnosticism (discussed in chapter 2) made that development inevitable, and its clearest representative is Irenaeus. In his treatise *Against Heresies,* Irenaeus pressed the case for the unity implicit in the fulfillment of various ancient prophecies in Christ: typology in Irenaeus's treatment became a general theory of the relationship between the Scriptures of Israel and Jesus. In effect, the reference to Israel's Scriptures consistently in this way defined them primarily as sources of types. It is no coincidence that the second century saw the rise and triumph of the use of the phrase "New Testament" to refer to the canon of the Gospels, the letters of Paul, and the other writings generally received within the church. That phrase implies another, "Old Testament," which embodies the theory that the Scriptures of Israel are to be understood as types that are fulfilled in Christ. Irenaeus contributed to that early Christian vocabulary of the Scriptures, and even more influentially to the early Christian theory of the Scriptures.

Although Irenaeus made great play of his skepticism of Gnostic speculations, he in fact contributed one of the most daring ideas that orthodox Christianity accepted, and he did so within his general theory of the Scriptures. Just as he argued for the unity of the Old and the New Testament on the basis of the typology of Hebrews, so Irenaeus developed the relationship between Adam and Christ on the basis of what he read in St. Paul (especially in Romans 5). The description offered by Henry Chadwick can scarcely be improved upon:

The divine plan for the new covenant was a "recapitulation" of the original creation. In Christ the divine Word assumed a humanity such as Adam possessed before he fell. Adam was made in the image and likeness of God. By sin the likeness became lost, though the image remained untouched. By faith in Christ mankind may recover the lost likeness. Because Irenaeus regarded salvation as a restoration of the condition prevailing in Paradise before the Fall, it was easy for him to accept Justin's terrestrial hopes for the millennium. Because he believed that in the Fall only the moral likeness to God was lost, not the basic image, he was able to regard the Fall in a way very different from the deep pessimism of the Gnostics.[3]

For all his stress on the authority of apostolic tradition, Irenaeus here shows himself to be one of the great synthetic philosophers of early Christianity. In a single theory he elevated the flesh to the realm of what may be saved, set out a general approach to the relationship between the Testaments of the Scriptures, and articulated a symmetrical theology of primordial sin and eschatological hope. "God became man that man might become divine" (*Against Heresies*, 3.10.2; 3.19.1; 4.33.4, 11).

✡
**195**
✝

Although there were more creative thinkers in the history of classical Christianity (such as Origen), and more accomplished theologians (such as Augustine), none was more influential than Irenaeus in his theory of recapitulation. It was a masterful advance along lines already laid down earlier,[4] and Christianity ever since, consciously and not, has been exploring its implications.

But for all the daring profundity of Irenaeus's contribution, he did not articulate a theory of what we could call history. The consequence of the Incarnation was absolute, but by definition it did not emerge from any sequence of events that were determined by the terms and conditions of this world. That point is sometimes difficult to grasp for modern readers, because it is generally assumed as a matter of course that Christianity operates within assertions about history.[5] But history speaks of sequence as well as of consequence: from the time of the Gospels until the present, Christian faith indeed speaks of events, but of events that are as unsequential as they are without precedent. Real time for Irenaeus dissolves the appearances of this world into the prophecies of the past, their fulfillment in Christ, and the totally restored humanity that recapitulation promises. Within such a perspective, history does not even have the significance of a footnote.

The explanation of Irenaeus's lack of historical curiosity is pursued by Lloyd Patterson:

> Irenaeus' lack of interest in *historia* is doubtless due largely to his position on the edge of the world of Hellenistic intellectual ideas in general. But more than this is to be discerned in his silence. Unwitting though it may have been on his part, he was involved in preparing the way for a renewal of the debate with contemporary philosophy in which accounts of human happenings as such were not likely to play any significant part.[6]

The position of Irenaeus comported with his own background. Unlike Justin before him and Augustine after him, but like Origen in the third century, he was not a convert to Christianity but a product of Christian culture.

A native of Smyrna in Asia Minor (present-day Turkey), he knew Bishop Polycarp, a great martyr and hero of the faith. Irenaeus's move to Lyons involved him in an embassy to Pope Eleutherus to seek tolerance of the Montanists in Asia Minor. Irenaeus was no Montanist: Montanus, after all, claimed personally to fulfill Jesus' promise of the coming of a Paraclete (a "Comforter") in the Gospel according to John (see John 14:16–17, 26; 15:26; 16:7).[7] But Irenaeus was nurtured in a milieu that anticipated the immediate fulfillment of biblical promises in Christ, and his theory of recapitulation is no historical survey, but an answer to the single question: How is it that faith in Jesus Christ will ultimately transform humanity?

Because recapitulation, like typology, is a theory of salvation, rather than a historical argument, Irenaeus is able to make statements about Jesus without recourse to information about him, even in contradiction of the Gospels. Because Jesus is held to sum up our humanity in his flesh, Irenaeus holds he must have died around the age of fifty, the supposed time of complete human maturity (*Against Heresies,* 2.22.1–6). The only reference in the New Testament to Jesus' age comes in the Gospel according to Luke, where he "began to be about thirty" (Luke 3:23) at the start of his ministry. Although that statement is vague, only speculation can turn Jesus' age at his death into fifty. Evidently, the Gnostics were not the only thinkers in the second century who were inventive.

The operative point in the distinction between Irenaeus and the Gnostics he opposed is not that he was historically minded while they embraced philosophy. That once fashionable generalization has virtually no merit. The contrast between them is at once more basic and more interesting. Irenaeus's speculation involved the flesh in its beginning in types, in its recapitulation in the case of Jesus, and in its fulfillment in paradise. Gnostic speculation, by contrast, referred to flesh as an ancillary accident in the overall unfolding of spiritual essence. It is for that reason that Jesus, for Irenaeus, must have been fifty when he died, much as Hebrews can invent elements in Jesus' struggle for obedience. Hebrews' invention of circumstance (the "loud cry" in Gethsemane) is less substantial than Irenaeus's, but each is motivated by the concern for what must have been the case. And what must have been in the flesh is a projection of what eternally is in heaven.

197

The procedure of thinking on the basis of God's nature, and relating that to human nature, is perhaps best instanced by Origen. The discussion in the last chapter showed that the increasing emphasis upon the flesh, characteristic of orthodox Christianity in its resistance to Gnosticism (see chapter 2), was radically questioned by Origen. He insisted rather on the transformation of the idiom of existence from earth to heaven as one imagined the body in which resurrection occurred. The line of demarcation between millennial expectations of eschatology (such as Justin's and Irenaeus's) and spiritual expectations of eschatology (such as Clement's and Origen's) is quite clear in classical Christianity, and the difference has yet to be resolved, even in modern theology.

On the side of those who were sympathetic with Origen, however, the role of history was severely limited. He himself was inclined to see the writings of Moses as an example of *historia,* a matter for literal reading. The aim of deeper interpretation was to find the allegorical or spiritual meaning that provides insight into the restoration (*apokatastasis*) of all things in Christ, a transformation that can only occur outside the terms and conditions of this world.[8] Any limitation to the realm of literal history was for Origen the most dangerous self-deception.

The difference between Irenaeus and Origen is instructive on several levels. Although they both invested what happened to Jesus in the flesh with profound meaning, each understood the proper medium of that meaning characteristically. In the more millennial perspective of Irenaeus, what happened in the case of one person of flesh has consequence for all people of flesh, and vice versa. In the more philosophical mode of Origen, Jesus' flesh is important as the occasion to reveal the divine nature of the spiritual body, a reality that only the restoration of all things will manifest fully.

The difference between the *recapitulatio* of Irenaeus and the *apokatastasis* of Origen is more than a matter of nomenclature. It also reflects the dividing line between millennial and philosophical views of eschatological transformation, and distinctive assessments of the value of the flesh. Because history is also a matter of what happens to flesh and blood, for Irenaeus the speculations of theology may take on an almost historical form, while for Origen history only provides a possible occasion for philosophical reflection.

Yet for Irenaeus as for Origen, the appropriate interests of theology are only quasi-historical. Flesh is the medium of revelation in Irenaeus, while it is related to revelation in Origen. Those are two ways of recognizing the flesh of Jesus and one's own flesh as consequential, but not as sequential. Neither writer imagines history as being started and then methodically pushed along by God in order to lead up to the kingdom of heaven. During the twentieth century, some Christians of a liberal caste of mind adhered to a movement called "the social Gospel," and that movement did (and does among its current successors) invoke the pattern of a linear development of progress in divine revelation.[9]

But in classical Christianity there could be no such simplistic picture of the unfolding of history, because there was not even an agreement that history existed as a category of divine action. God had given flesh consequence: that followed immediately from any understanding of the Incarnation, whether along the lines of an Irenaeus or of an Origen. But the consequentiality of flesh had been donated by God himself in the case of Jesus. Flesh was not held to have an inherent value, such that one human event leading to another could produce revelation. In early Christianity sequence proved to be a much more elusive aspect of history than consequence.

The discovery of the significance of historical sequence within Christianity was perhaps the most radically influential result of the Constantinian settlement. In most of the areas of its life, the church had at least some slight preparation for the transformations that were involved after 312. In politics, Christians had no experience of leadership, but they had already thought through the relationship between secular power and eternal salvation. In their values, they had faced up to the question of the goods of this world, so that they could react to the blandishments of the empire with the thriving movements of asceticism that multiplied from the fourth century onward. Teleologically, whatever grandeur the empire might offer could only pale into insignificance in comparison with the glory that was to come. But history—specifically, history as a sequence of events—could scarcely be ignored or slighted when it seemed actually to validate the claims of the gospel. There was a before Constantine and an after Constantine in a way there has not been a before and after Marcus Aurelius, or even Augustus. Something happened that demanded a sequential explanation.

199

### EUSEBIUS OF CAESAREA (263–339)

That explanation, and the beginning of Christian history, came with Eusebius, bishop of Caesarea. Through Pamphilus, his teacher and model, Eusebius had been deeply influenced by the thought of Origen. So before there was a consciously Christian history, there was an irony of history: starting from the least historical perspective there was provided the first comprehensively historical account of the meaning of Christ. His prominence in the ecumenical church at various councils from Nicea onward, as well as his friendship with Constantine, go a long way toward explaining why Eusebius should have made the contribution that makes him the Herodotus of ecclesiastical history.

As he attempted to express the startling breakthrough under Constantine, Eusebius portrayed the new emperor as chosen by God himself. The most famous result of his meditation on the significance of the new order is his *History of the Church,* a vitally important document that takes up the Christian story from the time of Christ. The settlement under Constantine is his goal, however, and his portrayal of the emperor is perhaps most vividly conveyed in his *Praise of Constantine.* After speaking of Christ as the Word of God, which holds dominion over the whole world, Eusebius goes on to make a comparison with Constantine (*Praise of Constantine,* 1.6):

> Our Emperor, beloved of God, bearing a kind of image of the supreme rule as it were in imitation of the greater, directs the course of all things upon earth.

Here the old Stoic idea of the rule of the emperor as commensurate with the divine rule is provided with a new substance: the emperor who obeys Christ himself imitates Christ's glory. Eusebius was inclined to describe himself as moderately capable,[10] and that may be an accurate assessment of him as a theologian and historian. But as a political theorist, he is one of the most influential thinkers in the West. He provided the basis upon which the Roman Empire could be presented as the Holy Roman Empire, and the grounds for claiming the divine rights of rulers. At the same time, his reference to the conditional nature of those rights, as dependent upon the imitation of Christ, has provided a basis upon which political revolution may be encouraged on religious grounds.

Part of Eusebius's argument was that Constantine restored the united form of the empire, which had been the ideal of Augustus.[11] After a preface that sets out Christ's divine and human natures, Eusebius carefully places Christ's birth during Augustus's reign, after the subjugation of Egypt (*History of the Church,* 1.5). The pairing of Augustus and Christ, Christ and Constantine is therefore symmetrical, and defines the scope of the work. The result is to present a theologically structured political history.

The extent of that history is determined by its political horizon, much as in the case of Eusebius's predecessors in classical history. Whether we think of Herodotus in his explanation of the Persian Wars, or of Thucydides in the case of the Peloponnesian War, the impetus of writing history seems to be the experience of political change and dislocation. The scope of such work would be extended by such writers as Polybius (the apologist for Rome) and Josephus (the apologist for Judaism), but the desire to learn from the past in the effort to construct a more politically viable present is evident throughout.

Most readers of Eusebius feel uncomfortable at his apology for Constantine. Although the form is political history, the substance seems embarrassingly like flattery. How could Eusebius so thoroughly fail to be critical, whether as historian or as theologian? As a historian, he knew that kings and their flatterers were transient; as a theologian in the line of Origen, he knew that perfection eluded human flesh. The key to this riddle lies in Eusebius's conviction that Christ was at work in Constantine's revolution (*History of the Church*, 10.1):

> From that time on a day bright and radiant, with no cloud overshadowing it, shone down with shafts of heavenly light on the churches of Christ throughout the world, nor was there any reluctance to grant even those outside our community the enjoyment, if not of equal blessings, at least of an effluence from and a share in the things that God had bestowed on us.

The sharp change from persecution and all it involved was as disorienting for Eusebius as the Peloponnesian War had been to Thucydides, and an explanation was demanded. In that explanation, ecclesiastical history was born: that is, not simply the anecdotes of experience, but a rational account of God's activity within human events. The sequence of flesh met the consequence of flesh, and history was the offspring.

The intervention in the case of Constantine and his colleague Licinius (who at first reigned with Constantine) was nothing less than the appointed plan of God within a definite sequence of events.

Eusebius reminds the reader of the terrible tortures Christians had experienced, and then proceeds (*History of the Church,* 10.4):

> But once again the Angel of the great counsel, God's great Commander-in-Chief, after the thoroughgoing training of which the greatest soldiers in his kingdom gave proof by their patience and endurance in all trials, appeared suddenly and thereby swept all that was hostile and inimical into oblivion and nothingness, so that its very existence was forgotten. But all that was near and dear to Him He advanced beyond glory in the sight of all, not men only but the heavenly powers as well—sun, moon, and stars, and the entire heaven and earth.

Only the language of apocalypse, of the sequenced revelation of God himself in Christ, can explain to Eusebius's satisfaction how the former agony can so quickly have been transformed into festivity. In Constantine, the promised future had begun, and there was no room for a return to the past.

The picture that Eusebius draws of the contemporary scene might have been drawn from an apocalyptic work in Hellenistic dress (10.9, after the narrative of the removal of Licinius):

> Men had now lost all fear of their former oppressors; day after day they kept dazzling festival; light was everywhere, and men who once dared not look up greeted each other with smiling faces and shining eyes. They danced and sang in city and country alike, giving honor first to God our Sovereign Lord, as they had been instructed, and then to the pious emperor with his sons, so dear to God.

History for Eusebius was not just an account of the past, it was an apocalypse in reverse. His account was designed to set out the sequence of events that brought about the dawn of a new age. Long before Eusebius, Origen had written that Rome would prosper better by worshiping the true God than even the children of Israel had (*Against Celsus,* 8.69). For Origen, the argument was hypothetical; for Eusebius, it had become a reality. The new unity of the empire, under God, in Christ, and through the piety of the emperor himself, constituted for Eusebius a divine polity (*politeia* or *politeuma*), literally a breath away from paradise. It is as if the millenarianism of Justin and Irenaeus had been made the prelude to the spiritual transformation of Clement and Origen. *Recapitulatio* contributed the sequence, and *apokatastasis* represented the aim, of Eusebius's theology of history.

### AUGUSTINE OF HIPPO (354–430)

If Christian history was born under the pressure of success, its baptism of fire was the experience of an unimaginable failure. In 410 C.E., Alaric sacked the city of Rome itself. That event was a stunning blow to the empire generally, but it was a double blow to Latin Christianity. First, the pillage occurred while the empire was Christian; two centuries before, Tertullian had argued that idolatry brought about disaster (see *Apologeticus,* 41.1), and now Christianity could be said to do so. Second, Latin Christianity— especially in North Africa—had been particularly attracted to a millenarian eschatology. How could one explain that the triumphant end of history, announced by Eusebius and his followers, seemed to be reversed by the Goths? The explanation of that dilemma occupied Augustine in his *City of God,* a tremendous work of twenty-three books, written between 413 and 426. From the outset, he sounds his theme, that the city of God is an eternal city that exists in the midst of the cities of men; those two cities are both mixed and at odds in this world, but they are to be separated by the final judgment (*City of God,* 1.1). That essentially simple thesis is sustained through an account of Roman religion and Hellenistic philosophy, including Augustine's critical appreciation of Plato (books 1–10).[12]

In the central section of his work, Augustine sets out his case within a discussion of truly global history, from the story of the creation in Genesis. On the basis of the fall of the angels, which Augustine associates with the separation of light from darkness in Genesis 1:4, he speaks of the striving between good and evil. But the distinction between those two is involved with the *will* of certain angels, not with any intrinsic wickedness (*City of God,* 11.33). People, too, are disordered in their desire, rather than in their creation by God (*City of God,* 12.8).

The difference between the will God intends for God's creatures and the will they actually evince attests the freedom involved in divine creation. But the effect of perverted will, whether angelic or human, is to establish two antithetical regimes (*City of God*, 14.28):

> So two loves have constituted two cities—the earthly is formed by love of self even to contempt of God, the heavenly by love of God even to contempt of self. For the one glories in herself, the other in the Lord. The one seeks glory from man; for the other God, the witness of the conscience, is the greatest glory. . . . In the one the lust for power prevails, both in her own rulers and in the nations she subdues; in the other all serve each other in charity, governors by taking thought for all and subjects by obeying.

By Book 18, Augustine arrives at his own time, and repeats that the two cities "alike enjoy temporal goods or suffer temporal ills, but differ in faith, in hope, in love, until they be separated by the final judgment and each receive its end, of which there is no end" (*City of God*, 18.54).

That commits Augustine to speak of eschatological issues, which he does until the end of the work as a whole. It is in his discussion of eschatology that Augustine frames classic and orthodox responses to some of the most persistent questions of the Christian theology of his time. He adheres to the expectation of the resurrection of the flesh, not simply of the body (as had been the manner of Origen). In so doing, he refutes the Manichaean philosophy that he accepted prior to his conversion to Christianity. In Manichaeanism, named after a Persian teacher of the third century named Mani, light and darkness are two eternal substances that struggle against each other, and they war over the creation they have both participated in making.[13] As in the case of Gnosticism, on which it was dependent, Manichaeanism counseled a denial of the flesh. By his insistence on the resurrection of the flesh, Augustine revives the strong assertion of the extent of God's embrace of God's own creation in the tradition of Irenaeus.

At the same time, Augustine sets a limit on the extent to which one might have recourse to Plato. Augustine had insisted with

Plato against the Manichaeans that God was not a material substance, but transcendent. Similarly, evil became in his mind the denial of what proceeds from God (see *Confessions,* 5.10.20). When it came to the creation of people, however, Augustine insisted against Platonic thought that no hard and fast division between soul and flesh could be made (so *City of God,* 22.12). Enfleshed humanity was the only genuine humanity, and God in Christ was engaged to raise those who were of the city of God. Moreover, Augustine specifically refuted the contention of Porphyry (and Origen) that cycles of creation—involving a series of lives—could be included within the entire scheme of salvation. For Augustine, the direct power of the resurrection within the world was already confirmed by the miracles wrought by Christ and his martyrs: God did not have to create the world again in order to effect God's ultimate purpose. He gives the example of the healings connected with the relics of St. Stephen, recently transferred to Hippo (*City of God,* 22.8).

Even now, in the power and influence of the Catholic Church, God is represented on earth, and the present, Christian epoch (*Christiana tempora*) corresponds to the millennium promised in Revelation 20 (*City of God,* 20.9).[14] This age of dawning power, released in flesh by Jesus and conveyed by the church, simply awaits the full transition into the city of God, complete with flesh itself. It is interesting that, where Origen could cite a saying of Jesus to confirm his view of the resurrection (as discussed in the last chapter, see Matt. 22:30; Mark 12:25; Luke 20:36), Augustine has to qualify the same saying (*City of God,* 22.18): "They will be equal to angels in immortality and happiness, not in flesh, nor indeed in resurrection, which the angels had no need of, since they could not die. So the Lord said that there would be no marriage in the resurrection, not that there would be no women."

In all of this, Augustine is straining, although he is usually a straightforward interpreter of Scripture. But he is wedded to what the Latin confession of "the resurrection of the flesh" implies, and therefore cannot follow Origen's exegesis. There is a double irony here. First, Origen the sophisticated allegorist seems much simpler to follow than Augustine, the incomparable preacher. Second, Augustine's discussion of such issues as the fate of fetuses in the resurrection sounds remarkable like the Sadducees' hypothesis, which Jesus argues against in the relevant passage from the synoptic Gospels. The direct correlation of flesh with resurrection, which Jesus disputed, seems axiomatic to Augustine.

Augustine is well aware, as was Origen before him, that Paul speaks of a "spiritual body," and acknowledges that "I suspect that all utterance published concerning it is rash." And yet he can be quite categorical that flesh must be involved somehow: "The spiritual flesh will be subject to spirit, but it will still be flesh, not spirit; just as the carnal spirit was subject to the flesh, but was still spirit, not flesh" (*City of God,* 22.21). Such is Augustine's conviction that flesh has become the medium of salvation now and hereafter. As in the case of Irenaeus, the denial of a thoroughly abstract teaching leads to the assertion of greater literalism than may have been warranted.

In his adherence to a kind a millenarianism and to the resurrection of the flesh in the Latin creed, Augustine is very much a product of North Africa and of Italy, where he was active (chiefly as a teacher of rhetoric) prior to his conversion and his return to North Africa. But his *City of God* creatively offers the great frame, primordial and eschatological, within which history becomes a theological discipline. Here, he argues, is more than a lesson in how to avoid war and create order. And here there is certainly more than the superficial enthusiasm that comes of histories written by the winners. Rather, history for Augustine—and from Augustine—is the interplay of those two forces that determine the existence of every society, every person.

Augustine died in Hippo while the city was actually under siege by the Vandals. His passing, and the passing of his church and his city, was a curious witness to his *Christiana tempora.* But his conception that his history and every history reflected the struggle between the two cities prepared him and the global church for those disappointments, and for much worse. He had turned back to the Eusebian model of history as apocalypse, and he took it even more seriously than Eusebius himself had. No apocalyptic seer ever promised an easy transition to the consuming reign of Christ, and on to that moment when God would be all in all (so 1 Cor. 15:28, which Augustine quotes). Smooth, unhampered progress is a model of history that recommends itself only to those in the line of Eusebius and liberal historians since the nineteenth century. If history is apocalyptic, because the times of the church are millennial, then our flesh has indeed been blessed, but our history is equally dedicated to struggle.

The struggle, however, is not ultimately between good and evil, but between the love of God and the love of self. That is the key to Augustine's ceaseless, pastoral ministry, as well as to his remarkably broad intellectual horizon. In every time and in every place, there is the possibility that the city of God will be revealed and embraced; now, in the *Christiana tempora*, we at last know its name, and can see the face of that love that would transform us all. The city of God is a present as well as eternal reality; the rule of the saints has already begun.

History after Augustine could be painted on canvasses of indeterminate size, because he established the quest to integrate the historical task with philosophical reflection. At the same time, in his *Confessions* (completed in 400), he established the genre of autobiography as an investigation of the dynamics of universal salvation within the life of the individual he knew best, himself. Written large in nations and written small in persons, history attested the outward-working and inward-working power of God, if only one's eyes could see with the love of God, and be freed of the blindness of self-love.

✿
✞

Eusebius and Augustine together provided the classical program for Christianity's survival of the decay of the Roman Empire. A political theory of divine right and a historical perspective of the two cities would provide the matrix for the remains of the empire in the east and the petty kingdoms in the west to construct successive, variant, sometimes conflicting models of Christ's dominion on earth. Without reference to those two ideologies, an understanding of the Middle Ages is simply impossible.

The contribution of Eusebius is frequently overlooked because the "Constantinian triumphalism" of which he was the chronicler has long been out of fashion, whether within the church or without. But a commitment to a monarch who is Christ's regent in fact survived both the Reformation and the Renaissance; only the age of the Enlightenment saw it superseded. Even that supersession involved a cognate commitment: to the idea that nationally constituted people could and should assert their inherent rights, as "endowed by their Creator," in the words of the Declaration of Independence.

Two factors especially have tended to obscure the religious grounds of political thought. First, the Enlightenment represented an appeal to universal reason apart from any engagement of faith. In the light of events since the eighteenth century, that appeal—with its naive corollary that people act out of enlightened self-interest—has lost plausibility. The second factor is related to the first. The Soviet Union represented what was perceived as a threat to the "West" in essentially secular terms. That Cold War (which indeed involved the resources of a major war) resulted in the elevation of the ideologies of "capitalism" and "communism" to the realm of religious commitment. Now that the Soviet Union is a thing of the past, it is obvious that the West's "capitalism" was no purer than the East's "communism," and that neither constitutes a comprehensive account of a way of life, of social order, and of the significance of the world in the manner of religion. Discussion of government along explicitly religious lines—particularly among Christians in the United States—may be expected to increase for the foreseeable future.

Augustine's influence is more widely recognized than Eusebius's, and it is unquestionably deeper. Global history and personal history have perennially been seen as revelatory; echoes of the *City of God* and the *Confessions* are heard in books, seen in movies, resonant in political arguments and personal disclosures. It may not be too much to say that with Augustine the human being in historical experience was invented. And he nuanced what he meant by history; its time was for him not so many atomistic segments. Time for Augustine was rather our remembrance of the past, our expectation for the future, our attention in the present (see *Confessions,* 11). History, in today's jargon, was "constructed" in his understanding.

Considerable attention has been given this century to the eclipse of the view of history as objective events, the story of what "really happened." Facts, to be sure, remain at the end of this debate: there are data which can be verified, and there are mistakes that cannot be verified. But the arrangement of verifiable data into a sequenced account, and the determination of the scope of the inquiry, those cannot be decided by anything approaching an objective standard.[15] Augustine provides self-conscious answers to the questions of the sequence (including the scope), and the consequence of history. And he shows how confronting the past belongs to the human task, personal and collective, of living in the present and fashioning a future.

# 5

# Two Successful Religions: The Reason Why

## The Successful Transaction

The criteria for the success of a religious system for the social order may be set forth in these questions:

1. Does that religious system for the social order long govern the society that to begin with it identified and addressed, or do books form the principal monuments to the theory? Neither Rabbinic Judaism nor orthodox and catholic Christianity reaches us only through the medium of books; books do not constitute religious systems, only expositions of ideas.

2. Does that religious system define the character of its enemies—e.g., that which is embodied in heresy—or does the social group addressed by that theoretical system produce heresies out of phase with that system? Both Rabbinic Judaism and orthodox Christianity would over time define the character of their enemies.

3. Does that religious system exhibit the power to make its own modes of thought that are not represented in its initial doc-

uments, and does it contain media of religious experience not encompassed by them? Both religious systems met the challenge of renewal, not once but many times through time.

4. Does that religious system possess the inner resources to produce, in line with its single mythic system and symbolic structure and in communication with its canonical writings, continuators and secondary developments over time? Or does the original statement appear to have delivered the entire message? Is its canon closed or open? Both Rabbinic Judaism and the catholic, orthodox Christianity of ancient times precipitated an exegetical process that explored possibilities beyond all imagining at the outset.

Neither religion ever stagnated; both solved the problems that confronted them. Each showed the capacity so to shape imagination as to force the everyday to conform to the shape of intangible faith. Each accommodated to changing times on its own terms, and neither merely reacted to them. A successful religion is one that shows the capacity to realize its theory of the social order over a long time among those to whom that theory is set forth. A Judaism that endures through time and through change, imposing on history its interpretation of what things ought to mean (a worldview), maintaining among its faithful the patterns of a holy way of life it prescribes (a way of life), and able to define "Israel" for believers (and outsiders) alike, may be declared successful. Above all, a Judaic religious system that shows the power to deal with changing circumstances and maintain a cogent and coherent statement for itself—linking past, present, and future within a claim of timeless and enduring truth—such is a highly successful Judaism.

The reason we deem Rabbinic Judaism and mainstream Christianity—orthodox, catholic Christianity, such as produced the Bible and defined Christianity in the West—highly successful religious systems emerges in the story, here told, of how each one found the way to accommodate change and adapt to circumstance without for one moment conceding that anything was altered.

Rabbinic Judaism alone emerges from ancient times; no other Judaism competed. The Judaic systems that took shape to contend with that Judaism defined themselves by reference to that Judaism, declaring disbelief in its beliefs, or belief in what it denied. Karaism spoke up for the written Torah without the oral one; Sabbateanism maintained that the Messiah would not only not be a sage but would violate the laws that sages exemplified and enforced. That same Rabbinic Judaism also showed the capacity to take over and draw strength from sources of religious vitality not originally its own—Qabbalistic doctrine and practice, for one, and the renewal of Greco-Roman philosophy, for another. Later history would show, therefore, that that Judaism possessed, within its mythic and symbolic structure and its generative convictions and conduct of life, resources for renewal and, above all, for resilience.

What trait marked Rabbinic Judaism for success in the formative age? The power of Rabbinic Judaism lay in its capacity to confront not the destruction of the Temple so much as the long-term despair accompanying failure to reconstruct it. That same Judaism forms the only Judaic system reaching us from antiquity that met the challenge of triumphant Christianity, and indeed turned that challenge to its own advantage. This it did by turning to its own advantage each component of the Christian case to constitute Israel—the Messiah has come, to us; we are the true Israel, the one after the spirit; the Bible, Old and New Testaments, is the complete word of God, which we understand but you counterfeit. Pretending Christianity had not appeared, and rarely according explicit recognition to Christian presence (not to say, appeal to Israel), Rabbinic Judaism reaffirmed precisely the points of contention. The Messiah will be a sage; yours was no sage. Israel comprises a genealogy, after the flesh, of the family of Abraham and Sarah, Isaac and Rebecca, Jacob and Leah and Rachel—but a genealogy anyone may adopt for himself or herself. And the Torah comes to us not only in the written form, accessible to you, but in the oral form that we alone possess from Sinai.

The challenges to Christianity and Judaism that account for their trading places left each religious tradition remarkably capable of accommodating change and adapting to circumstance. We

offer as a hypothesis for explaining the success of each religion—
on its own terms and in competition with the other—this initial experience of dealing with extraordinary changes in circumstance.

## JUDAISM BEYOND DESPAIR

Clearly, Rabbinic Judaism transformed itself over the three hundred
years from the advent of Christianity to its world-historical triumph in Rome. This documentary history, identifying the Yerushalmi and associated Midrash-compilations as the first written
statement of the emblematic traits of the Rabbinic-Judaic structure and system, points to fifth-century writings and therefore
fourth-century events as the occasion for systemic transformation.
Not only so, but the persistence of the system that came to expression in the fifth-century documents of Christendom and later
on in Islam, the systemic stability and cogency from that time to our
own day—as well as the difficulties the same system has met in
sustaining itself in worlds other than the classically Christian and
Muslim—point to a further fact. Where Christianity and Islam
flourished, there so did Rabbinic Judaism, and when and where
those great religious structures trembled, so did the system and
structure of Rabbinic Judaism.

The point of origin is easy to identify: the Land of Israel in the
fourth century. What happened at that time, in the empire that
controlled—and when Christian, greatly prized—that country, is
self-evident. Rabbinic Judaism took shape in response to the success of Christianity and dealt, for the Israel after the flesh to which
it addressed its statement, with the issues raised by the triumph of
Christianity. The birth of the Judaism under discussion here took
place in the year 312, the year of Constantine's vision at the Milvian Bridge of a cross and the words, "By this sign you will con-
quer." And from its formation in the century beyond that defining
moment to our own day, Rabbinic Judaism enjoyed truly astonishing success in that very society for which its framers proposed
to design a religious system of the social order: Israel.

The answers to all four questions set forth at the outset (and many like them that can be formulated) point in one direction and to one conclusion: Rabbinic Judaism takes its place among the most successful religious systems of the social order ever put forth by humanity. From the time the summa of Rabbinic Judaism, the Talmud of Babylonia or Bavli, reached closure to our own day, that document formed the court of final appeal among nearly all Jews who practiced (a) Judaism. It was subjected to systematic commentary; its laws were applied; decisions based on those laws were codified. As we noted, the heresies produced by Jews took as their principal issues the definitive convictions of this Judaism—e.g., Karaism, with its rejection of the oral part of the Torah, and Sabbateanism, with its rejection of the doctrine of the Messiah as a sage—and no recorded heresies stood entirely beyond the framework of this Judaism. Rabbinic Judaism made its own both the philosophical and the mystical approaches to thought and religious experience, deriving greater strength from the modes of inquiry of the former and the modes of knowing God of the latter. And, of greatest interest, Rabbinic Judaism maintained an open canon, classifying as "Torah" teachings, writings, and public statements of even the most current generation of sages (though diverse groups within Rabbinic Judaism certainly fight out their differences on which particular sages teach authentic Torah).

**215**

When we realize the human situation of the faithful of this Judaism's "Israel," we identify a further criterion of success: its power to confront the human situation of weakness, defeat, and failure. This was not a Judaism for a triumphant nation, but for a defeated people; not one for a nation secure in its own territory but for a dispossessed people; not one for a society uniform and coherent in its indicative traits, but for a vast number of societies, each with its own customs and traditions, language and economic system and setting. This Judaic system, indeed, commanded no politics of its own to support its position with power, had no economy of its own to sustain its communicants with comfort, called upon no single and agreed-upon cultural construction to validate its convictions by making belief into the premise of workaday relationships and routine transactions, whether of thought or feeling, whether of attitude or consequent action. What gave to Rabbinic Judaism its power to speak to people over long spans of time and great distances of space, over a broad range of languages and cultures, lay in the humanity of its message. It relinquished to others a hearing among the empowered possessors of the land, in favor of addressing the weak and the homeless. True, the message proved complex and particular; but the answers it conveyed responded to universal and commonplace questions.

The mark of this Judaism's success lies in a simple fact, right on the surface. At any point before our own century, any Jew who wished could opt out of the politics of holy Israel and join Christendom or Islam. But over time, enough decided to stick it out that holy Israel endured, and its Judaism retained its devoted faithful. In this context—evaluating, explaining success—we need not rehearse the painful history of subordination, contumacy, and humiliation, which tells the tale of the world in which this "Israel" gave itself over to the life that the Torah sets forth as the godly way. So far as a successful religious theory of the social order persuades individuals to stick it out and stay the course, before us is the documentary account of the founding of a religious system with scarcely a peer. For under ordinary conditions, it was easier to remain a Christian, whether Latin or Greek, or a Muslim, than to become something else; and the opportunities for change, e.g., conversion, were few and distant. But not a day went by, from the formation of this Judaism to our own time in which, for individual Jews, the easier way did not lead outward, and the distance covered by the step was only down the street, to a nearby church or mosque.

Nor was the movement to an alien world, it was actually toward a different, but quite congruent, social order, whether the Muslim or the Christian. Both of them defined orders of being that spoke of the same God and appealed to the same Scriptures, in the case of Christianity, or at least to the same God in the line of Abraham and Moses (not to mention Christ) in the case of Islam, and neither of them was unintelligible to Israel or uncomprehending of Israel. Not only so, but there were more than a few days on which the choice was not one or another way to God, but life of exile or even death, and when faced with the choice of death or apostasy, entire communities of Israel chose to leave their homes and all they had or even to die. Here, before us, is a truly successful religious system, one that exacted that last full measure of devotion that, in the name of God, a theory of the social order can demand.

## WHY JUDAISM SUCCEEDED

Sages' Judaism for a defeated people prepared the social order conceived to form a holy nation for a long future. Addressing the situation of that social order, that of a vanquished people, a brokenhearted nation that had lost its city and its Temple, that had, moreover, produced another nation from its midst to take over its Scripture and much else, this Judaism recast that reality. It turned defeat into the occasion for renewal, disappointment and despair into the media for social and personal regeneration. This was accomplished through the utilization of an appropriate message in the formation of a suitable doctrine. Specifically, a very particular way of seeing things was made to yield a doctrine of emotions or virtues that showed things were not what they seemed. Here is how Judaism succeeded: it imparted its vision of reality upon reality, not compromising but persisting, so that the dream became the norm, and the fantasy, normal. That is what, in the social order, religion accomplishes—when it works.

✡

**217**

✝

That defeated people, in its intellectuals, as represented in the Rabbinic sources, found refuge in a mode of thought that trained vision to see things otherwise than as the eyes perceived them. Among the diverse ways by which the weak and subordinated accommodate to their circumstance, the one of iron-willed pretense in life is most likely to yield the mode of thought at hand: things never are, because they cannot be, what they seem. The upshot was that Rabbinic Judaism's Israel was instructed on how to tame its heart and govern its wild emotions, to accept with resignation, to endure with patience, above all, to value the attitudes and emotions that made acceptance and endurance plausible.

The sages of Rabbinic Judaism taught not only what Israel was supposed to do or not do, but also what Israel is supposed to feel.

And that was how they accomplished their most difficult task, the transformation of the Jews to conform to the picture of "Israel" that the sages set forth and proposed to bring into being. From beginning to end, the documents of Rabbinic Judaism set forth a single, consistent, and coherent doctrine: the true Israelite was to exhibit the moral virtues of subservience, patience, endurance, and hope. These would translate into the emotional traits of humility and forbearance. And they would yield to social virtues of passivity and conciliation. The hero was one who overcame impulses, and the truly virtuous person, the one who reconciled others by giving way before the opinions of others.

All of these acts of self-abnegation and self-denial, accommodation rather than rebellion, required to begin with the right attitudes, sentiments, emotions, and impulses, and the single most dominant motif of the Rabbinic writings, start to finish, is its stress on the right attitude's leading to the right action, the correct intentionality's producing the besought decision, above all, accommodating in one's heart to what could not be changed by one's action. And that meant, the world as it was. Sages prepared Israel for the long centuries of subordination and alienation by inculcating attitudes that best suited people who could govern little more than how they felt about things.

The notion that sages teach feelings is hardly puzzling. Since Israelites are commanded to love God, it follows that an emotion, love, becomes holy. It is when the affection of love is directed to God. The same emotion, love, may become not only profane but sinful when it is directed to the wrong objects—self or power, for example. Accordingly, "our sages" in the definitive holy books of Judaism make plain their conviction that feelings too come to the surface as matters of judgment. Emotions constitute constructions for which, they hold, we bear responsibility.

The repertoire of approved and disapproved feelings remains constant through the half-millennium of the unfolding of the canon of Judaism from the Mishnah through the Talmud of Babylonia. The emotions that are encouraged—such as humility, forbearance, accommodation, a spirit of conciliation—exactly correspond to the political and social requirements of the Jews' condition in that time. The reason that the same repertoire of emotions persisted with no material change through the unfolding of the writings of the sages of that formative age was the constancy of the Jews' political and social condition. In the view of the sages at hand, emotions fit together with the encompassing patterns of society and culture, theology and the religious life.

So the affective rules form an integral part of the way of life and worldview put forward to make sense of the existence of a social group. For sages it follows that how I am supposed to feel in ethos matches what I am expected to think. In this way, as an individual, I link my deepest personal emotions to the cosmic fate and transcendent faith of that social group of which I form a part. Emotions lay down judgments. They derive from rational cognition. The individual Israelite's innermost feelings, the microcosm, correspond to the public and historic condition of Israel, the macrocosm.

What Rabbinic Judaism teaches the private person to feel links her or his heart to what that same Judaism states about the condition of Israel in history and of God in the cosmos. All form one reality, in the supernatural world and in nature, in time and in eternity wholly consubstantial (so to speak). In the innermost chambers of deepest feelings, the Israelite therefore lives out the public history and destiny of the people, Israel. The genius of Rabbinic Judaism, the reason for its resilience and endurance, lies in its power to teach Jews to feel in private what they also must think in public about the condition of both self and nation. The world within, the world without, are so bonded that one is never alone. The individual's life is always lived with the people.

The notion of the centrality of human feelings in the religious life of Israel presents no surprises. Scripture is explicit on both sides of the matter. The human being is commanded to love God. In the biblical biography of God, the tragic hero, God, will despair, love, hope, feel disappointment or exultation. The biblical record of God's feelings and God's will concerning the feelings of humanity—wanting human love, for example—leaves no room for doubt. Nor does the Judaism that emerges from late antiquity ignore or propose to obliterate the datum that "the merciful God wants the heart." The Judaism of the rabbis of late antiquity makes explicit that God always wants the heart. God commands that humanity love God with full heart, soul, mind and might. That is the principal duty of humanity.

So without the Rabbinic canon and merely on the basis of knowledge that that canon begins in the written Torah of Scripture, the facts about the critical place of religious affections in Israel's religion would still prove clear and one-sided. Just as the sages framed matters of the Written Torah in a fresh and original way, all the time stating in their own language and categories the teachings of the written Torah, so here too, we ask where, when, how, and for what purpose, did Rabbinical authorships draw upon the legacy of the written Torah, in concluding, as they did, that "the Merciful God wants the heart."

## THE TORAH OF SOUND EMOTIONS

An epitome of the sages' treatment of emotions yields a simple result. From the first to the final document, a single doctrine and program dictated what people had to say on how Israel should tame its heart. So far as the unfolding components of the canon of Judaism portray matters, emotions therefore form part of an iron tradition. That is, a repertoire of rules and relationships handed on from the past, always intact and ever unimpaired, governed the issue. The labor of the generations meant to receive the repertoire and recipe for feeling proved one of only preserving and maintaining that tradition. As successive documents came to closure, we see each one adding its improvements, while leaving the structure basically the same. Like a cathedral that takes a thousand years to build but, throughout the construction and not only at the end, always looks uniform and antique, so the view of the affective life over centuries remained not only cogent but essentially uniform.

The sources, read sequentially, do not. So while the formative centuries of the history of Judaism overall mark a period of remarkable growth and change, with history consisting of sequences of developments in various substantial ideas and generative conceptions, here, in the matter of emotions, it does not. The single fact emerging from a canonical survey is that the sages' doctrine of affections remained a constant in an age of change.

While the Mishnah casually refers to emotions—e.g., tears of joy, tears of sorrow—where feelings matter, it always is in a public and communal context. For one important example, where there is an occasion of rejoicing, one form of joy is not to be confused with some other, or one context of sorrow with another. Accordingly, marriages are not to be held on festivals (M. M.Q. 1:7). Likewise mourning is not to take place then (M. M.Q. 1:5, 3:7–9). Where emotions play a role, it is because of the affairs of the community at large, e.g., rejoicing on a festival, mourning on a fast day (M. Suk. 5:1–4). Emotions are to be kept in hand, as in the case of the relatives of the executed felon (M. San. 6:6). If one had to specify the single underlying principle affecting all forms of emotion, for the Mishnah it is that feelings must be kept under control, never fully expressed without reasoning about the appropriate context. Emotions must always lay down judgments.

We see in most of those cases in which emotions play a systemic, not merely a tangential, role, that the basic principle is the same. We can and must so frame our feelings as to accord with the appropriate rule. In only one case does emotion play a decisive role in settling an issue, and that has to do with whether or not a farmer was happy that water came upon his produce or grain. That case underlines the conclusion just now drawn. If people feel a given sentiment, it is a matter of judgment, therefore invokes the Law's penalties. So in this system emotions are not treated as spontaneous, but as significant aspects of a person's judgment. It would be difficult to find a more striking example of that view than at M. Makh. 4:5 and related passages. The very fact that the Law applies comes about because the framers judge the farmer's feelings to constitute, on their own and without associated actions or even conceptions, final and decisive judgments on what has happened.

The reason that emotions form so critical a focus of concern in Rabbinic Judaism is that God and the human being share traits of attitude and emotion. They want the same thing and respond in the same way to the same events. They share not only ownership of the land but also a viewpoint on the value of its produce. For example, in the law of tithing, the produce becomes liable to tithing—that is, giving to God's surrogate God's share of the crop of the Holy Land—when the farmer deems the crop to be desirable. Why is that so? When the farmer wants the crop, so too does God. When the householder takes the view that the crop is worthwhile, God responds to the attitude of the farmer by forming the same opinion. The theological anthropology that brings God and the householder into the same continuum prepares the way for understanding what makes the entire Mishnaic system work.

It is the matter of the intention and will of the human being as we move from theological to philosophical thought in the Mishnah's system. "Intention" stands for attitude, and, as we have already noted, there is no distinguishing attitude from emotion. For the discussion on intention works out several theories concerning not God and God's relationship to humanity but the nature of the human will. The human being is defined not only as sentient but also as a volitional being, who can will with effect, unlike beasts and, as a matter of fact, angels (who do not, in fact, figure in the Mishnah at all). On the one side, there is no consideration of will or attitude of animals, for these are null. On the other side, will and attitude of angels, where these are represented in later documents, are totally subservient to God's wishes. Only the human being, in the person of the farmer, possesses and also exercises the power of intentionality. And it is the power that intentionality possesses that forms the central consideration. Because a human being forms an intention, consequences follow, whether or not it is given material expression in gesture or even in speech. The Mishnah and the law flowing from it impute extraordinary power to the will and intentionality of the human being.

How does this bear practical consequences? The attitude of the farmer toward the crop, like that of the Temple priest toward the offering that he carries out, affects the status of the crop. It classifies an otherwise unclassified substance. It changes the standing of an already-classified beast. It shifts the status of a pile of grain, without any physical action whatsoever, from one category to another. Not only so, but as we shall now see, the attitude or will of a farmer can override the effects of the natural world, e.g., keeping in the status of what is dry and so insusceptible to cultic uncleanness a pile of grain that in fact has been rained upon and wet down. An immaterial reality, shaped and re-formed by the householder's attitude and plan, overrides the material effect of a rainstorm.

## HUMILITY AND ACCOMMODATION IN THE TWO TALMUDS

What is most interesting in the Yerushalmi is the recognition that there are rules descriptive of feelings, as much as of other facts of life. These rules tell us how to dispose of cases in which feelings make a difference. The fact is, therefore, that the effects of emotions, as much as of opinions or deeds, come within the rule of law. It must follow, in the view of sages, the affective life once more proves an aspect of society. People are assumed to frame emotions, as much as opinions, in line with common and shared judgments. In no way do emotions form a special classification, one expressive of what is private, spontaneous, individual, and beyond the law and reason.

223

The Bavli carried forward with little change the now traditional program of emotions, listing the same ones cataloged earlier and no new ones. The authors said about those feelings what had been said earlier. A leader must be someone acceptable to the community. God then accepts him too. People should be ready to give up quarrels and forgive. The correspondence of social and personal virtues reaches explicit statement. How so? The community must forbear, the individual must forgive. Communal tolerance for causeless hatred destroyed the Temple; individual vendettas yield miscarriages. The two coincide. In both cases people nurture feelings that express arrogance. Arrogance is what permits the individual to express emotions without discipline, and arrogance is what leads the community to undertake what it cannot accomplish.

A fresh emphasis portrayed in the Bavli favored mourning and disapproved of rejoicing. We can hardly maintain that that view came to expression only in the latest stages in the formation of the canon. The contrary is the case. The point remains consistent throughout. Excessive levity marks arrogance, deep mourning characterizes humility. So many things come down to one thing. The nurture of an attitude of mourning should mark both the individual and the community, both in mourning for the Temple, and also in mourning for the condition of nature, including the human condition, signified in the Temple's destruction.

A mark of humility is humble acceptance of suffering. This carried forward the commonplace view that suffering now produces joy later on. The ruin of the Temple for example served as a guarantee that just as the prophetic warnings came to realization, so too would prophetic promises of restoration and redemption. In the realm of feelings, the union of opposites came about through the same mode of thought. Hence God's love comes to fulfillment in human suffering, and the person who joyfully accepts humiliation or suffering will enjoy the appropriate divine response of love. Another point at which the authors of the Bavli introduce a statement developing a familiar view derives from the interpretation of how to love one's neighbor; it is by imposing upon one's neighbor the norms of the community, rebuking the other for violating accepted practice. In this way the emotion of love takes on concrete social value in the norms of the community. Since the verse invites exactly that interpretation, we can hardly regard as innovative the Bavli's paragraph on the subject. Stories about sages rang the changes on the themes of humility, resignation, restraint, and perpetual goodwill. A boastful sage loses his wisdom; a humble one retains it. Since it is wisdom about which a sage boasts, the matching of opposites conforms to the familiar mode of thought. The strikingly fresh medium for traditional doctrines in the Bavli takes the form of prayers composed by sages. Here the values of the system came to eloquent expression. Sages prayed that their souls may be as dust for everyone to tread upon. They asked for humility in spirit, congenial colleagues, goodwill, good impulses. They asked God to take cognizance of their humiliation, to spare them from disgrace. The familiar affective virtues and sins, self-abnegation as against arrogance, made their appearance in liturgical form as well. Another noteworthy type of material, also not new, in which the pages of the Bavli prove rich, portrayed the deaths of sages. One dominant motif is uncertainty in face of death, a sign of humility and self-abnegation.

The basic motif—theological as much as affective— encompassing all materials is simple. Israel is estranged from God, therefore should exhibit the traits of humility and uncertainty, acceptance and conciliation. When God recognizes in Israel's heart, as much as in the nation's deeds and deliberation, the proper feelings, God will respond by ending that estrangement that marks the present age. So the single word encompassing the entire affective doctrine of the canon of Judaism is "alienation." No contemporary, surviving the Holocaust, can miss the psychological depth of the system that joins the human condition to the fate of the nation and the world, and links the whole to the broken heart of God.

We therefore find ourselves where we started, in those sayings that state that if one wants something, he or she should aspire to its opposite. Things are never what they seem. To be rich, accept what you have. To be powerful, conciliate your enemy. To be endowed with public recognition in which to take pride, express humility. So too the doctrine of the emotional life expressed in law, scriptural interpretation, and tales of sages alike turns out to be uniform and simple. Emotions well up uncontrolled and spontaneous. Anger, vengeance, pride, arrogance—these people feel by nature. So feelings as much as affirmations and actions must become what by nature they are not. If one wants riches, seek the opposite; if one wants honor, pursue the opposite. But how do people seek the opposite of wealth? It is by accepting what they have. And how pursue humility, if not by doing nothing to aggrandize oneself?

So the life of the emotions, in conformity to the life of reflection and of concrete deed, will consist in the transformation of what things *seem* into what they *ought* to be. No contemporary psychologists or philosophers can fail to miss the point. Here we have an example of the view—whether validated by the facts of nature or not—that emotions constitute constructs, and feelings lay down judgments. So the heart belongs, together with the mind, to the human being's power to form reasoned viewpoints. Coming from sages, intellectuals to their core, such an opinion surely coheres with the context and circumstance of those who hold it.

## SEEING THINGS AS OTHER THAN WHAT THEY SEEM

This theory of the emotional life, persistent through the unfolding of the canonical documents of Judaism, fits into a larger way of viewing the world. We may call this mode of thought an *as-if* way of seeing things. That is to say, it is *as if* a common object or symbol really represented an uncommon one. Nothing says what it means. Everything important speaks symbolically. All statements carry deeper meaning, which inheres in other statements altogether. So too each emotion bears a negative and a positive charge, as each matches and balances the other: humility, arrogance, love, hate. If a negative emotion is natural to the heart, then the individual has the power to sanctify that negative, sinful feeling and turn it into a positive, holy emotion. Ambition then must be tamed, and so transformed into humility; hatred and vengeance must change into love and acceptance.

What we see in the surveyed doctrine of emotions is an application of a large-scale, encompassing exercise in analogical thinking—something is like something else, stands for, evokes, or symbolizes that which is quite outside itself. It may be the opposite of something else, in which case it conforms to the exact opposite of the rules that govern that something else. The reasoning is analogical or it is contrastive, and the fundamental logic is taxonomic. The taxonomy rests on those comparisons and contrasts we should call parabolic. In that case what lies on the surface misleads. What lies beneath or beyond the surface—there is the true reality. How shall we characterize people who see things this way? They constitute the opposite of ones who call a thing as it is. Self-evidently, they have become accustomed to perceiving more or less than is at hand. Perhaps that is a natural mode of thought for the Jews of this period (and not then alone), so long used to calling themselves God's first love, yet now seeing others with greater worldly reason claiming that same advantaged relationship. Not in mind only, but still more, in the politics of the world, the people that remembered its origins along with the very creation of the world and founding of humanity, that recalled how it alone served, and serves, the one and only God, for hundreds of years had confronted a quite difference existence.

The radical disjuncture between the way things were and the way Scripture said things were supposed to be surely imposed on Jews an unbearable tension. It was one thing for the slave born to slavery to endure. It was another for the free man sold into slavery to accept that same condition. The vanquished people, the brokenhearted nation that had in 586 B.C.E. and again in 70 C.E. lost its city and its Temple, that had, moreover, in the fourth century produced another nation from its midst to take over its Scripture and much else, could not bear too much reality. That defeated people, in its intellectuals, as represented in the sources we have surveyed, then found refuge in a mode of thought that trained vision to see things otherwise than as the eyes perceived them.

Among the diverse ways by which the weak and subordinated accommodate to their circumstance, the one of iron-willed pretense in life is most likely to yield the mode of thought at hand: things never are, because they cannot be, what they seem. The uniform tradition regarding emotions persisted intact because the social realities of Israel's life proved permanent, until, in our own time, they changed. The affective program of the canon—early, middle, and late—fits tightly in every detail with this doctrine of an ontological teleology in eschatological disguise. Israel is to tame its heart so that it will feel that same humility within, that Israel's worldview and way of living demand in life at large. Submit, accept, conciliate, stay cool in emotion as much as in attitude, inside and outside—and the Messiah will come.

## Forbearance or Aggression: The How of Judaism's Success

The profound program of emotions, the sages' statement of how people should feel and why they should take charge of their emotions, remained quite constant. No one can imagine that Jews in their hearts felt the way sages said they should. The repertoire of permissible and forbidden feelings hardly can have defined the broad range of actual emotions, whether private or social, of the community of Israel. In fact, we have no evidence about how people really felt. We see only a picture of what sages thought they should, and should not, feel. Writings that reveal stunning shifts in doctrine, teleology, and hermeneutical method form from beginning to end the one picture of the ideal Israelite. It is someone who accepts, forgives, conciliates, makes the soul "like dirt beneath other peoples' feet." These kinds of people receive little respect in the world we now know; they are called cowards. Self-assertion is admired, conciliatory attitudes despised. Ours is an age that admires the strong-minded individual, the uncompromising hero, the warrior whether on the battlefield or in the intellect. Courage takes the form of confrontation, which therefore takes precedence over accommodation in the order of public virtue.

Why sages counseled a different kind of courage we need hardly ask. Given the situation of Israel, vanquished on the battlefield, broken in the turning of history's wheel, we need hardly wonder why wise men advised conciliation and acceptance. Exalting humility made sense, there being little choice. Whether or not these virtues found advocates in other contexts for other reasons, in the circumstance of the vanquished nation, for the people of broken heart, the policy of forbearance proved instrumental, entirely appropriate to both the politics and social condition at hand. If Israel had produced a battlefield hero, the nation could not give him an army. If Jewry cultivated the strong-minded individual, it sentenced such a person to a useless life of ineffective protest. The nation required not strong-minded leadership but consensus.

The social virtues of conciliation, moreover, reinforced the bonds that joined the nation lacking frontiers, the people without a politics of its own. For all there was to hold Israel together to sustain its life as a society would have to come forth out of sources of inner strength. Bonding emerged mainly from within. So consensus, conciliation, self-abnegation and humility, the search for acceptance without the group—these in the literary culture at hand defined appropriate emotions because to begin with they dictated wise policy and shrewd politics.

Vanquished Israel therefore would nurture not merely policies of subordination and acceptance of diminished status among nations. Israel would also develop, in its own heart, the requisite emotional structure. The composition of individuals' hearts would then comprise the counterpart virtues. A policy of acceptance of the rule of others dictated affections of conciliation to the will of others. A defeated people meant to endure defeat would have to get along by going along. How to persuade each Jew to accept what all Jews had to do to endure? Persuade the heart, not only the mind. Then each one privately would feel what everyone publicly had in any case to think.

That accounts for the persistence of the sages' wise teachings on temper, their sagacious counsel on conciliating others and seeking the approval of the group. Society, in the canonical writings, set the style for the self's deepest sentiments. So the approved feelings retained approval for so long because emotions in the thought of the sages of the canon followed rules. They formed public, not personal and private, facts. Feelings laid down judgments. Affections therefore constituted not mindless effusions but deliberate constructions. Whether or not the facts then conformed to the sages' view (or now with the mind of psychology, philosophy, and anthropology) we do not know. But the sages' view did penetrate deeply into what had to be. And that is so, whether or not what had to be ever would correspond with what was.

The sages of the formative age of Judaism proposed for Israel the formation of exactly that type of personality that could and did endure the condition and circumstance of the Exile. The doctrine of the Messiah makes this point as well. In rejecting the heroic model of Bar Kokhba for the Messiah-general's arrogance and affirming the very opposite, the sages who defined Judaism in the first seven centuries C.E., and whose heirs expanded and developed the system they had defined, made the right choice. Living in other peoples' countries and not in their own land, meant for Israel, as Judaism conceived Israel, a long span of endurance, a test of patience to end only with the end of time. That required Israel to live in accord with the will of others. Under such circumstances the virtues of the independent citizen, sharing command of affairs of state and having the gifts of innovation, initiative, independence of mind, proved beside the point. From the end of the second revolt against Rome in 135 C.E., to the creation of the State of Israel in 1948, Israel, the Jewish people, faced a different task.

The human condition of Israel therefore defined a different heroism, one filled with patience, humiliation, self-abnegation. To turn survival into endurance, pariah status into an exercise in godly living, the sages' affective program served full well. Israel's hero saw power in submission, wealth in the gift to be grateful, wisdom in the confession of ignorance. As with the Christian cross, ultimate degradation was made to stand for ultimate power. Like Jesus on the cross, so Israel in exile served God through suffering. True, the cross would represent a scandal to the nations and foolishness to some Jews. But Israel's own version of the doctrine endured and defined the nation's singular and astonishing resilience. For Israel did endure and endures today.

If, then, as a matter of public policy, the nurture of the personality of the Israelite as a person of forbearance and self-abnegation proved right, within the community too the rabbis were not wrong. The Jewish people rarely enjoyed instruments of civil coercion capable of preserving social order and coherence. Governments at best afforded Jews limited rights over their own affairs. When, at the start of the fifth century, the Christian Roman government ended the existence of the patriarchate of the Jews of the Land of Israel, people can well have recognized the parlous condition of whatever Jewish authorities might ever run things. A government in charge of itself and its subjects, a territorial community able routinely to force individuals to pay taxes and otherwise conform where necessary—these political facts of normality rarely marked the condition of Israel between 429 and 1948. What was left was another kind of power, civil obedience generated by force from within. The stress on pleasing others and conforming to the will of the group, so characteristic of sayings of sages, the emphasis that God likes people whom people like—these substitutes for the civil power of political coercion imparted to the community of Israel a different power of authority.

Both sources of power, the one in relationship to the public world beyond, the other in respect to the social world within, in the sages' rules gained force through the primal energy of emotion. Enough has been said to require little explication of that fact. A system that made humility a mark of strength and a mode of gaining God's approval, a social policy that imputed ultimate virtue to feelings of conciliation, restraint, and conformity to social norms had no need of the armies and police it did not have. The heart would serve as the best defense, inner affections as the police who are always there when needed. The remarkable inner discipline of Israel through its exacting condition in history from the beginnings of the sages' system to today began in those feelings that laid down judgments, that construction of affections, coherent with beliefs and behavior, that met the match of misery with grandeur of soul. So the vanquished nation every day would overcome the onetime victors. Israel's victory would come through the triumph of the broken heart, now mended with the remedy of moderated emotion. That union of private feeling and public policy imparted to the Judaic system of the dual Torah its power, its status of self-evidence, for the long centuries during which Israel's condition persisted in the definition imparted by the events of the third crisis in the formation of Judaism.

In the view of the sages of the dual Torah, attitudes or virtues of the heart—e.g., emotions—fit together with the encompassing patterns of society and culture, theology and the religious life. The affective rules formed an integral part of the way of life and worldview put forward to make sense of the existence of the social group. That simple fact accounts for the long-term world-creating power of Judaism in Israel, the Jewish people. How Jews were supposed to feel in ethos matched what they were expected to think. In this way the individual linked the deepest personal emotions to the cosmic fate and transcendent faith of that social group of which he or she formed a part. Emotions laid down judgments. They derived from rational cognition. The individual Israelite's innermost feelings, the microcosm, correspond to the public and historic condition of Israel, the macrocosm.

That accomplishment of Rabbinic Judaism accounts for its power not only to respond to, but itself to define and shape, the condition of Israel, the Jewish people. What the dual Torah taught the private person to feel linked the individual's heart to what Judaism stated about the condition of Israel in history and of God in the cosmos. All formed one reality, in the supernatural world and in nature, in time and in eternity wholly consubstantial (so to speak). In the innermost chambers of deepest feelings, the Israelite therefore lived out the public history and destiny of the people, Israel. The genius of Judaism, the reason for its resilience and endurance, lay in its power to teach Jews to feel in private what they also in any event had to think in public about the condition of both self and nation. The world within, the world without, are so bonded that one is never alone. The individual's life always was lived with the people.

The sages' repertoire of approved and disapproved feelings remained constant through the four centuries' unfolding of the canon of Judaism from the Mishnah through the Talmud of Babylonia, 200–600. Beyond that point, moreover, that same doctrine of virtue persisted in molding both the correct attitudes of the individual and the public policy of the community. The reason is clear. First, the emotions encouraged by Judaism in its formative age—such as humility, forbearance, accommodation, a spirit of conciliation—exactly correspond to the political and social requirements of the Jews' condition in that time. Second, the reason that the same repertoire of emotions persisted with no material change through the unfolding of the writings of the sages of that formative age was the constancy of the Jews' political and social condition.

In successfully joining psychology and politics, inner attitudes and public policy, sages discovered the source of power that would sustain their system. The reason that Judaism enjoyed the standing of self-evident truth for so long as it did, in both Islam and Christendom, derives not from the cogency of its doctrines, but principally from the fusion of heart and mind, emotion and intellect, attitude and doctrine—and the joining of the whole in the fundamental and enduring politics of the nation, wherever it located itself.

The sages' notion of the centrality of human feelings in the religious life presents no surprises. Scripture is explicit on both sides of the matter. The human being is commanded to love God. God's emotional life likewise registered. In the biblical biography of God, the tragic hero, God, will despair, love, hope, feel disappointment or exultation. The biblical record of God's feelings and God's will concerning the feelings of humanity—wanting human love, for example—leaves no room for doubt. Nor does Rabbinic Judaism ignore the datum that "the merciful God wants the heart." The Judaism of the rabbis of late antiquity makes explicit that God always wants the heart. God commands that humanity love God with full heart, soul, mind, and might. That is the principal duty of humanity. So without the Rabbinic canon and merely on the basis of knowledge that that canon begins in the written Torah of Scripture, the facts about the critical place of religious affections in Israel's religion would still prove clear and one-sided. But the sages' contribution, from the Mishnah forward, proves distinctive and definitive. For they impart the distinctive pattern of their mind upon the doctrine that emotions matter: they define just which ones must register.

233

In Christendom and Islam, Israel could survive—but only on the sufferance of others. But those others ordinarily accorded to Israel the right of survival. Judaism endured in Christendom because the later-fourth-century legislators distinguished Judaism from paganism. Judaism lasted in Islam because the Muslim law accorded to Judaism tolerated status. Israel therefore would not merely nurture policies of subordination and acceptance of diminished status among nations, but Israel would also develop, in its own heart, the requisite emotional structure.

How to persuade each Jew to accept what all Jews had to do to endure? Persuade the heart, not only the mind. Then each one privately would feel what everyone publicly had in any case to think. That accounts for not the mere persistence of the sages' wise teachings but for their mythopoeic power. The sages' views on temper, their sagacious counsel on conciliating others and seeking the approval of the group—these not only made life tolerable, they in fact defined what life would mean for Israel. Society, in the canonical writings, set the style for the self's deepest sentiments. So the approved feelings retained approval for so long because emotions, in the thought of the sages of the canon at hand, followed rules. Feelings laid down judgments. Affections therefore constituted not mindless effusions but deliberate constructions. Whether or not the facts then conformed to the sages' view we do not know. But the sages' view did penetrate deeply into what had to be. And that is so, whether or not what had to be ever would correspond with what was.

Life in "exile," viewed as living in other peoples' countries and not in their own land, meant for Israel, as Judaism conceived Israel, a long span of endurance, a test of patience to end only with the end of time. That circumstance required Israel to live in accord with the will of others. Under such circumstances the virtues of the independent citizen, sharing command of affairs of state, the gifts of innovation, initiative, independence of mind, proved beside the point. From the end of the Second Revolt against Rome in 135, to the creation of the State of Israel in 1948, Israel, the Jewish people, faced a different task.

It was to make use of the power of the weak, the force available to the humble and forbearing. Both sources of power, the one in relationship to the public world beyond, the other in respect to the social world within, in the sages' rules gained force through the primal energy of emotion. Enough has been said to require little explication of that fact. A system that made humility a mark of strength and a mode of gaining God's approval, a social policy that imputed ultimate virtue to feelings of conciliation, restraint, and conformity to social norms had no need of the armies and police it did not have. The heart would serve as the best defense, inner affections as the police who are always there when needed. The remarkable inner discipline of Israel through its exacting condition in history from the beginnings of the sages' system to today began in those feelings that laid down judgments, that construction of affections, coherent with beliefs and behavior, that met the match of misery with grandeur of soul. So the vanquished nation every day would overcome the onetime victors. Israel's victory would come through the triumph of the broken heart, now mended with the remedy of moderated emotion.

The human being, "in our image, after our likeness," created male and female, is counterpart and partner and creation, in that, like God the human being has power over the status and condition of creation, putting everything in its proper place, calling everything by its rightful name. And that brings us to the meeting of theology and philosophy in the Mishnah's judgment of the nature of the power of the human being in relationship to God. The human being and God are the two beings that possess the active will. The human being is like God in that both God and the human being not only do things, but also form attitudes and intentions. That theory of the human being, a philosophical issue concerning the nature of will and attitude, meets the theory of God's relationship with humanity, a theological concern with regard to the correspondence of God's and humanity's inner being. And all of this deep thought is precipitated by the critical issue facing Israel, the Jewish people, defeated on the battlefield and deprived of its millennial means of serving God in the Temple in Jerusalem: what, now, can a human being do?

235

Addressing an age of defeat and, in consequence of the permanent closure of the Temple in Jerusalem, despair, the Mishnah's principal message, which makes the Judaism of this document and of its social components distinctive and cogent, is that the human being is at the center of creation, the head of all creatures upon earth, corresponding to God in heaven, in whose image the human being is made. The way in which the Mishnah makes this simple and fundamental statement is illustrated on nearly every page of the document. It is to impute the power, effected through an act of sheer human will or intentionality, to the human being to inaugurate and initiate those corresponding processes, sanctification and uncleanness, which play so critical a role in the Mishnah's account of reality. The will of the human being, expressed through the deed of the human being, is the active power in the world.

As matters would be phrased in later writings, "Nothing whatsoever impedes the human will." But looking back on the age at hand, we know that everything did. The "Israel" of the Mishnah never achieved its stated goals, for example, in once more setting up a government of priests and kings, in once more regaining that order and stasis that, in mind at least, people imagined had once prevailed. But, the key is in the "once more," for these were things that, in point of fact, had not been at all. The will for "once more" encompassed nowhere and never.

So, stated briefly, the question taken up by the Mishnah and answered by Judaism is, What can a person do? And the answer laid down by the Mishnah is that the human being, through will and deed, is master of this world, the measure of all things. But that world of all things of which the human being is the measure is within: in intellect, imagination, sentient reality. Since when the Mishnah thinks of a human being, its authorship means the Israelite, who is the subject and actor of its system, the statement is clear. This is the Judaism that identifies at the center of things Israel, the Israelite person, who can do what he or she wills. In the aftermath of the two wars and defeats of millennial proportions, the message of the Mishnah cannot have proved more pertinent— or poignant and tragic. And yet the power of the message shaped the entire history of Israel, of the Jewish people, and of Judaism, from then to now. For Israel, the Jewish people, understood as the answer to the ineluctable questions of frailty and defeat in society and death for everyone who walked the earth the self-evident truth that everything that matters depends on the human will and intention: we are what in mind and imagination and sentiment and heart we hope, believe, insist, above all by act of will persist in being.

## TRADING PLACES, COMPARING SYSTEMS OF RELIGION

The relationship between Judaism and Christianity in their classic formulations has yielded, at each stage of our study, a clear appreciation of the social entity addressed, the way of life set out, the view of the world involved. At each stage, moreover, we have seen changes within each system of religion that are sometimes dramatic in nature. The "Israel" of Mishnah differs from the "Israel" of the Talmuds, and "Christ" in Romans is a long way from the Nicene Creed.

Such shifts occur frequently and necessarily, as the religious system concerned forms and transforms culture, and also appropriates that cultural reality within itself. The destruction of the Temple, for example, was indirectly brought about by the eschatological expectations of the first century. The belief that only a pure Temple was acceptable to God led teachers such as Jesus to interfere with the ordinary operation of the cult to prepare the way for God's definitive intervention. Expectations of that kind were common among Jews, including that branch of "Israel" that was also called Christian.

By the year 66 C.E., and again by the year 132 C.E., changes in the conduct of worship in the Temple were correctly interpreted by Rome to represents threats to the imperial order, and the reaction was catastrophic (from the points of view of Judaism and of Christianity). The destroyed Temple, ruined on the ground, was replaced in Hebrews by Christ's changeless, eternal priesthood in heaven, and in Mishnah by the ideal of ceaseless memory of how correct sacrifice was to be conducted. In those different appropriations of the same dreadful event they had contributed to producing, Christianity and Judaism set themselves up to become unalterably distinct systems, each claiming the name of Israel under a different definition and for characteristic purposes.

## SYSTEMS OF RELIGION AND HISTORY

Because systems of religion develop in time, evolve, change and mutate, it is often difficult to say how we know when we are dealing with a single system, and when several are at issue. Is the shift from Jesus to Paul, or from *The Shepherd of Hermas* to Nicea, a transition or a radical break? We may likewise ask: is the difference between Exodus, Mishnah, and Talmud so great, that from the point of view of actual content there is no single "Torah" among them?

Yet in some way or another, Judaism always claims a single Torah, just as Christianity always claims a single Christ. But those claims are by definition theological: they are most certainly not descriptions that critical study can validate. There is only a single Torah *if* God gave Moses and the sages the same disclosure on Sinai; there is only a single Christ *if* he is the same yesterday, today, and forever. Apart from the continuity that faith attributes, systems of religion in their histories appear to fragment before the student's eyes into a functionally endless number of discrete systems, each distinct within its particular historical setting.

Theologians during the last century and the present century, Judaic and Christian, reflexively resisted historical methods in the study of their systems, and with good reason. Typically, history is corrosive of faith, in that it reduces the quest for belief to the comparatively dull verification of fact. Instead of asking whether Jesus is the Son of God, history will demand proof that he turned water into wine. Instead of asking how to rule our hearts according to the Torah, history will question whether that was what Moses (if he existed) was interested in. Just as history corrodes faith by reducing it to the mere assertion of fact, so history shatters a single religious system into a thousand shards, each viable only within a particular setting.

The whole idea of constructing a "history of religion" (which remains fashionable in some quarters) is a contradiction in terms. "History" and "religion" occupy different and competing places within the realm of how people might explain and react to the world around them. A religion brings with it its distinctive view of the world, and history insists upon its own characteristic perspective. The same world that is awaiting obedience to the Torah in Judaism is reflecting the transformation of Christ in Christianity, while liberal history sees the world as a closed system in which human actors vie with one another on the grounds of self-interest.

History since the Enlightenment has been attempting to provide a global explanation of humanity from a secular point of view. History in that project is a curious hybrid of Augustine's ambition (discussed in chapter 4) in its breadth with the rational emphasis of René Descartes (1596–1650)[1] in its method. For better than a century, historians and philosophers of history have expressed the concern that the hybrid may in fact be a mismatch, and continuing debate concerning the nature of history remains a part of our intellectual inheritance. That is one reason for which the question of history occupied us in chapter 4.

However that debate proceeds, it seems evident that a "history of religion" in the old sense can only be recommended to the extent that one might also read about "the Torah in history" or "Christ through the ages." In each case, a particular point of view (of self-interested people in history, or Torah, or Christ) is being used to order and evaluate the events of the past. The exercise is less an inquiry than an apologetic defense of the relevant point of view. "History" from the time of the Enlightenment has functioned as the ideological equivalent of theology among intellectuals in the West. Doubt that history can be as comprehensive as religion has grown in exact proportion to the doubt that people respond to their world in a fundamentally rational way. The Enlightenment's faith in reason has eroded, and with it a confidence that history will do the work of theology. The "history of religion" can today only be practiced as apologetics or indulged as nostalgia.

The present book is an experiment. In addition to offering an elucidation of classic Judaism and classic Christianity in their mutual relations, we have explained them on the hypothesis that each is a system, not just a collection of systems. What is experimental in our work is that we have not claimed a theological justification for associating Mishnah with the Talmuds or Paul's letter to the Romans with Origen. We have rather claimed that, alongside the changes we have traced, a demonstrable continuity emerges on the basis of analytic comparison.

To put our experiment in somewhat paradoxical terms, where others have attempted histories of religion, we have analyzed religions in history. There is a single system of religion that stretches from before Mishnah to the Midrash Rabbah, and there is a single system of religion that stretches from Jesus to the Council of Chalcedon.[2] We can now say that, not simply on grounds of faith, but on the basis of critical comparison. Because the two systems traded places while they maintained contact with one another within the Roman world, there must have been two comparable (and sometimes competing) systems the entire time.

Our comparative analysis accepts the methods of history as a matter of course, but denies history the power to reduce religion to local, momentary expressions. The analytic study of religions in history has revealed the influence of religious systems through history. Each system shapes itself and impinges on its world, even as it enters into relations with other systems and adapts itself to its environment.

## ROMAN RELIGION, MODERN RELIGION

The politics of the Judeo-Christian exchange also involved the Roman government's awareness that it was dealing with two distinct—and distinctly troublesome—religions. Imperial policy, in all its astonishing swings, was at least consistent in calibrating encouragement or persecution to the degree to which the prosperity of the empire might be served by Christianity or Judaism. By courting Judaism at the beginning of the period, and then by embracing Christianity at the end of the period, the empire defined religion in a new way.

Religion by the time of Constantine was no longer simply the ancestral way of the Romans, including the common sense of the gods, but a conscious choice of which system served the empire best. Religion became, quite consciously, both a matter of choice and a question of policy. Each chapter of the present volume traces how that new attitude toward religion emerged.

Defined as an option, religion becomes impervious to understanding. I am a Christian or a Manichaean or a Jew because I wish to be, and I believe what I want to believe. The system of religion no longer creates me: I choose it in the marketplace of ideas. The treatment of religions as commodities was typical of the syncretism of the Roman world, and it has remained a part of our culture today. But in order to understand any religion, the bureaucratic stance of the Roman functionary must be abandoned. A system of religion orders and interacts with the culture it informs; it is not simply an accoutrement that is chosen after culture has been formed.

Rome correctly identified Judaism and Christianity as distinct systems of religion, but it never understood them, not even in embracing Christianity. Indeed, the belief that it could accept Christ's triumph without his cross proved a grave mistake on Rome's part, and Augustine explained that error even as the empire was being sacked.

The experience of reversal meant the demise of Rome in the western part of the empire.[3] By then, both Judaism and Christianity had proven their vitality as systems of religion by overcoming the sort of reversals of fortune that would have destroyed or corrupted other systems. The value of a land correctly ordered survived the pillage of that land in Judaism, and the emphatic call to self-conscious poverty survived Christianity's inheritance of unimaginable wealth.

What national state could have survived what Judaism did; what organized ideology could have converted the empire—and then, could have survived the conversion—in the manner of Christianity? What Rome took to be options proved to be more profound than that, and the resilience of both systems was demonstrated by their ability to cope with what seemed to contradict their respective expectations. The politics of the traded places (surveyed in chapter 1) shows that religion was more than Rome thought it was, and not the mere matter of taste some people still take it to be.

241

In fact, the confrontation with circumstances, which obviously contradicted the supreme values of each system, only caused each of them to redouble its insistence on what was truly supreme. For that reason, it is not surprising that—as we have seen in chapters 2 and 3—the development of teleology comports with the articulation of values.

The apocalyptic eschatology of classic Christianity's early years corresponds to conditions of physical oppression that threatened to extinguish the movement. The later emphasis on a more philosophically conceived transcendence was embraced by teachers whose asceticism was freely chosen, not forced upon them. The Mishnah's silence in regard to eschatology reflects its concentration on the land in itself; the Talmudic recourse to eschatology represents the yearning to acquire that same land again. Values and teleology prove to be mutually defining in Judaism and Christianity, and each takes value to the point that it can describe as ultimate, even in the face of opposition from the world outside.

The trading of histories proved to be a complex exchange to describe. But that complexity was for the most part a function of the modern belief that history is a simple matter. We saw, on the contrary, that history involves the claim of the consequence and sequence of events in the past as they impinge on the present. Christianity always insisted on the consequence of events, and of the human beings (in human flesh) through whom they occurred, but sequence only entered its idiom after Constantine's conversion seemed to vindicate apocalyptic expectations. Conversely, paradigmatic thinking among the sages removed sequence from the story of Israel; every moment now could become any moment then, and what was of consequence was the moment, not the event.

Politics, values, teleologies, and histories were all traded, and they were redefined in the exchange. Two systems, then, become apparent in their symmetrical differences, which speak far more eloquently of what they are than their obvious similarities. Systems of religion, it turns out, may be described as interacting over time. The degree of their interaction demonstrates that (1) they are discrete systems, and (2) they are not locked into particular circumstances of history. We claim, then, that our experiment has been productive at a theoretical level, and may fruitfully be repeated within the critical study of religions: systems of religion operate through historical time, as well as in historical time. We have access to them only in history, but comparative analysis reveals their influence through history, and their transcendence of any Rome that might try to contain them.

## CENTERING CHRISTIANITY

If the systemic center of Judaism is the Torah, understood as God's measure of the human being as master of the world, what is the systemic center of Christianity? Answering that question is difficult, because Christianity transformed itself so radically over time. It claimed from an early stage to preserve "the faith once for all delivered to the saints" (Jude 3), and insistence upon the continuity of the tradition has been a persistent feature of Christianity. Such claims, however, are of a theological order; we must pursue an answer to the question of continuity along the lines of our analytic experiment.

Because our thinking is analytic, it will not do to resort to tautology. To say, "The systemic center of Christianity is Christ" is not only obvious, it is also misleading, since the definition of "Christ" varies significantly over time and from place to place. When we apply theological terms of reference such as "Christ" and "faith" to describe what holds Christianity together, we assume that there is an unvarying essence over time that Christianity expresses. But the analytic continuity we seek to describe is not an essence derived from theology. Rather, our quest is for a stable feature that consistently lies at the generative heart of the system.

The practice of eucharist in Christianity—in its primitive, early, and classic periods—provides a demonstration of the range of variety and change that we must account for within a systemic analysis. Among Jesus' followers in Galilee, the common meal was an occasion to participate in a celebration of the kingdom of God, for which one prayed every day. In the circumstances of his confrontation with the authorities in Jerusalem, Jesus transformed that practice into a replacement for sacrifice in the Temple (see Preface, pp. xv–xviii).

✡
**243**
✝

That transformation of practice, initiated by Jesus, set in motion a continuous transformation of the meaning of the meal within Christian practice. In the Preface and Introduction to this book, we have already seen how Peter's circle domesticated the meal into a renewal of the covenant within one's household, and how James's circle attempted to limit the full practice of eucharist to circumcised men at Passover. Paul, of course, insisted on a more inclusive practice, a demonstration of the body of Christ (see 1 Cor. 11:23–32), while the synoptic Gospels aim to provide for a variety of practice within their respective communities (in the stories of the feedings of the 5,000 and the 4,000; see pp. xviii–xix, 27–29).

The transformations of meaning, of course, went on from there. The paschal meaning of eucharist was developed in the Gospel according to John, so that Jesus was seen as giving himself as the bread of heaven for the life of the world. The feeding of the 5,000—understood as occurring at Passover—is taken up in John 6 in just such a fully paschal sense. Jesus himself is identified as the manna, miraculous food bestowed by God on his people (see Exodus 16). The motif was already articulated by Paul, but John develops it to construe the eucharist as a Mystery, in which Jesus offers his own flesh and blood. Any crude misunderstanding is avoided, because Jesus defines himself as the true bread of life, which is given by God, the surety of eternal life and of resurrection on the last day (6:32–40). The Johannine Gospel associates the synoptic story of the feeding of the 5,000 with Passover (6:4) and then fully develops the quasi-magical exposition of the eucharistic bread as manna, which Paul in 1 Corinthians 10 only tentatively indulged (John 6:26–59). That autobiographical reading of Jesus' words—as giving his personal body and blood in eucharist—had probably already occurred to Hellenistic Christians who followed synoptic practice. The Johannine practice made that meaning explicit.

That meaning involved an implication of the healing qualities of the eucharist, which was taken up and developed by Irenaeus. Irenaeus's appreciation of the eucharist is essentially of the Johannine type, based on the miraculous provision of bread in chapter 6 (see *Against Heresies,* 2.22.3; 3.9.5): here is a blessing for the last times that compares with the miraculous sustenance of Israel. But where eating the bread of life in John results in having eternal life in oneself, for Irenaeus the result is a transformation of one's own flesh (for reasons that will be evident from a reading of chapters 2 and 4).

Irenaeus's insistence on this notion is inexorable. He is keen to point out that Jesus took bread that had been produced from the earth in order to give thanks in John 6:11 (*Against Heresies,* 3.9.5); the same God who creates also redeems, and what God redeems is the flesh of which the bread is a symbol. When Irenaeus speaks of the eucharist itself, he returns to the same theme. Jesus says "This is my body" of bread that had been created in the ordinary way, and its offering is "the new oblation of the new covenant" (*Against Heresies,* 4.17.5). The theological significance of this sacrifice is explicated powerfully and simply (*Against Heresies*, 4.18.5):

> For as the bread, which is produced from the earth, when it receives the invocation from God, is no longer common bread, but the eucharist, consisting of two realities, earthly and heavenly, so also our bodies, when they receive the eucharist, are no longer corruptible, having the hope of resurrection to eternity.

Explicitly and deliberately, Irenaeus makes resurrection into a transformation of human flesh, and eucharist announces "consistently the fellowship and union of the flesh and spirit."

But when precisely did eucharistic bread and wine come to be identified with the personal body and blood of Jesus, offered on the cross? In his recent study of the history of the sacraments, Bernhard Lang suggests that first occurred within the eucharistic theology of Cyprian of Carthage. Cyprian was bishop of Carthage, and arguably the most influential ecclesiastic of his day. The systematic persecution under Decius, which lasted one vicious year (250–251) forced Cyprian into hiding, and then confronted him with the most difficult question for the church during the third century: how to deal with lapsed Christians.

Much as Irenaeus proceeded on a Johannine basis, Cyprian grounded his theology of the eucharist in the synoptic Gospels. The theme of solidarity with Jesus the martyr reaches its classic expression in Cyprian, along martial lines (*Letter*, 58:1):[4]

> The end of the world and the time of the Antichrist draw near, so that we must all stand prepared for the battle. Do not consider anything but the glory of life eternal, and the crown of the confession of the Lord; and do not regard those things which are coming as being such as were those which have passed away. Now a more serious and ferocious battle threatens, for which the soldiers of Christ ought to prepare themselves with uncorrupted faith and sturdy courage.

Martyrdom here finds its power in the imitation of Christ, in struggling as he struggled, and it exerts an impact within the final travail of the world as a whole.

In his study of the eucharist, Lang has identified Cyprian as the founder of the classical catholic theology:

> For the bishop of Carthage, the eucharist is a ritual repetition and imitation of the Last Supper of Jesus. Since the subsequent development of the Lord's Supper follows Cyprian's conception, this statement may appear as a banality. However, the novelty of Cyprian's understanding deserves to be highlighted. Before Cyprian, the eucharist was not so much a repetition of the Last Supper of Jesus as it was a ritual producing and consuming of sacred food. With Cyprian, the biblical context of the Last Supper and the connection with Jesus' death are given prominence. Like the original Last Supper, the eucharist was now celebrated in an atmosphere of "tribulation," the foes assault upon Christ and his followers.[5]

In precisely this sense, Cyprian would routinize the use of the verb *sacrificare* in order to refer to the celebration of the eucharist: it was after all *oblatio et sacrificium nostrum* (see, for example *Letter,* 63.9):

> Whence it appears that the blood of Christ is not offered if wine is lacking in the chalice and that the sacrifice of the Lord is not celebrated with lawful sanctification unless the oblation and our sacrifice correspond to the passion.

In the eucharist, believers offered the sacrifice of Jesus, so that they also might be an acceptable sacrifice.

Within the practices of eucharist we have reviewed, people eat and drink, their affections are engaged, and an overall ideology explains what is happening. But within each of those categories of eucharistic practice—pragmatic, affective, and ideological[6]— significant, sometimes dramatic change occurred within Christianity. Throughout the period, Christians framed their communities to comport with their eucharistic practices, excluded enemies from their tables, explained their practices in new ways, and produced fresh theologies.[7] But their self-definitions, their designations of enemies, their explanations and theologies of eucharist, were often contradictory. Again: What is the systemic continuity within such variety?

At each stage, and in every place, Christianity has been practiced as final humanity: the last attempt of God to shape and call the people of God. The model of Jesus has been invoked to say who finally we are as God's children—eschatologically, transcendentally, or both. For that reason, transformation has always been involved, and change has been actively embraced.

Christians classically look at the world from its end in Christ backwards, not from the beginning. Their hope is also their ground of engagement with other people, who are themselves created to be God's children. Their engagement will sometimes look like politics to others, but systemically it is faith working through love (Gal. 5:6). Their values will always look askew from the point of view of those who believe things in themselves matter, because Christians cherish only what will effect (and affect) their final humanity in Christ.

That teleology will speak of what is to come, not simply as a future continuous with the present, but as that place where our ultimate transformation is to occur. And Christians' history will be the story of salvation, written in their own hearts and in the lives of their own people. Such is classic Christianity, then and now, effective as system within history and through history, oriented on the dawn of a kingdom that it already rejoices in on the grounds of the humanity discovered in Christ.

247

# Notes

## Preface

1. See Hershel Shanks, ed., *Parallel Histories* (Washington, D.C.: Biblical Archaeology Society, 1993).

2. Judaism the religion and Christianity the religion, not the institutions of the Jews as an ethnic group compared with the doctrines and structures of Christianity as a religion, as is the case in Shanks's book.

3. The description of the contrasting Judaic systems, the first represented by the Mishnah and related Midrash-compilations, the second, by the Talmud of the Land of Israel and related Midrash-compilations, depends on substantially revised and rewritten parts of several works by Jacob Neusner. These works are as follows: Chapters 1 and 2 draw upon *Transformation of Judaism* (Urbana: University of Illinois Press, 1992). Chapter 3 reviews *The Foundations of Judaism: Method, Teleology, Doctrine* (Philadelphia: Fortress Press, 1983–85). I–III. II. *Messiah in Context: Israel's History and Destiny in Formative Judaism* (Lanham, Md.: University Press of America, 1988). Studies in Judaism series, and *Judaism and Christianity in the Age of Constantine: Issues of the Initial Confrontation* (Chicago: University of Chicago Press, 1987); and Jacob Neusner and William Scott Green, eds., *Judaisms and Their Messiahs in the Beginning of Christianity* (New York: Cambridge University Press, 1987). Chapter 4 recapitulates some of the findings of *Judaism: The Evidence of the Mishnah* (Chicago: University of Chicago Press, 1981) and *The Presence of the Past, the Pastness of the Present: History, Time, and Paradigm in Rabbinic Judaism* (Bethesda, Md.: CDL Press, 1995). Chapter 5 goes over the main points of *Death and Birth of Judaism: The Impact of Christianity, Secularism, and the Holocaust on Jewish Faith* (New York: Basic Books, 1987; second printing, Atlanta: Scholars Press for South Florida Studies in the History of Judaism, 1993); *Judaism and Christianity in the Age of Constantine: Issues of the Initial Confrontation* (Chicago: University of Chicago

Press, 1987) and further, *Self-Fulfilling Prophecy: Exile and Return in the History of Judaism* (Boston: Beacon Press, 1987; 2d printing: Atlanta: Scholars Press for South Florida Studies in the History of Judaism, 1990); and *Vanquished Nation, Broken Spirit: The Virtues of the Heart in Formative Judaism* (New York: Cambridge University Press, 1987).

4. See Bruce Chilton, *A Galilean Rabbi and His Bible* (Wilmington, Del.: Glazer, 1984).

5. The particulars of the dispute are detailed in Bruce Chilton, *The Temple of Jesus: His Sacrificial Program with a Cultural History of Sacrifice* (University Park: Penn State Press, 1992), 91–111.

6. See Bruce Chilton, *Pure Kingdom: Jesus' Vision of God* (Grand Rapids, Mich.: Eerdmans, 1996).

## INTRODUCTION

1. Any more than a single, unitary "Jewish people," from before 587 B.C.E. has formed an actual presence in time and space, not only in the imagination of theologians and ideologists. The representation of "Israel" as unitary and encompassing, beginning with origins in a single family from a single mother and a single father, likewise serves diverse theological purposes, but in no way belongs to a historical account of real people, who actually made history. For an account of the theories of "Israel" in various ancient Judaisms, see J. Neusner, *Judaism and Its Social Metaphors: Israel in the History of Jewish Thought* (New York: Cambridge University Press, 1988).

2. Except on theological grounds, but the history of religion cannot undertake a theological assignment.

3. See J. Neusner, *The Transformation of Judaism: From Philosophy to Religion* (Champaign: University of Illinois Press, 1992).

4. He is quoted in *Eusebius' History of the Church* 6.25. A discussion of the significance of Hebrews within the development of the canon is available in Bruce Chilton, *Beginning New Testament Study* (London: SPCK, 1987), 12–20.

5. A fine, recent commentary is available in William L. Lane, *Hebrews 1–8* and *Hebrews 9–13:* Word Biblical Commentary 47A, 47B (Dallas: Word, 1991). Also see the helpful discussion in Brooke Foss Westcott, *The Epistle to the Hebrews* (London: Macmillan, 1909 [from 1889]), lxii–lxxxiv.

6. See Lane, lxix–lxxxiv.

7. In his recent monograph on Hebrews, Barnabas Lindars considered the possibility that 2:17 presupposed some previous awareness of the theme on the part of the readership of the epistle. But he wisely came to the conclusion that, in fact, the author was simply preparing the way for the closer analysis of Jesus as great high priest that was to come; cf. *The Theology of the Letter to the Hebrews: New Testament Theology* (Cambridge: Cambridge University Press, 1991), 40–41.

8. His name has not yet been changed to Abraham, which is related in Genesis 17:5.

9. See also Hebrews 5:6, 10; 6:20.

10. The link with the practice of eucharist is so obvious in the mind of the author, he does not even elaborate upon it. Cf. the discussion in Lindars, *The Theology of the Letter to the Hebrews*, 76–77.

11. For a consideration of the terminological problems, cf. Harold W. Attridge, *The Epistle to the Hebrews: Hermeneia* (Philadelphia: Fortress, 1989), 230, and Westcott, *The Epistle to the Hebrews* (London: Macmillan, 1909), 244–252.

12. Attridge, *The Epistle to the Hebrews*, 232–35, follows other commentators in taking the *thumiaterion* as an alter, and so charges Hebrews with a "minor (sic!) anomaly," but he points out himself that "censer" would be a more straightforward rendering, with the diction of the Septuagint.

13. Cf. Westcott, *The Epistle to the Hebrews*, 258–60.

14. See Hebrews 8:1–6. Hebrews' usage of the language of typology is quite complex, although the underlying conception is fairly simple. Paul reflects an earlier form of typological interpretation in 1 Corinthians 10.

15. The mention is in reference to Joseph's command for the disposal of his own bones, a fitting context for the attitude toward "Israel" in Hebrews!

16. The angelic mediation of the Torah was a common belief in the period. See Galatians 3:19, Acts 7:53; Josephus's *Antiquities,* XV § 136. Cf. Lane, 37–38.

17. See Lindars, *The Theology of the Letter to the Hebrews,* 38. Lindars also presents a careful characterization of how Hebrews' approach to Scripture might (and might not) be called typological; see 53–55.

18. Indeed, the epistle in its present form is designed to pass as a late letter of Paul's. His imprisonment is assumed (13:18–19), and the naming of Timothy is an indirect attempt to claim Pauline authorship (13:23). The famous reference to Italy in 13:24 is similarly part of the strategy of a Pauline presentation, and not a criterion of the actual provenience of the epistle.

19. Local apostolic writings were clearly available, but the emergence of the canonical New Testament would await the second century, largely under the impetus of the veneration of such traditions that Hebrews displays. Cf. *Beginning New Testament Study,* 12–18.

20. Politics: *Rabbinic Political Theory: Religion and Politics in the Mishnah* (Chicago: University of Chicago Press, 1991). Economics: *The Economics of the Mishnah* (Chicago: University of Chicago Press, 1989). Philosophy: *Judaism as Philosophy: The Method and Message of the Mishnah* (Columbia: University of South Carolina Press, 1991).

21. See J. Neusner, *Judaism and Christianity in the Age of Constantine: Issues of the Initial Confrontation* (Chicago: University of Chicago Press, 1987).

22. For what follows, cf. Bruce Chilton, *Profiles of a Rabbi: Synoptic Opportunities in Reading about Jesus,* Brown Judaic Studies 177 (Atlanta: Scholars Press, 1989).

23. John, of course, is presented as a prophetic figure in the synoptics. See Matthew 3:1–12; Mark 1:1–8; Luke 3:1–18.

24. See Marinus de Jonge, "Messiah," *Anchor Bible Dictionary,* vol. 4 (Garden City, N.Y.: Doubleday, 1993), 777–78.

25. See Matthew 3:15; 5:17; 23:32; 26:54, 56; Mark 14:49; Luke 4:21; 24:44.

26. Charles Taylor cited Psalm 72:16 in order to instance the imagery of grain growing on mountains. See *The Teaching of the Twelve Apostles* (Cambridge: Deighton Bell, 1886), 129, 130.

27. Verse 43 specifies 100 men, which in the synoptic transformation is multiplied by 10 and by 5. The number "10" is of symbolic significance within the biblical tradition (cf. Jöram Friberg, "Numbers and Counting," *Anchor Bible Dictionary,* vol. 4, ed. D. N. Freedman (New York: Doubleday, 1992), 1139–46, 1145. The number "5," however, is better taken of the Pythagorean number of man, the pentagram; cf. Annemarie Schimmel, "Numbers: An Overview," *Encyclopedia of Religion,* ed. M. Eliade (New York: Macmillan, 1987), 13–19.

28. Cf. Chilton, *A Galilean Rabbi,* 95–96.

29. Cf. Friberg, "Numbers and Counting," 1145.

30. See Paul J. Achtemeier, *Mark: Proclamation Commentaries* (Philadelphia: Fortress, 1986), 29, who rightly observes that the statement attributed to Jesus "presupposes not only the present order of events in Mark, but also the present form of the Greek prose." His conclusion of particularly Markan authorship, however, is not warranted.

31. *Against Apion* I.37–43.

32. See Yigael Yadin, *The Ben Sira Scroll from Masada* (Jerusalem: Israel Exploration Society, 1965).


# 1. TRADING POLITICS

1. The phrase itself comes from Tertullian, *Apology* 21.1, and has been applied generally to refer to the Roman settlement with Judaism. See Amnon Linder, *The Jews in Roman Imperial Legislation* (Detroit: Wayne State University Press, 1987), 54–90, 101 n. 7.

2. For a cautious discussion, see C. K. Barrett, *The Acts of he Apostles: The International Critical Commentary* (Edinburgh: Clark, 1994), 556.

3. See E. Mary Smallwood, *The Jews under Roman Rule: Studies in Judaism in Late Antiquity* 20 (Leiden: Brill, 1976), 371–76.

4. See E. A. Judge, "Judaism and the Rise of Christianity: A Roman Perspective," *Tyndale Bulletin* 45.2 (1994): 355–68.

5. See Smallwood, *The Jews under Roman Rule,* 428–66.

6. See Linder, *The Jews in Roman Imperial Legislation,* 99, 101–2.

7. See Lee I. Levine, ed., *The Galilee in Late Antiquity* (New York: Jewish Theological Seminary, 1992).

8. See Henry Chadwick, *The Early Church* (London: Penguin, 1993), 29.

9. Manichaeanism is discussed in chapter 4, within our assessment of Augustine of Hippo.

10. Cited by R. G. Mulgan, *Aristotle's Political Theory* (Oxford: Clarendon Press, 1977), 3.

11. The details are spelled out in J. Neusner's *Judaism and Society: The Evidence of the Yerushalmi* (Chicago: University of Chicago Press, 1984), chap. 3. Note also Neusner's *Foundations of the Theology of Judaism,* vol. 2, *Israel* (Northvale: Jason Aronson, 1991).

12. The polemical purpose of the claim that that abstraction, "Israel," was to be compared to the family of the mythic ancestor lies right at the surface. With another "Israel," the Christian church, now claiming to constitute the true one, Jews found it possible to confront that claim and to turn it against the other side. "You claim to form 'Israel after the spirit.' Fine, and *we* are Israel after the flesh—and genealogy forms the link, that alone." (Converts did not present an anomaly, of course, since they were held to be children of Abraham and Sarah, who had "made souls," that is, converts, in Haran, a point repeated in the documents of the period.) That fleshly continuity formed of all of "us" a single family, rendering spurious the notion that "Israel" could be other than genealogically defined. But that polemic seems to me adventitious and not primary. At the same time the metaphor provided a quite separate component to sages' larger system.

13. Within their context, systems never take risks, since always at stake is self-evidence.

## 2. TRADING VALUES

1. For Plato the issue was episodic and bore no important systemic message; for Christian thinkers, economics makes its first consequential appearance in medieval times, with the renewal of Aristotelianism.

2. Polanyi, "Aristotle Discovers the Economy," in Karl Polanyi, Conrad M. Arensberg, and Harry W. Pearson, *Trade and Market in the Early Empires: Economies in History and Theory* (Glencoe, Ill.: Free Press, 1957), 79.

3. Davisson and Harper, *European Economic History*, 130.

4. Ibid., 131.

5. Polanyi, "Aristotle Discovers the Economy," 79.

6. Ibid., 88.

7. Ibid., 90. Also Karl Polanyi, *The Lifelihood of Man*, ed. Harry W. Pearson (New York: Academic Press, 1977), in particular 145–276.

8. The borders of the Land of Israel were notoriously difficult to specify; they did not coincide with any political boundaries to which we can now point. In general, what was meant by "the Land of Israel" seems to me to have been land settled and held by the immigrants in the time of Joshua, on the one side, and those in the time of the return to Zion on

the other, with the former real estate more deeply sanctified, more fully comprising land of the Land of Israel, than the latter. So the holiness of the Holy Land depended on the joint ownership of that particular property between God and (an) Israeli(ite), and the longer the Israelite held the land, the holier the land became. So the Holy Land is not an absolute, geographical fact, but a relative (in our terms), social one. Israelites outside the Land of Israel did not impart holiness to the land on which they lived, and gentiles within the Land of Israel also did not impart holiness to the land on which they lived. And all real estate outside the Land of Israel was held to be cultically unclean in the level of corpse-uncleanness, than which there is no more virulent source of uncleanness. So the entire matter of "land as wealth," or "land is the only form of wealth," which was an absolute commonplace in ancient economics, has to be recast in the context of (a) Judaism. There are numerous details of the law that rest on precisely that supposition. Then Israelites living on land nearby, e.g., in Syria, imparted to that land holiness as well, though less holiness inhered in that land than in land in the Land of Israel occupied by Israelites. So from the viewpoint of the system, not surprisingly, the land is in gradations, that is to say, it is both classified and also hierarchized. That hierarchical classification seems to me yet another striking piece of evidence for the philosophical character that permeates the Mishnah's system; it is surely a conception of which the priestly authors of Leviticus and Numbers, after 500, were entirely oblivious.

9. And that must govern our definition of wealth when we follow the expansion of the category at hand, that is, rational disposition of scarce resources. When we speak presently of scarce resources of another type, we will not identify virtue as a scarce resource in the way in which land is a scarce resource, but we will identify scarce resources that produce worldly comfort and ease and other benefit, as valuable as land, as desired as gold, as productive as a vineyard or a field; and that may prove "spiritual" or "immaterial" or "metaphorical," but systemically wealth throughout is understand as palpable and real and consequential for the material well-being of the owner of wealth in that form. I cannot overemphasize the danger of our assuming that wealth is either material or spiritual; in this system's secondary phase, there is wealth that is entirely palpable and produces precisely the same good life that owning fields and

villages does, but it is not wealth in real estate at all, and, all the more so, assuredly not wealth in the form of liquid capital. I think no form of wealth identified by us proved so incomprehensible to the system builders before us as capital.

10. For a recent and succinct discussion, see S. J. Hafermann, "Corinthians, Letters to the," *Dictionary of Paul and His Letters,* ed. G. F. Hawthorne and R. P. Martin (Downers Grove, Ill.: InterVarsity, 1993).

11. That contrast of light and darkness, in turn, manifests the influence of Zoroastrianism upon Judaism, but that is an entirely separate topic.

12. See George W. MacRae's presentation in *The Nag Hammadi Library,* ed. J. M. Robinson (San Francisco: Harper and Row, 1978).

13. See Stephen Benko, *Pagan Rome and the Early Christians* (Bloomington: Indiana University Press, 1986), 54–78.

14. See Henry Chadwick, *The Early Church* (London: Penguin, 1993), 29, 74–79.

15. Marcion has already been mentioned in the Introduction, pp. 31–32.

16. The reading in the Sourcebook provides an example of Clement's theology in regard to the point. Clement also wrote a *Protrepticus,* an exhortation to join the Christian philosophical school, as well as the *Paedagogus.* A third volume was to have been called the *Didaskalos* ("Teacher"), but instead Clement was in the process of writing his *Stromateis* ("Miscellanies") at the time he died, perhaps near the year 215.

17. See Henry George Liddell and Robert Scott, *A Greek-English Lexicon* (Oxford: Clarendon, 1901), 724.

18. See *Against Heresies* 4.33.7. For a discussion of Irenaeus's theology of the church, see Gustaf Wingren, *Man and the Incarnation* (Edinburgh: Oliver and Boyd, 1959), 147–80.

19. See *Against Heresies* 3.9.8.

20. See J. N. D. Kelly, *Early Christian Creeds* (New York: Longmans, Green, 1949), 163–66. As he conclusively shows, the creeds developed over centuries, and there was considerable local variation. Our citation of the Apostles' Creed in its traditional form is intended as a point of departure, rather than as a claim for its originality.

21. These terms of reference emerged gradually during the course of debate throughout the century. Only with the Council of Chalcedon in 451 was the matter settled for catholic and orthodox Christianity.

## 3. TRADING TELEOLOGIES

1. Chapter 4 takes up the broader question of the conception of history in Rabbinic Judaism and in Christianity in the formative age.

2. *The Christian Tradition: A History of the Development of Doctrine* 1 (Chicago: University of Chicago Press, 1971), 124.

3. That is the title of his next section, 132–41, following "The Apocalyptic Vision and Its Transformation," 123–32. For a detailed analysis of Jesus' eschatology, see Bruce Chilton, *Pure Kingdom: Jesus' Vision of God* (Grand Rapids, Mich.: Eerdmans, 1996).

4. *The Christian Tradition*, 126.

5. See Jean Daniélou and Henri Marrou, *The Christian Centuries* 1, trans. V. Cronin (New York: McGraw-Hill, 1964), 87. The relevant source is Minucius Felix, *Octavian* 9; 31.1-2. They give further examples of the charges of intellectuals on pp. 88–90.

6. See F. L. Cross, *The Early Christian Fathers* (London: Duckworth, 1960), 26. Still, his remark is kinder than Streeter's dismissal of *The Shepherd* (which he cites) as "the pottering mediocrity of the timid little Greek." For a more appreciative assessment, see Carolyn Osiek, "The Genre and Function of the *Shepherd of Hermas,*" *Early Christian Apocalypticism:* Semeia 30 (Decatur: Scholars, 1986), 113–21.

7. See Cross, *The Early Christian Fathers,* 24; Pelikan, 125–26.

8. By the same token, the theme in Mark that has been called "the messianic secret" is best explained as Christology with a low profile. Jesus has no doubt about who he is, and neither does the reader or hearer of the Gospel, but it is also clearly understood that such knowledge is dangerous to all who have it (whether Jesus himself, or those who follow him).

9. See Jean Daniélou, *Origen,* trans. W. Mitchell (New York: Sheed and Ward, 1955), 13.

257

## 4. MARCHING IN PLACE

1. See Bruce Chilton and Jacob Neusner, *Judaism in the New Testament: Practices and Beliefs* (London and New York: Routledge, 1995).

2. *II Corinthians:* Anchor Bible 32A (Garden City, N.Y.: Doubleday, 1984), 330.

3. *The Early Church* (London: Penguin, 1993), 80.

4. For a discussion of that issue, see M. Widman, "Irenaüs und seine theologischen Väter," *Zeitschrift für Theologie und Kirche* 54 (1957): 155–66, and Jean Daniélou and Henri Marrou, *The Christian Centuries*, vol. 1, *The First Six Hundred Years* (New York: McGraw-Hill, 1964), 112.

5. That is the theme of the brilliant work by Lloyd G. Patterson, *God and History in Early Christian Thought: Studies in Patristic Thought* (New York: Seabury, 1967).

6. Ibid., 45.

7. See Daniélou and Marrou, *The Christian Centuries*, 100–103. Tertullian's acceptance of a Montanist stance shows the extent to which Montanism represented an emphasis on the active spirit of prophecy, which went well beyond Montanus personally.

8. See Patterson, *God and History in Early Christian Thought*, 55.

9. See Walter Rauschenbusch, *A Theology for the Social Gospel* (New York: Abingdon, 1960 [from 1917]), and the discussion in Bruce Chilton, ed., *The Kingdom of God in the Teaching of Jesus: Issues in Religion and Theology* 5 (Philadelphia: Fortress, 1984), 6.

10. See Eusebius: *The History of the Church*, trans. G. A. Williamson (Minneapolis: Augsburg, 1975), 8, and *History of the Church* 1.1; 10.4.

11. See his *History of the Church* 10.9.6–9 and Patterson, *God and History in Early Christian Thought*, 84.

12. For a brief discussion of the *City of God*, see E. R. Hardy, "The City of God," *A Companion to the Study of St. Augustine*, ed. R. W. Battenhouse (New York: Oxford University Press, 1969), 257–83.

13. See Stanley Romaine Hopper, "The Anti-Manichean Writings," *A Companion*, 148–74.

14. See Lyford Paterson Edwards, *The Transformation of Early Christianity from an Eschatological to a Socialized Movement* (Menasha, Wisc.: Banta, 1919), 17.

15. For a succinct and illuminating account of the most important issues involved, see Bernard Lonergan, *Method in Theology* (New York: Herder, 1972), 175–234.

## 5. TWO SUCCESSFUL RELIGIONS

1. See Geneviève Rodis-Lewis, *Descartes* (Paris: Calmann-Lévy, 1996).

2. And, perhaps, beyond, but that remains to be analyzed in our fashion.

3. A new order gradually emerged on a fresh basis, but that is another story, which must include the rise of Islam.

4. For this translation, and for his analysis of Cyprian, we are indebted to Bernhard Lang, *Christian Worship: A Cultural and Historical Study* (New Haven, Conn.: Yale University Press, forthcoming). See Rose Bernard Donna, *Saint Cyprian: Letters* (1–81): *The Fathers of the Church* (Washington, D.C.: Catholic University of America Press, 1964). The epistle is numbered 55 in A. Roberts and James Donaldson, *Ante-Nicene Christian Library*, vol. 8, *The Writings of Cyprian* (Edinburgh: Clark, 1868).

5. Lang, *Christian Worship*, 62.

6. These dimensions of the typology of sacrifice, and therefore of eucharist, are developed in Bruce Chilton, *The Temple of Jesus: Jesus' Sacrificial Program within a Cultural History of Sacrifice* (University Park: Penn State Press, 1992), 27–42, and *A Feast of Meanings: Eucharistic Theologies from Jesus through Johannine Circles* (Leiden: Brill, 1994).

7. See the criteria for the success of a religious system at the beginning of this chapter.

✡
### 259
♰

# $\mathsf{S\cup BJECT\ INDEX}$

# Index to Biblical and Talmudic References